STRANG

The Impacts of Internet Culture and Modern Communication Technology on Society and the Christian

Benjamin Clark

ISBN: 978-1-945774-99-7

Trust House Publishers
P.O. Box 3181
Taos, NM 87571 USA
www.trusthousepublishers.com

Ordering Information: Quantity sales. Special discounts are available on quantity purchases by churches, associations, and others. For details, contact the publisher at the address above.

Orders by U.S. trade bookstores and wholesalers. Please contact the publisher.

2 3 4 5 6 7 8 9 1

Preface

This all started in a revival meeting in the early 2000s. Back when Myspace was the thing that everybody was talking about. I don't know exactly what revival meeting it was, but an evangelist got up and preached an entire sermon on why Myspace was bad. At the time, middle-school aged me thought what every typical, public schooler would of thought. Ok, sure, whatever. That's just what old people do. He went on a 45-minute rant before closing, and all of the adults agreed with him after the service that Myspace, whatever it was, was a very bad thing that children should not be on. The problem, at least in my mind, was that none of these people actually understood what they were talking about. A common sentiment, that still comes out of pulpits today, goes something like this: I don't know what a Facebook is, but you don't need one.

This was the where the seed for this book was planted, and it illustrates the fundamental problem with how independent, fundamental, Bible-believing Baptist churches are handling the cultural revolution brought about by the internet. The problem is, they don't understand the problem. Social media and smartphones exploded onto the scene in the early 2000s. While most good pastors and preachers had enough spiritual discernment to see what was going on, they had no idea why it was happening or really, what all of this stuff even was. All they knew was that they could recognize a foul spirit by its stink, and they could see the damage that it caused. And thus began the ongoing conflict between the church and the latest virus to infect the Bride of Christ. They could diagnose the disease through the symptoms but couldn't bridge the gap of why this particular thing caused the damage that it did.

The problem manifests itself like this: a preacher preaches against something wicked on the internet, the Holy Spirit convicts the hearts of the hearers that the old preacher is correct, but they reason their way out of quitting because, in their minds, even though they know that they have a virus, and they know that they have symptoms, they don't want to connect that cause the effect. It is an intellectual and spiritual dishonesty that the flesh creates to protect itself from quitting its favorite sins. Sin has a defense mechanism to divert blame away form itself in order to preserve its continuance. Pastors and preachers can lob Bible verses about gossip and backbiting at it all day long, but the layman simply deflects by saying that they don't use it for that, and they can handle it and that preacher should just mind his own business and run his own life. Sure, he preaches against Facebook, but Reddit is fine. After all, he can't prove that Instagram is the reason they aren't getting anything out of their Bible reading, so why should he tell them to stop?

When I started doing research on this topic, I wanted to answer the question, what does the internet really do to the human soul? Is it actually good for us? Should it be used by churches to grow their ministries, both through outreach and development of the Christians within the local assembly? Does spending time on Twitter actually hurt my walk with God, even if I am not using it to say wicked things or read things I shouldn't?

I also wanted to make sure that I didn't just quote a bunch of preachers who hated on things for the sole sake of hating on things. Some preachers preach against things because they love their flock and have seen the evils it has done to others, and they want their people to thrive as Christians. Other preachers preach against things because they need something need to hate on every three weeks. It can be difficult to tell the difference sometimes. When I started doing my research, I spent most of my time looking for unsaved authors to say what the internet was doing to humanity, and they apply their findings spiritually to determine if the outcomes could be beneficial to Christians. I understand that the world is not the best place to look for information, but the church tends to shy away from subjects like psychology and sociology. This is understandable, since these are two of the most corrupted fields of study, but the problem with avoiding it completely is that now most people don't know how to fight it. Interestingly enough, many of these authors approached their work sincerely and actually, accidentally arrived at solutions that were more biblical than some sermon outlines I have heard. It bears record that true science aligns with the Bible.

That isn't to say that I didn't reach Christian authors at all. I went looking, and the results were startling. Out of all the research I found about the internet, cell phones, smart devices and social media, I only found one book by a Christian author, and it had been written in the last year. I found a few other sources about television that applied to the modern age, but in reality, there was not much there. There is a noticeable absence of Christian resources that discuss the internet, cell phones, and social media.

I grew up inside the internet. I signed up for Facebook in seventh grade. I got an Instagram in college to keep up with my friends. When I wasn't gaming online, I was watching videos about it on YouTube. I lived and breathed through the household dialup connection, and when I finally got a smartphone, it was a relief that I didn't have jump from wi-fi hotspot to wi-fi hotspot anymore. I didn't start writing this as an outsider looking in. I wrote it from being raised in the culture brought about by the internet and seeing that it did affect my walk with God, but not being exactly sure how.

That is how this whole work started. With one, backwoods hick preacher from Kentucky who never graduated from high school. And even though he was a fool in the ways of the world (I Corinthians 1:25), he was 20 years ahead of the department heads of Harvard and MIT who have spent their lives studying this particular subject. It would seem, that the wisdom of God, contained within the Bible and given through walk with Jesus Christ jumps the gap and lets the rest of the world come in behind to fill in the seams.

This book will not be new to some people. It is going to tell you what you already know, based on studying your Bible, walking with God, and working with people. This book is designed to tell you the why. It is written to explain the concepts though a biblical lens and help Christians maintain a walk with God in a rapidly changing world. It is not written to give a specific list of things that are good and bad. If that were the case, it would be outdated before it was finished. In fact, it already is. After I finished writing, I realized that I never once mentioned TikTok, which is now one of the biggest social media platforms in the world. But that isn't the point. The point is to explain why certain features cause you to react in certain ways so that you can take these concepts and apply them to whatever comes down the pike next. This is written to help you understand how the internet changes you so that you can prevent it from damaging your Christian walk. The goal is to explain why.

> *Oh soul, are you weary and troubled,*
>
> *No light in the darkness you see*
>
> *There's light for a look at the Savior,*
>
> *And life more abundant and free...*[1]

1 *Turn Your Eyes Upon Jesus* | Helen H. Lemmel | Words: Public Domain

TABLE OF CONTENTS

Introduction

Genesis 3:1 – Now the serpent was more subtil than any beast of the field with the LORD God had made…

II Thessalonians 2:8-12 – And then shall that Wicked be revealed, whom the Lord shall consume with the spirit of his mouth, and shall destroy with the brightness of his coming: Even him whose coming is after the working of Satan with all power and signs and lying wonders, And with all deceivableness of unrighteousness in them that perish; because they received not the love of the truth, that they might be saved. And for this because God shall send them strong delusion, that they should believe a lie: That they all might be damned who believed not the truth, but had pleasure in unrighteousness.

I Timothy 6:10 – For the love of money is the root of all evil: which while some coveted after, they have erred from the faith, and pierced them selves through with many sorrows.

It is undisputed within the premillennial, Bible-believing circles that the world will grow more and more sinful as the rapture of the church approaches. The Bible describes the moral condition of mankind at the second coming of Jesus Christ after the tribulation as having degraded to meet that which was prevalent during the days of Noah and Lot (Luke 17:26-29). With the Scriptures in mind, the sinful decline of this world should not come as a shock to any active reader of the word of God. While the specific instances will grieve the Spirit of God in the heart of a Christian, in a morbid sense, it can also be seen as encouragement that the end of the age is approaching and that the "countdowns getting lower every day!" But what has remained somewhat ambiguous throughout the Church Age is not what the world will become, but how the god of this world will direct it into that state. While the world is incredibly vile, corrupt, ungodly, etc., we still have a little ways to go before we get to the sins of Sodom are dominant on a global scale.

The Bible has long warned of the coming moral decay, but it seems that now, it is doing so at an accelerated pace beyond what any Christian may have ever predicted. To state that the world is changing in any other manner, such as that a Kingdom is continuing to grow, and will continue until all the world is converted demonstrates a total lack of biblical knowledge and refusal to define sin through a biblical context. The greater question to be dissected is not what the condition of man is or will be (although this certainly is profitable to discuss), but how did humanity reach this position? We may be commanded to be "simple concerning evil" (Romans 16:9), but we should be experts in preventing ourselves from partaking in it. This issue should be at the forefront of the mind of every Christian. The reason behind this assertion can be explained through two main points of discussion.

The first of these is that there is a spirit that is driving the course of this world in a very specific direction, and the majority of the lost souls in this world are under its direction without their awareness or consent. In order to evangelize a lost soul, a Christian must be able to empathize with the condition of the sinner to show that the love of Christ is able to reach any that will call on him (Revelation 22:17). Empathy is key during personal work, and nearly all sound winning is done through one-on-one personal work. It may come after a great deal of plowing and watering by the Word of God, preaching, or personal witness, but in the majority of cases, the conversion of a sinner requires a one-on-one conversation to help make sure the lost person knows what they are doing and to help provide assurance of salvation. During that time, empathy and compassion from the soulwinner are critical. It helps to eliminate the gap between what a lost person believes a Christian is and who they are, showing them that salvation is attainable for a "whosoever" just like them.

The second reason for a Christian to consider the spirit of the age is to make a Christian consciously aware that no man is immune from the driving spiritual forces that encompass the masses with which he interacts on a daily basis. No man can live in this world in such a totally sanctified manner he is entirely immune from the spiritual influence that society has on his walk with God. Ephesians 5 talks about the battle and no Christian is so strong in their walk that the world around them goes down without a fight. Our culture permeates every detail of our daily interactions through subconscious transactions that we are not even vaguely aware of. While any born-again child of God who is serving God and seeking to grow in their walk with Him knows that the constant influence of the world on their life does impact their walk with God, if they do not properly understand the methods Satan employs to hinder a Christian's spiritual walk, they will fail to maintain that walk. In fact, given the nature of the current deceptions enveloping the world, it is entirely possible (and fairly common) for a saved Christian to be totally deceived as to the condition of his walk with Christ. It is paramount for a Christian wishing to develop and maintain a healthy walk with Jesus Christ that they comprehend the spiritual devices the Devil will use to hinder this walk (II Corinthians 2:11).

Through ages past, bold, bloody tools such as inquisitions, crusades, and revolutions have been used to suppress the influence of the Bible. While these tools are still used today in some parts of the world, these are not prevailing methods used against the vast majority of modern Christianity, especially against Christianity in America. These are highly aggressive means that have easily understood effects and implications. But Satan, in staying true to the subtlety of his nature (Genesis 3:1), has in these last times unleashed his most powerful weapon on humanity yet. This weapon, which is both prevalent in our society and rapidly encroaching on the cultures of every other society on the planet, contains its most lethal aspects, not in its visible, tangible promotion of sin, but in its passive degradation of humanity's natural desire to seek spiritual fulfillment. It is a biblical testament to the nature of Satan as a serpent. When bitten by a cobra, it is not the puncture wound left by the fangs that kills the man, but the unseen venom that slips into the blood which stops the heart and kills the body. The venom he has unleashed on humanity in these last days has spread across the globe and has set in motion the final stages of the darkening of the heart of man. It spreads a new form of chaos across the Earth, to which the antichrist will be uniquely adapted to thrive in, and will eventually contribute to elevating him to his position as the globally recognized god of this world. This venom has infected every continent and now, as it grows beyond infancy and into its adolescence, has begun to demonstrate its lethal power over an unprepared people. And once again, true to the nature of venom, the longer it stays in the system, the more it becomes evident that greater damage has been done than the obvious fang marks in the skin. The lingering effects of this venom will continually weaken the body of the human race until it is unable to seek after any spiritual attention to stop its effects, long before the death of the soul in Hell takes place.

The venom which this book will attempt to illuminate is delivered to the body of the saved and lost alike through the use of a cultural shift brough about by an invention. A key point in this book will be to show that the dangers do not lie in the inventions itself, but in the passive, subconscious, and spiritual impact that the system has on how people think. These two great afflictions seeking to encompass the entire world in these last days of the Church are the invention of the smartphone and the development of Internet Culture. These two influences are each sustained and strengthened by the existence of the other, are actively rewriting the rules of human consciousness and interaction. The fact that humanity is largely unaware of their effects, or that their introduction to mankind is Satanically orchestrated does not detract from their efficacy. The end goal of their Satanic inspiration is to convert the global population into a condition that will allow for the antichrist to set up his kingdom during the Great Tribulation. It has long been the speculation of biblical scholars, ever since the apostle John penned the book of Revelation in A.D. 90, as to how the world would devolve into such a depraved condition as to accept the antichrist as its God and king. The general concept is largely understood, as it is clearly laid out in II Thessalonians chapter 2 and quoted at the beginning of this section (because they received not the love of the truth), but the method of how to make the world not love truth has not been extracted from the Scriptures, as God has not yet seen fit to shine his light on this subject. Since God is bound to uphold the promises given in the Scriptures (Psalms 138:2, Numbers 23:19), he must show those who look to him how to escape the snare of the Devil as he deploys new tactics to ensnare Christians. As this book delves deeper into the inner workings and passive effects of cell phones and Internet Culture, it will become increasingly obvious that they are the engine that drives the acceleration of the depravity of man.

As the reader begins to understand the nature of this engine, it will become clear that the problems do not come from willful rejection of the commandments of God, but through a passive erosion of understanding the workings of the spiritual realm. This is why it is necessary to develop a deeper understanding of the complicated world we live in. By taking into account that all laws given by God were created for the good of mankind (Deuteronomy 6:21), it can be understood that God gives his commandments to protect his people from things that are detrimental to them. An understanding of this concept is crucial to the development of a Christian as it allows one to cultivate their understanding of what sin beyond the explicitly given examples, such as "thou shalt not kill" (Exodus 20:13) . God does not simply pass down arbitrary laws and expect all to follow them for no discernable reason. God, having created mankind and possessing a complete understanding of the inner workings of the human body, soul, and spirit, has directed mankind in a manner that protects him from the harmful effects that sin has on the individual. God directs man not to sin out of a love for man and a desire to prevent man from destroying himself, "as sin when it is finished, bringeth forth death" (James 1:15). The less sin that a man haw in his life, the better he is able to fellowship with his Creator. This brings to light the biblical principal that everything present in a Christian's life must be examined to determine the complete impact that each item, thought or action will have on their relationship with God. The walk with God of a New Testament believer is not determined by a long list of explicit commands such as those rigidly adhered to by the Pharisees of the intertestamental period and the gospels, but in a personal relationship with Jesus Christ as an individual who shows his heart on in our decisions on a moment-by-moment basis. In attempting to maintain a mutually joyful relationship with an indwelling savior who is "of purer eyes than to behold evil, and canst not look on iniquity:" (Habakkuk 1:13), a Christian must evaluate every action, thought, or deed to determine if it is a benefit or detriment to their overall relationship with Jesus Christ, though it may not be initially evident.

Any God-called, spirit-filled, Bible-believing pastor with any hint of a walk with God has, within the last fifteen years, preached at some point against the many vices of the internet. This may have been due to the dangers present online, as well as the problems caused by smartphones. The job of any shepherd over a flock is to identify potential hazards that may harm his sheep ensure that they are protected from them. While the internet and smartphones have indisputably caused damage to local churches through the vast quantity of easily available pornography, the inundation of the liberal news media, and an overwhelming spirit of covetousness are only a few examples of the myriad of undeniably sinful and anti-biblical content contained within the World Wide Web. The easy accessibility of the smartphone to the user at every moment of the day makes the act of viewing, creating, and distributing sinful content easier than it has ever been. This saturates the holder with unbiblical practices that actively hinder the drive of a Christian to walk in purity.

The abundance of sinful content on the internet, made perpetually available through the use of smartphones, is obvious to anyone defining sin through a biblical perspective. However, were the problematic content and convenient availability of the internet the only dangers of this lethal duo, it could be intentionally and successfully circumvented. The internet could, within a small sphere of self-isolating, God-fearing users, be maintained as a tool to assist in the spiritual growth of believers. This could be further enhanced by the perpetual presence of a smartphone, which has been attempted by some Christians who have created a tool that does provide some spiritual benefit. The unfortunate reality of the situation though, is that the passive effects of this system, not the obvious sinful content, reach far beyond the surface and convey a far greater portion of harm to the user. The unfortunate reality is that, as is shown through the metaphor of an iceberg, the actual dangers lie beneath the surface. While some activities may seem to be entirely harmless, they possess their greatest strength in the persistent erosion of the human spirit and mind. This does in no way discredit the evident, despicable sins and their damage done to the saved and lost alike. It is never the intent of this thesis to undermine the reality of the tangible damage done by online gambling, gossip and griping, and a considerable amount of time will be spent bringing these sins to light. The purpose though will be to expound on the greater and more lethal dangers that lie beneath the surface. These passive sins have, in their greater power, enabled these more obvious sinful practices to reach the level of prominence that they have achieved in our society. The goal is to determine and treat the cause, not the symptoms.

The majority of time will be spent analyzing the passive effects that the internet and smartphones have had on lost and saved individuals, as well as the lost world as a collective whole. This will begin with the recent history of communication technology and how it came to be known in its current form. This will include some minor excavation into the effects of each step on the individual, and also on society. Moving forward, it will delve into the operations and inner workings of the internet to show its inherently corrupt nature that feeds on the core of humanity's sinful condition to sustain its exponential and unchecked growth. Having established the foundational working of this system, this book will analyze the active effects of the internet and smartphones, and how they operate in tandem to passively disable the intellectual thought and force-feed emotional decision making. It will then evaluate the present and future state of the human condition from which parallels will be drawn to the biblical description of mankind's moral, emotional and mental condition during the Great Tribulation. Although the Church will not be present for this dispensation, the Church will see the kingdom of the antichrist begin to develop, and understanding the future will help to show the believer what to expect as the rapture draws nearer. An understanding of the coming global climate is also vital to Christians to prevent us from supporting the setup of the antichrist's kingdom, which many "churches" today are a part of. As the purpose of this book is to analyze the effects of these two inventions on the lost and the saved, it will conclude with the basic biblical guidance for the Christian living in the end of our current age, as well as how to navigate the oncoming deluge of societal and technological development, so that as the culture continues to shift and our technology changes, the principals put in place can effectively guide the reader to fruitful walk with Jesus Christ.

Section 1 ⟩ What

CHAPTER 1 ⟩ THE WORLD ON A WIRE

During the Kingdoms of Israel and Judah in the Old Testament, God made one fact abundantly clear to his people: if they continue to break His commandments and serve other gods, He will temporarily banish them from the promised land. This sermon is echoed across hundreds of years and is preached about by nearly every prophet of the age. If the Jews continued to move farther from God, He would send in the King of Assyria and the King of Babylon (both Kings are strong types of the antichrist) to punish the Jewish nation. Despite the warnings of the prophets, the message is largely ignored, and God, being just, eventually had to punish them severely. What is notable about this is that the generation of people who are punished did not become wicked and choose false gods in a matter of months, or even years. It took generations of religious and cultural decay to reach a level of depravity that demanded the intervention of God's divine justice. It is made clear that the continual degeneration of Israel and Judah eventually culminates in their separate invasions, with Judah's occurring much later due to the following God more closely than their neighbors to the north. Eventually, God had to remove them from the land of Judah for 70 years to allow the land to keep her sabbaths, as was required under the law (II Chronicles 36:21, Exodus 23:10-11). The importance of this allegory lies in the fact that the people did not change quickly. The unrepentant sin of generations of Israelites eventually filled up the limits of God's longsuffering. It took 490 years of Israelites skipping the land's sabbaths to amass a debt of 70 years of rest, which was eventually paid in full.

This brief excerpt in history bears a great deal of relevance today in understanding the Lord's dealings with mankind.

In order to understand the impacts of Internet Culture and smartphone use on humanity, it is vital to understand the history of communication technology. This foundational work must be laid because, as in the case of the Jewish kingdoms, the world as a global society did not develop a universal plan to end up in the condition we are today. A study of how communication methods have changed over time shows that the core mechanics of the technology have subtly degraded the quality of information provided, which has in turn altered how the people who consume it think.

Once free from the grip of the Dark Ages, European culture was able to begin developing into an industrial machine that fostered an environment fertile for invention known as the Enlightenment. As it continued to progress throughout the fledgling years of the modern era, the drive to interact with other people planted the seeds for the progressive development of communication technologies. Little did humanity know that these seeds had been planted by Satan to direct us to a desired end, and that these seeds would produce such a bitter fruit as we find ourselves subsisting on now. As Satan is the god of this world (II Corinthians 4:4) it would be foolish to assume that his machinations for the total deception of the entire world did not begin to root into the hearts of men until the 20th century. He has labored continuously in the realm of communication technology to utilize it for his own will and has quite successfully contorted for his greatest purpose: the introduction of his kingdom to the whole world (Revelation 13:3.)

Each major technological breakthrough in the realm of communication will be evaluated in terms of what it produced and how that specific invention altered the minds of the world. While not abundantly clear at the time, the changes that each development brought about to society are clearly visible in hindsight when viewed through a biblical lens, and also with an understanding of the current state of affairs. The past trends in technology predict the future outcomes to a high degree of accuracy, as well as the aspects of technology that will be developed in the future. These trends also prove that, while every generation claims that people have changed for the worse, this complaint is not solely the favorite pastime of the elderly. The information provided will establish that the qualities which contribute to a sinner's need for salvation as a Christian's spiritual growth are declining. This assertion is supported by empirical scientific data that has been collected across generations, which will be explored in a later chapter. The important feature to note is that Satan has gradually corrupted the human condition over the last 300+ years by progressively weakening each generation spiritually with new technologies, and then using the ground he has gained to introduce new ideas that serve his cause.

It is important to note that these inventions are not inherently evil, nor is it sinful to use them (Romans 14:14). If one takes the stance that, since technological development can have negative effects on a person, then all forms of modern convenience should totally be avoided at all costs, then that would indicate that biblical Christianity would need to resemble the approach taken by the Amish, who are not known for their evangelistic nature. Jesus, when praying for the disciples and also the Church when he went to Gethsemane, prayed not take them out of the world, but that they would be able to walk with God despite being in the world (John 17:15, I Corinthians 5:9-10). Christians are commanded to be aware of the devices that the Devil uses to influence them so that they can become aware of the spiritual implications and adapt to the circumstances given to them so that they might please God in a better manner. This prevents Satan from gaining an advantage over the Christian with these devices, as per II Corinthians 2:11.

THE PRINTING PRESS

The Printing press may be the most historically significant invention of man since the development of written language. Developed around 1440 by Johannes Gutenberg (Powers, 2010, p. 131) the printing press fundamentally altered the course of history in Europe. The general understanding is that this invention made the production of books easier, faster, cheaper and more accurate, ultimately making them more accessible to the common people, facilitating a cultural explosion of knowledge that kickstarted The Enlightenment. While this is true, it glosses over several key factors that underlie this statement.

Until reading became a key factor in the daily life of the common man, all information had to pass from person to person orally. The lack of literacy in society meant that the most impactful words came from an auditory source because it was the only source. The reliability of the information depended entirely on the reputation of the speaker and the circumstances surrounding the delivery. It also explains the slow rate of theological development of the early church, as most of Christianity depended entirely on words that they had heard preached and could remember to deepen their understanding of the heart of God. The only method for delving deeply into the words of God was through an extensive education to become literate, and then the dangerous, lengthy, and expensive procurement of a Bible. This was largely unavailable to most of humanity at the time, and the result was a general inability to thoroughly exposit the Scriptures in a doctrinal manner by the common man.

The difference in auditory and literary cultures is expounded upon in depth in Marshall McLuhan's work "The Gutenberg Galaxy," where he typifies these cultures through the example of European and African children when he states "Whereas for Europeans, 'seeing is believing,' for rural Africans reality seems to reside far more in what is heard and what is said" (McLuhan, 1962, p. 19). It is key to understand the intended meaning of this statement. A society in which there is little written culture places more importance on spoken words, while a literary culture places more importance on written words. This moves the focus of the Scriptures from the preaching of the words, spoken by men, to the studying of the words, literally as they were preserved by God. It is much more profitable to grow your relationship from the source (the Bible) than it is through another man's exposition of those words (preaching). The written word helps keep the speaker in check since anybody with a Bible can examine his theology and determine if what he is saying is truly of God.

The greatest impact of this was that a deeper understanding of the words of God facilitated a much deeper and more theologically correct walk with God. This is reflected best through the preaching of Jonathan Edwards. Widely regarded as one of the greatest preachers in American history, he deployed little to no oratory skill in his delivery of sermons, often reading them verbatim from his notes. The driving force behind his preaching (aside from the obvious intervention of the Holy Ghost) was that he "read his sermons, which were tightly knit and closely reasoned expositions of theological doctrine" (Postman, 1986, p. 55). This comprehension of the Scriptures was only made possible by his fervent study of the word of God. It was a fervent study of the word of God by Martin Luther that resulted in his eventual conversion to Jesus Christ in a Catholic monastery and dealt a blow to the power of the Catholic Church (Ruckman P. , The History of the New Testament Church, Volume 1, 1982, p. 472).

While the invention of the printing press was an overwhelmingly positive event in the timeline of humanity, there is nothing that the Devil cannot manipulate to further his own agenda. Gutenberg's Bible brought about a revolution in public literacy in Europe by reducing the amount of time and money required to procure a Bible, allowing the supply of Bibles to catch up with the demand. Since two of the major blocks to achieving Bible literacy were now eliminated, a greater proportion of the population could now undergo the training to become literate and therefore be able to read the words of God. Literacy, though, is not limited to the ability to comprehend a single written volume, but an entire written language, in which anything can be written. As quickly as Bibles could be produced, so could everything else. Important textbooks on physiology, medicine, and mathematics provided the public with a greater understanding of the world around them. The downside to this is that literature could also begin to heavily influence culture in favor of those who the world determined to be the greatest writers. False teachings, frivolous information, and smut could also be produced. In time, human nature would prevail, and would set up over itself the basest of men in its pantheon of great writers. Over the years, the battle for control of the human consciousness would wage between the great philosophers, theologians, and creative writers, but none would anticipate the damage that would be done, not through the devolution of man's religious adherence, but the evolution of the means of communication.

THE NEWSPAPER

The newspaper in America entered the scene with a dramatic flair of fury, justice, and dedication to the public. It is now exiting the stage in an awkward, embarrassing shuffle that is mercifully hidden beneath a smothering cloak of irrelevance. Although the first American newspaper was founded in 1690, the importance of the newspaper agency in America did not become apparent until the embers of revolution began to grow in the hearts of the soon to be American public (Tebbel, 1969, p. 35). A key element, which will be discussed in Chapter 2, is that this institution is founded on rebellion against authority in the name of public good. Newspapers became a mainstay of American life, although they did not begin to override the influence of the book until much later in the 19th century.

The most significant impact of a newspaper comes in its functional contrast to that of a book. An informative book presents a thought and then establishes that thought through a logical progression across, usually, hundreds of pages. Fictional works establish themes that are echoed throughout their stories that tie the entire novel together and form a cohesive thought. Depending on the story or concept being explored, consistency and logic must be maintained across the entire medium. A failure to do so will cause a contradiction than can undo the premise of the author or confuse the reader.

Newspapers are much shorter. Articles can explore events or thoughts through only a few pages at the most. This means that an idea must be expressed, supported, and concluded in less than ten percent of the length of an average book. No sources need to be named in a newspaper unless they are direct quotations, and the authority of the speaker in that field is rarely established fully. The key difference is that a newspaper is published on a bi-weekly, weekly, or daily basis, meaning that the work put into these articles cannot involve a significant amount of scrutiny or iteration. Books often represent the culmination of a lifetime of work and study while newspapers reflect the daily happenings, with little reflection deep enough to demonstrate importance.

This difference cannot be overlooked. The change represents a decline of the attention span of the reader as they move from long, logical thoughts to quick, emotional expositions. The daily news must be printed "on the daily" to stay current with whatever happened yesterday. Putting a considerable amount of time and effort into an article would constitute a substantial waste of resources as it will be washed away in the swathe of news that will be reported on in the next 24 hours. This also requires a much more emotional marketing approach, since a book needs only to sell once and can gain traction based on its merit. A newspaper must sell itself on a daily basis. Books are often purchased as part of a logical conclusion, based on a reader's enjoyment of a certain style, subject, or author. A book can be researched, recommended, vetted, and then purchased. Prior to purchase, a newspaper can be none of these things, and therefore must grab the attention of the passerby and convince them through a single headline that they are worthy of being purchased. While research can be done to determine the trustworthiness of a publisher or journalist, the daily paper becomes outdated 24 hours after being printed, and only allows for a much less informed decision to be made.

With the decline of intellectual investment, there comes an expectation in the decline of the return. The motivation for purchasing these smaller quantities of information must stem from emotions rather than logic. The daily news is generated perpetually, and by not purchasing it, you run the risk of having information that is a day behind the rest of the world that did purchase the paper. And so, the motivation for reading is altered from a desire to understand to a fear of being left behind. When this is combined with a gripping title and the idea that it requires much less time to be invested from the reader, the emotional hook is set. Logical readings were pushed gently aside for the emotional sustenance of the daily paper. As was discussed before, time limits what we are able to do in a day. When one item begins to require more time, that time must be taken from something else. The combination of the decrease of logical content and increase of emotional content has led to a passive decline in the intellectual capacity of the literate public. After all, you are what you eat, and it is much more tempting to fill up on junk food.

THE TELEGRAPH

The telegraph and the newspaper serve two very different purposes, and although the actual outcome likely varies greatly from the effects intended by the inventors, both have fulfilled their unique roles as communication technologies. The telegraph provided the world with a method of communicating instantly with any person within a reasonable distance of a telegraph station. This effectively eliminated the concept of space and time in regard to the spread of information (Postman, 1986, p. 66). Both space, the distance between two parties, and time, the duration it would take to transport that information, provided a massive constraint on the flow of information and ideas. When an event transpired, a messenger of some sort, be it a merchant, traveler, or common man, would have to record or remember the details of the event, and then they would spread it along their travels to the individuals with whom they would decide to share it with. Up-to-date information could only spread across short distances, and the longer that it took for that information to reach the destination, the less likely it was to actually be relevant. Communicating ideas happened in niches of society, and gossip at a public gathering place was the most reliable source of information from abroad. Both time and space served to dull the allure and potency of faraway news.

Until this point, newspapers would report only information that had relevance to the local inhabitants, or that was significant enough to bear an impact on the public despite its age and distance. This could include events such as the succession of a king or the start of a foreign war (Tebbel, 1969, p. 34). Building on the implications of the newspaper that were discussed in the last section, the invention of the telegraph served to exacerbate the nature of the content provided. An industry that thrived on emotional material was previously contained to sourcing its information from a localized population, and only so much reportable drama can happen in a sleepy town. With the increased availability of new and salacious information, celebrity gossip was born. It should be simple to deduce that an emotional industry would begin to immediately flourish when presented with the ability to grasp at emotionally charged material from all over the world. This unfettered flow of information began innocently enough, but rapidly decayed into a pointless flow of completely useless information. Henry David Thoreau commented on this when he stated "We are eager to tunnel under the Atlantic and bring the Old World some weeks nearer to the New; but perchance the first news that will leak through into the broad, flapping American ear will be that Princess Adelaide has the whooping cough" (Thoreau, 1949, p. 49).

Thoreau was dead on point with this observation, as the American public is still fascinated with the lives of the British Royal Monarchy, the details of which are entirely irrelevant to the life of any person who is not a citizen of Great Britain. Based on the current political position of the royal family as national figureheads and little more, the impact that their opinion, even on the average British citizen is tangential at best. To the American, their impact on daily life is roughly the same as that of a mascot for a team that you like but don't follow that closely. Consider momentarily how knowing the gender of Duchess Kate Middleton's next child the day after she knows it herself contributes any meaningful impact to the lives of the American public beyond giving it the ability to discuss the existence of this fact.

This also introduces another important concept which will be explored later, which is that the availability of a thing contributes massively to the draw that it will likely have on a person. The telegraph eliminated space and time, and with it, it "made irrelevance relevant" (Postman, 1986, p. 67). To quote directly from him, "What steps do you plan to take to reduce the conflict in the Middle East? Or the rates of inflation, crime, and unemployment? What are your plans for preserving the environment or reducing the risk of nuclear war... I shall take the liberty of answering for you: You plan to do nothing about them. You may, of course, cast a ballot for someone who claims to have some plans, as well as the power to act. But this you can do only once every two or four years by giving one hour of your time, hardly a satisfying means of expressing the broad range of opinions you hold...The news elicits from you a variety of opinions about which you can do nothing except to offer them as more news, about which you can do nothing." (Postman, 1986, p. 69)

The invention of the telegraph ultimately served to help cheapen the quality of literary material that people could consume. People began with books, which produced The Enlightenment,

The Philadelphia Church Age, and The Great Awakening. They then moved to newspapers since they were easier to read, shorter, more entertaining, and always up to date, thanks to their daily printings. By consuming a lower quality material that had been made readily available to the public, people began to crave this over the rich, nourishing information provided in books. The telegraph allowed for newspapers to gather information regarding irrelevant events, making their product consist of the most scandalous information they can find, with considerably less tangible value to the reader. While technology has been evolving, the quality of ideas that it has been transmitting has been steadily declining.

THE RADIO

From the era of The Enlightenment until the invention of the radio, the developed world was largely a society of readers. Following the invention of the radio, that fact remained, but introduced an additional channel for information to flow through. The information being funneled to the public from journalists was now delivered through visual means, like the newspaper, and audible means, being the newly minted radio. The implications here are more impactful than what may initially be apparent. Our literature-based society places more emphasis on information that is written than information that is heard. We trust the accuracy of written information because written information is established on a physical document that can be compared to other documents. It is permanent, and the thought progress of the writer can be analyzed in depth over a long period of time. This leads to dissection and analysis, determining the foundational accuracy.

Spoken words are much more difficult to break down. Once words have been spoken, they only exist within the limited memory of the hearers unless they are transcribed verbatim, in which case they become written words. Analyzing a speech for logical consistency and accuracy in real time is nearly impossible. Recollecting the exact wording is equally unlikely. This makes speech, as a medium, much less reliable as a source of accurate information due to its nature. This is why God chose to preserve his words physically in the form of The Holy Bible, rather than choosing to pass the information down verbally through storytelling like so many cultures do, or even audibly from Heaven to each believer (II Peter 1:19.) It also explains why Bible preaching is the most spiritually effective way to preach. The power of the words spoken comes from the written words of the Bible in the laps of the hearers, and it allows the Holy Spirit to confirm the validity of the preacher in real time as he delivers the sermon.

The invention of the radio allowed for news to be spread to large groups of people at a fraction of the cost that a newspaper could. Radio stations would broadcast their signal over a wide area, and anybody who has a radio and is in range can tune in and hear that signal. This was incredibly problematic when it comes to making money, because, after all, there is no way to charge people and make money off of a system that, due to its nature, must be made freely available to the public. Since the newspapers had already changed their primary source of income from subscriptions and sales to advertisers (Tebbel, 1969, p. 125), the source of revenue for radio stations was settled before the invention was even completed. Radio stations had to be fully funded through means of advertising. This means that the foundation for sustaining the existence of public radio is based on impressing a spirit of covetousness onto the listeners. Advertisers will only fund the ads if the return on investment is anticipated to be profitable. The radio has profitably executed this business model from the day of its creation until now, and lives on in spirit through the inventions following it. It cannot be overemphasized that the funding behind all freely accessible media in production today is advertising. Commercialism, consumerism, and covetousness are the gearbox of the modern communication machine.

The Television

"Television is the strongest drug we've ever had to dish out. Maybe that's why our hands shake a little when we take the cork out of the bottle, but we'll get over that." (Tungate, Adland: A Global History of Advertizing, 2013, p. 31). These words were stated rather bluntly by a man by the name of Leo Burnett in 1949. Burnett was an advertising kingpin who was notable for his work in propaganda during World War 2. Mr. Burnett understood a very basic principle of television, and that was that it was unlike anything else humanity had ever dealt with. As opposed to every medium that came before it, television was not based on words, but pictures. Every spoken word now had an image to provide context, with the context bearing greater relevance than the message. Modern society had moved into thinking with their eyes instead of their minds.

Until now, the majority of intellectually significant information was read or heard and had to be processed mentally. The words relied on their own weight to be stimulating, and the reader had to exert a mental effort to process all of the information into a cohesive thought. The radio forced you to use your imagination. The television did all of the imagining for the viewers. A producer could provide an image that would frame the information in whatever context he wanted to. This would allow him to manipulate the viewer to arrive at whatever conclusion that the producer wanted them to, before the information was even fully given. The ultimate result is that it caused the mind to relax and allowed the television to do all of the thinking, or, in its own words, programming for them.

The introduction of the screen to the world has allowed for all information to be framed, quite literally, in a different light. Cognitive studies have shown that information that is read from a digital screen is processed in a fundamentally different way than information printed on a physical piece of paper (Carr, 2010, p. 90). A book, once printed, can never be altered without damaging the pages or doing a considerable amount of work to remove or obscure the ink. Because of this, our brain assigns a greater level of depth and credibility to the work, since blank pages have been permanently altered to present the information given. This is all further confirmed through the senses of touch and smell, as paper is a physical item with specific characteristics. Books and papers also carry direct monetary links, as they must be individually purchased and preserved until they can be read. All of these concepts are grounded in a physical item that is unchanging.

The television is none of these things. A single screen displays all the information that can be channeled through it, be it sports, movies, the news, family videos, or sitcoms. All information is expressed in a visual picture and audible words that fade instantaneously and can be replaced in the blink of an eye with anything else being broadcasted. Televised information has no permanence and only engages the senses at the moment it is perceived. Mentally, your brain subconsciously interprets this as information that is less reliable.

Unlike viewing an event in reality, watching television totally neutralizes all information presented. Serious, life-altering news is portrayed through the same medium as cartoons, the NFL, and Tide commercials. As was discussed in the section on radios, there was initially no way to limit who could receive broadcast signals, so all of the revenue had to be drawn from either donations, advertising, or paid subscriptions. The subscriptions were a set amount that watching the programming costed every month, meaning that the primary goal of the broadcasters would be to addict you to the product. The more you watch, the more expensive their ads could be.

The need to present advertisements meant that, no matter how serious the information was that was being presented, it would have to be intermittently interrupted by a word from the sponsors. Unlike information presented in a book or newspaper that was paid for initially with a purchase, the information distributed by a television had to be paid for passively by advertisers. It is like being able to have a book for free but every other page you have to read an article about McDonalds. There are two major effects that this has on the human mind.

The first is that it breaks down the cohesive thought process that is presented to the viewer. No information presented can be longer than the time spent between the commercials. An idea must be presented, defended, and concluded in only a short amount of time. If it must span the gap of a commercial break, the concept must be reintroduced. This programs the viewer to try to comprehend complicated issues in short periods of time and assume that this is sufficient to reach the appropriate conclusion. The ugly reality of this is that providing a spin on information is now easier than ever. News anchors can introduce a topic, explain it in the way that they want to interpret it, and then close the argument without fully expounding the idea. If the argument is based on faulty information, follows an incorrect logical sequence, or lacks a reliable source, there is not enough time for the viewer to break down the fallacies of the ideas before being distracted with the reminder that some departments store has started their mid-spring sale with fashion for the whole family. The ability to present information in this manner is due entirely to the format in which the information is presented in.

The second effect is that all information presented is emotionally equated to the context in which it is presented. Since television must include frequent advertisements to maintain its revenue, any information presented in any light is interrupted frequently with emotionally based advertisements. As we will explore later, emotion is the most effective way to ensure a lasting mental effect on a consumer (Postman, 1986, p. 60). This means that each commercial break bombards the viewer with different ads to emotionally draw them to their product. The lasting effect of this is that each television show, which is highly emotional in its own right, straps the viewer down and launches them through an emotional roller coaster. Too much of anything is a bad thing (also know as excess, Matthew 23:25,) and when that thing is emotional response, too much of desensitizes the viewers. This is why all advertising, programming, movies, etc. has to constantly grow in intensity. The TV brain has to constantly consume content that is darker, grittier, funnier, sadder, and/or angrier than ever before because programming grounded by reality no longer stimulates it the way that it used too. As each company, be they advertisers or programmers, tries to raise the bar, they all make it much higher than what reality can keep up with. As the brain continually tries to reach each bar, it becomes more emotionally exhausted. The result is that, in the end, everything viewed on television gets brought to the same level of triviality that is still much more entertaining than real life.

Television, like all forms of media before it, changes the way we interpret information due to the nature of how it presents information. This is a critical concept that must be understood. The greatest influence that television has had over the world is not in that it glamourizes sin, thrives on covetousness, or brings the culture of the world into the home of the viewer (Pyle, 1792, p. 7). These are all serious problems, but none so great as the fact that television, although seemingly stimulating, subconsciously dulls all the information that it feeds to the viewer due to the manner in which the mind absorbs and processes the information. The television is, in its most basic form, a pair of sunglasses that makes the world that comes through it a little bit darker. The information is less informative, less developed, and more emotionally charged than anything before it.

ANALYZING THE PROGRESSION

These five inventions: the printing press, the newspaper, the telegraph, the radio, and the television have all fundamentally altered the manner in which humanity communicates over the past 500 years. The key to understanding how this has changed the world lies in understanding how the human mind has changed the way it understands information. This will allow a Christian who is actively trying to live independent of the influences of this world to understand the obstacles in their way to spiritual growth.

The Enlightenment began because of the new availability of books to the common man. Books fundamentally altered the cognitive process through which the public consumed information, creating a much more logical population that was able to process long progressions of deeper information. Much later, time spent reading books began to be shared with time spent reading the newspaper, which was only able to provide information in shorter bursts that had to constantly appeal to emotion on a daily basis. Emotional gratification, rather than cognitive engagement, was the only way to keep sales up. The newspaper served its purpose to dull the intellectual capacity of readers and introduce them to a form of entertainment that was more appealing and less helpful. The telegraph amplified the source material of the newspaper, allowing it to enhance the appeal while providing information that was less impactful to the daily lives of the readers. The radio could then come along to present the same kind of information in a way that stunted the impact of the information presented because it removed the physical aspects of the information and only allowed it to be consumed in the moment that it was presented. Despite this, it was still able to enhance the emotional pull on the target audience. This marked a regression in the human consumption of media back to before the invention of the printing press, where information was shared audibly, and not through written words.

Furthermore, entertainment as a selling point was now necessary because in-depth logical progression was, once again, impossible to express. An emotional stimulation was the only way to justify the time spent listening rather than reading. This was exacerbated by the perpetual interspersing of advertising, meaning that information was subject to perpetual interruption and constant decontextualization. Keep in mind, that any subject can be considered entertaining if it is presented in the correct light, meaning that the entertainment (be it fantastical, economical, political, or religious) was for children and adults. This paved the way for the television, which allowed the producers to frame all information with visual cues, allowing the producers to direct the readers to a desired end, rather than allowing the facts to speak for themselves. Furthermore, the continued distancing of information from words on a physical page to solely audio-visual presentations served to dismantle the validity and weight of information provided.

The common denominator in all of these changes is that all of these effects are purely passive due to the nature of the medium through which the information is transmitted. The form that the information took changed, not because man decided to move in that direction, but because it was the most efficient, effective, and lucrative way to use communication technology. If the news media had only reported on biblically sound principals since the creation of the first newspaper, humanity would still decay in its ability to walk with God. This is not because of the content, but because of the way that it is presented. God gave humanity a book to read so that we could understand him, and all media communication since the development of the newspaper has served to hinder our ability to know Him as He is on a subconscious level.

This is not to say that no good could come of these inventions. Many people have come to know Jesus Christ via Billy Graham radio crusades, Chick Tracts, and televised sermons. Each of the listed mediums have successfully lead souls to Jesus Christ. The point that is being made is that the nature of each medium is less effective at conveying complicated issues such as salvation and doctrine. While salvation is a simple concept, it must be handled carefully as to not instill a false sense of security into a misunderstanding sinner. The doctrines in Scripture that govern the growth a Christian are anything but simple to explain and internalize and take a lifetime of study to internalize and display.

The prominent communication tools of each era are less and less effective and accurately transmitting this information in a way that does the source material justice.

It is also prudent to understand from Matthew 7:20, that "Wherefore by their fruits ye shall know them." Fruit is not produced by a tree the moment a seed is planted in the ground. In some cases, after years of growth, watering, pruning, and fertilizing does a tree begin to produce fruit. What is quite unfortunate to human development is that the men who created these inventions had no idea what kind of seed they were planting in the ground when they released their inventions to the world. It is important to understand that none of these inventions are inherently evil, nor is it likely that the actual effect was the intention of the inventor. Many of them intended for their inventions to bring about prosperity, and believed that they would bring about peace on earth.

The unfortunate reality of these inventions is that it is an indisputably documented fact that biblical morality has globally decayed since the end of the Philadelphia church age (roughly 1885 in Europe and 1901 in the United States) (Ruckman, The History of the New Testament Church, Volume 2, 1982, p. 222) Little time will be spent proving that humanity has declined in its generally accepted understanding of accountability to a Holy God, especially as this is a biblical prophecy of the end of the Church Age (II Thessalonians 2:3, Luke 17:28-30, II Timothy 3:13, Proverbs 30:11-14.) While understanding "what" is happening helps a person to escape from the snares in their own life, understanding "why" it is happening will keep them from being ensnared again.

The church has long preached of apostacy within its ranks and the continual decline of the world, but fully expositing on what has caused this has long been the subject of debate. While many sinful practices have infiltrated the churches, the examination often stops short by stating that the cause of this issue is sin. While overt sin is undoubtedly detrimental, Satan has worked his most effective work through passive means, as he always has (Genesis 3:1.) Sin in the church is not nearly as effective as acceptance of sin in the church. By using the influences of communication technology to reduce the analytical capacity of the modern Christian, the devil has been able to passively reduce the scriptural adherence of the New Testament local church. Through years of passive erosion, what was once the great bastion of biblical truth has been reduced to the fully realized age of Laodicea. The correlation of the decline of the church and the rise of communication technologies cannot be ignored.

SIGNIFICANT DEVELOPMENTS

While the world has been connecting itself with wires and signals, it has also been fundamentally changing the way that it communicates with itself. As we are humans that exist within a finite space for a definable amount of time, when we alter the methods of our communication, it does more than enable more of the same communication with each other. Changing the media changes the message, which, in turn, changes the man. The fundamentals of these alterations are outlined below.

THE SPACE BETWEEN US

The invention of the telegraph eliminated the existence of distance in relation to information. People and goods could not move through the wires that spread across the world like wildfire, but ideas and information could. Thought could move at the speed of light across the Atlantic Ocean to connect North America with Europe, enabling conversation to occur at a rate that previously had been entirely impossible. Nothing was preventing the free flow of information from one side of the globe to the other, besides the availability of a person to gather and send it out. Now, events that had little or no bearing on an audience due to their proximity from the consumer could be read about with ease and accuracy. Any information from any corner of the globe could be made accessible.

While the initial intent of this development may have been the coordination of governments or economic prospects, it eventually decayed into its current form in which the transfer of totally useless information dominates. Although this may not have fully manifested itself during the time of the telegraph, electronic communication today provides more trivial information to its end users than anything else. The only information that will have any influence on the actions of most consumers today will be the weather and traffic reports.

While our mental outreach may have expanded, we are still contained to our physical bodies that cannot exist in more than one place or travel with any great speed. The information that we receive expands beyond our social circles, and relates to people, concepts and causes that extend far beyond what we will interact with in person on any given day. Our knowledge expands so far beyond our physical presence that humanity has begun to lose its sense of individuality. The excessive amount of information presented in today's world causes the consumers to become concerned about problems that they are not capable of handling. As such, it removes the sense of impact, consequence, and importance of the individual in limited space in which they exist. The results of this are something called nihilism, which is incredibly detrimental to the human soul and psyche. The development of technology has made the world a lot smaller but has made our individual sphere of influence uncomfortably large and therefore, insignificant. We are larger but spread thinner. The full effects of this, as well as an examination of the greatest culprit, social media, will be analyzed later on.

AT THE SPEED OF THOUGHT

Similar to the concept previously presented, the invention of electronic communication eliminated the travel time of information. The telegraph works on electrical impulses traveling through a wire medium, meaning that the telegraph enabled people to communicate information with no delay. By connecting cities through telegraph lines, global information could inundate the local populace in a way that never had before occurred. Prior to this invention, information could only travel as fast as a person could carry it, be it through a letter or by word of mouth. Regardless of the media, it was constrained to the physical ability of a person to move it from one place to another, and thus all information moved at the rate that a person could. By communicating electronically, the delay caused by a person moving the information was eliminated.

This development contained within itself many unforeseen implications. More information could now be transferred with greater reliability to a larger audience, meaning that people now began to be more connected to the workings of the world as a whole. Time has a way of dulling the impact of information, and largely serves to keep it within perspective of the person receiving it. A message delivered from far away over a long period of time will, by nature, have less of an impact on the daily life of the person receiving it. A person who is separated from the source of this information can do nothing to alter the situation until they are able to physically transport themselves or a response in return. Important information had to be conveyed with the understanding that it would age considerably before reaching its target destination, and that there was little that the receiver could do to impact what had already transpired.

By removing this factor, the receiver of the information could now mentally and emotionally invest a greater amount of consideration into what was being received. But in light of the fact that information could literally come from the opposite side of the world, it meant that people would now be more concerned with information that was of literally no consequence to their daily lives. Removing duration increases impact and pushes the individual from the local scene to the global stage, forcing them to live their life in light of considerably more information.

While an informed populace may seem like an odd concept to consider detrimental to humanity, one must consider how this impacts the individual. By living on a global stage while only being able to cause an impact on a local level (a person's existence is still physically constrained to the location of their body), it introduces an aspect of helplessness, as well as a false sense of confidence in the human mind. The helplessness is derived from being knowledgeable of many global issues that a person can do almost nothing about. Consider the global issues of the day in which the general American populace is moderately informed: homelessness, disease, famine, the coronavirus, the looming threats of China, Russia, Iran, and North Korea, climate change, Brexit, the national debt, race relations, and the progressive gender revolution, to name a few. Each of these issues is highly complicated and cannot even be understood properly without a great deal of investigation. If an individual becomes informed on these subjects, through a life of dedication, hard work, sacrifice, and perseverance, they may be able to have a small impact on one of these issues in the manner that they deem appropriate. They will likely not make a major achievement that has a notable effect in any of these fields, much less provide a suitable, lasting solution.

When this reality is internalized, the human mind becomes much more susceptible to anxiety. There is a vast supply of potential afflictions, any of which could, in their mind, negatively impact their future, their family, or the entire world. Conversely, people do not develop anxiety over problems that they are not aware exist. The impact this new glut of panic-inducing information, as well as the anxiety introduced through social media will be discussed later. The problem that having immediate, worldwide communication creates is that people are too well-informed on issues which they have no influence over.

Furthermore, human nature is unabashedly opinionated. The human mind "first believes, then evaluates" (Holiday, p. 191). Rather than living within the small sphere of influence that the human body is confined to, the outreach of our consciousness into the bountiful supply of world politics, social issues, and current events causes the brain to develop an opinion about everything. This is further amplified by a news media that capitalizes on the creation of new and alarming crises on a daily basis. When the new problem is introduced, the formation of an opinion happens automatically. This will happen regardless of the quantity or reliability of the information presented. All information produces a reaction, and that reaction forms the bedrock of all future information given about that subject. Furthermore, according to a study by the University of Michigan, when contradictions arise that disprove the originally provided position, most people believed the original claims more firmly than those who did not receive a contradiction (Reifler). This is a biblically sound principal that is shown in Proverbs 18:17, where Solomon states that "He that is first in his own cause seemeth just; but his neighbor cometh and searcheth him." The first information presented always seems to be just and creates a frame into which all other information will be placed.

The only way to properly understand the entirety of the matter is to search it out and gather more facts that paint the whole picture. Unfortunately, "Much study is a weariness to the flesh" (Ecclesiastes 12:12), and humanity is not prone to determining the unbiased, absolute truth regarding most matters, much less every matter that they are exposed to, thanks to the marvels of modern technology. The antichrist is able to deceive the world during the Tribulation, not because he is able to create convincing lies, but "because they received not the love of the truth, that they might be saved" (II Thessalonians 2:10). The end result is that everybody ends up with a variety of differing opinions that causes them to disagree with everybody else about something, which has a profound impact on personal pride.

Personal pride that is generated from confidence in an inadequately informed decision (not surprisingly) creates an additional issue. When a judgmental nature combines with an overabundance of shallow information, distrust in authority abounds. Each opinion generated is inevitably in contradiction to the opinion provided of a person who is an expert in that field. As is the case in every scientific, religious, or political field, there are disagreements between the most educated and qualified authorities. When these disagreements are made ultra-visible (thanks to nigh omnipresence of the news media) to the public, the authority and credibility of the dissenting opinion is called into question. When this is combined with the sheer number of divisive issues presented to modern society, the end result that all authority begins to appear untrustworthy. As there are so many officials that are obviously wrong (in the opinion of the opinionated individual), the trust in any authority to be absolutely correct waivers.

The greatest detriment derived from this is that if nothing is absolutely true, the archaic Bible most certainly is not nearly as perfect as it claims to be. The erosion of the concept of absolute authority and truth has minimized the individual's consideration of their inevitable judgement by a perfect and holy God (Hebrews 9:27). All things are drawn into question, and the concept of an unchanging, dogmatic God, drawn from faith and a perfect book, seems just a little bit less of a possibility. Information traveling at the speed of light is not the only factor that contributes to the death of biblical spirituality in society, but it is certainly not irrelevant. And it certainly did not happen by accident.

ALL I SEE IS ME

Communicating with an exponentially larger group of people about an enormous spectrum of issues can be grounded

BENJAMIN CLARK

into a single, unifying factor. All communication technology developed by man, since the invention of the book, has enabled humanity to interact more with humanity. When the prophets of the Bible wrote the words of God, they communicated, though 66 books, the words of God to man. This permitted man, through the mediation of the Holy Spirit, to hold a conversation with God. Man could speak with God through prayer, and God could speak to man through His words that were preserved in a book. When humanity increased its capacity for human-to-human communication, it increased the amount of humanity that individuals could be exposed to.

As is the case with the introduction of anything new, when something is created, it impedes upon the current market of opportunities available within the constraints of time. This ever-increasing supply of manmade content all contains the underlying and unifying trait that it simply manmade. In a world where the competition for attention gets more aggressive on a daily basis, the appeal of spending that precious, limited time reading and rereading a repetitive, incredibly detailed Elizabethan book begins to diminish rapidly. By combining this influence with the massive quantity of useless and appealing information made available to people today, reading the Bible now has steeper competition from a larger crowd of competitors than ever before. This infringement of manmade influence into the spiritual fundamentally alters the thought processes of society. As God's communication to mankind diminishes through mankind's own volition, mankind has begun to ask council and guidance of itself to a far greater extent than ever before. God has, throughout the Bible competed with Baal, Dagon, and Jupiter for the worship and attention of his people. As humans look more and more to themselves to solve their problems, humanity has now placed Mankind on a pedestal the pantheon of false gods.

While mankind may not be openly sacrificing, praying, or calling their own works "Holy Scriptures," it is evident that man has replaced God in his approach to dealing with the world's issues. While in America God may be given a courtesy nod during great disasters, the will of God is never addressed in any broadcast or daily paper provided by any major news outlet in the world. The issues presented are issues that mankind must work together on and solve on its own. This incessant parade of the works of man removes God, and every god, from the picture entirely. The debate is no longer on which god is the true God, because the news media does not push us to look up when looking for solutions. It only holds up a mirror and tells the individual what man is doing to solve his own problems. This makes American a functionally atheistic society. At no point is the wrath or blessing of God, due to the spiritual bearing of a decision, addressed as the true source of any event by any news reporter, senator, sitting president, or most pastors. The spiritual realm has been eliminated in the hearts of the consumer of the modern media, not through a sword, but brutal silence. The more that humanity looks inward in all of its situations, the less it will seek after God. Or any god, for that matter.

When a Christian begins to invest a significant portion of their limited amount of time into the affairs of men, they begin to lose sight of the hand of God. The scriptural backing for this is indisputable. Jeremiah states that "mine eye affecteth mine heart" in Lamentations 3:51. The biblical principal of sowing and reaping comes into effect here, as it is defined in Galatians 6:7-8. Special attention should be paid to verse 8 as it speaks to sowing to the flesh. Any individual who invests a great amount of time in the current events of this life cannot spiritually realign themselves by reading a less Bible in the time that they have left. Paul made this entirely clear in II Timothy 2:4, when he stated "No man that warreth entangleth himself with the affairs of this life; that he may please him who hath chosen him to be a soldier." Nobody is able to please God by becoming entwined with the affairs of men. Furthermore, Jesus Christ gave the commandment to "Lay not up for yourselves treasures upon earth…But lay up for yourselves treasures in heaven…For where your treasure is, there will your heart be also" in Matthew 6:19-21. God promises to keep a person's mind at peace if that person keeps their heart on God (Isiah 26:3).

The goal of the modern media push is to generate emotional investment in the news of the day. Any individual who is entwined with these stories and has "spent their time in nothing else, but either to tell or to hear some new thing" (Acts 17:21) is not committed to spiritually developing their walk with Jesus Christ. These two forces are in direct conflict with each other, and "no man can serve two masters: for either he will hate the one, and love the other; or else he will hold to the one and despise the other" (Matthew 6:24). He goes on to say "Therefore take no thought saying, What shall we eat? or, What shall we drink? or, Wherewithal shall we be clothed?...for your heavenly Father knoweth that ye have need of all these things. But seek ye first the kingdom of God and his righteousness." This command, though given in the context of the Millennial Reign of Jesus Christ, enforces a direct order to seek the Kingdom of God. This command stays consistent throughout the transition of God's focus from Israel to the church throughout the Gospels and Book of Acts. The conclusion of Paul's ministry in Acts 28:31 ends with him preaching the Kingdom of God, which can only be attained through faith (Ephesians 2:8-9). Faith is the most important aspect of a person's spiritual walk, and it is defined in Hebrews 11:1, where it says "Now faith is the substance of things hoped for, the evidence of things not seen" and emphased through Ephesians 6:16, where it says "Above all, taking the shield of faith." The tangible issues of the modern world seek to ensnare the minds of the people with anxiety. To a Christian, this not only serves keep their minds fixed on carnal issues rather than spiritual, but also to cripple their faith that God is in total control of every situation.

CONCLUSION) GOING THE WRONG WAY
A LONG WAY

There is a fierce and painful irony that emerges from the study of how communication technologies have developed since the close of the Dark Ages. This tragedy becomes most noticeably apparent when a biblical perspective is taken, simply because the Bible takes a negative view of mankind and establishes the law of human collapse. This law is that humanity will, in the last days, continue to decline into a sinful state in which the entire world will embrace the sins of the days of Lot and Noah. Noah's days were marked by the destruction of every person in the world, except for Noah and his family (I Peter 3:20) since they chose to listen to God. The days of Lot are marked by open sodomy that was practiced aggressively. The combination of these two influences is a world that is not too far down the road from the one that we live in today. The Scriptures establish that the days of the coming of the Son of Man are marked by a global society (Noah) of openly sinful people (Lot & Noah, Luke 17:26-30).

The great irony of the age is that the nature of communication technology has eroded at the ability of the human mind to communicate effectively with the God who created them. The breakdown of cognitive functionality is fed by the problem it creates. It is self-serving. A population with an inability to think logically will struggle to solve the logical problem of being less logical. To put it simply, the problem feeds itself, and the longer it continues, the more difficult it becomes to solve. This demonstrates why society has exponentially decayed in recent years. Cumulative, or exponential, growth begins slowly, but grows faster due to the fact that it able to use the progress it has made to make progress faster. The most common example of this is long term monetary investment, in which money will accumulate to more than double the value if it is undisturbed for twice as long in an account with constant growth. The dividends of the Devil's investment are now beginning to mature, and his patience has yielded the exact result he is looking for.

To further the irony, the only solution for combating this movement is through the reading and growth in an understanding of the Scriptures, which are printed in a book. The only way back to a true knowledge of God is upstream, against the progress, against what is new, and against the rest of the world. If the world is preparing to worship the devil, then resisting that progress is the best thing that a Christian can do.

When God gave his laws to Israel, he made a very important and highly overlooked statement. Deuteronomy 6:24 says that God gave all of his statutes "for our good always." Every command given by God shows what a sin is and is not. His word bears two key benefits behind it. First, for one, by living according to God's laws, God will bless you spiritually and usually physically. Living by Gods laws keeps you in favor with the One who sustains existence (Colossians 1:17). The second benefit to following the laws of God, as it is shown in Deuteronomy, is that sin is detrimental to your overall quality of life. All sin has passive consequences that reduce your ability to live a meaningful life as God intended it. He wants us to live a life free of sin is free of guilt, bitterness, fear, and worry. A life with less sin in it invites fewer unnecessary problems into it. A life of sin is plagued by envy, strife, pride, and every other biblically wicked mindset that can be listed. All of these reduce the quality of life for the soul of man and his capacity to please God as he was intended to (Jeremiah 5:25, Revelation 4:11). Although a soul may derive short term benefits from sin (Hebrews 11:25), the end of the path is darker than the way God intended for it to be, as he is separated from the God of Light (James 1:17). Thus, as we progress towards the coming kingdom of the devil, the world will, in its biblical and intellectual ignorance, favor its sinful nature over its divine purpose.

The great failing of the church remains in that the majority of its preaching has been to attack the symptoms of moral degradation rather than the cause. Countless sermons have been preached on the wickedness of television, dirty movies, and useless tabloids. These sermons have all been correct in their identification of sinful practices, and the congregations around the world would have done well to heed these warnings with greater care. As was discussed before, the core issue does not lie in the content, but in the medium through which it is presented. The nature of these inventions assaults the God-given faculties of man, and, even if only wholesome content is consumed, the passive damage will continue to gnaw away at the mind of the believer. The Devil does not need to get everybody to stop praying, he just needs to hinder your ability to pray. Only the "effectual, fervent prayer of a righteous man availeth much" (James 5:16). While the Devil certainly has made great progress by making men pray less, his greatest work has come through making the church to pray less effectively. The same goes for reading the Scriptures and any other meaningful spiritual transaction that a Christian can take part in. Satan's most damaging work has been in the decay of the capacity of men to know God. Everything else stems from that naturally.

Ultimately, the only possible outcome for this situation is a societal collapse into a morally defunct and emotionally dysfuntional dystopia. This will result in the instigation of the kingdom of the antichrist, followed shortly thereafter by the second coming of Jesus Christ. A scripturally competent Christian must be aware of the fact that this end is inevitable. This end will come about because it must, and the Bible documents this future since it is authored by the One who inhabits eternity (Isiah 57:15). The condition of the world is prophesied in the Bible, and the Scriptures cannot be broken (John 10:35). The Bible prophesies that each dispensation will end with the failings of mankind, which God must address in a new means of dealing with them. In the case of the church age, the end will come with the apostacy of the local church and the world's acceptance of the antichrist as their god and king (II Thessalonians 2:3-4, Revelation 3:14-22). The church has understood this since John and Paul finished their writings, and there is no point in trying to establish or refute this fact by any author. The key lies in understanding, biblically, where the world is heading, and then viewing the world to determine exactly how it will arrive at that position. The Bible provides the address, and an understanding of communication technology creates the road map.

Satan, the god of this world (II Corinthians 4:4), may have lost his beauty in his fall, but not his wisdom (Ezekiel 28:12). Since before the fall of man, he has had a plan to unite the world under him and receive the worship of all men. His end is foretold throughout the book of Revelation, and he will fulfill his role exactly as the word of God details it. A Christian must, as this time draws near, be aware of the devices that Satan is using to bring about this end. In doing so, a Christian can avoid contributing to the damnation of the human race, point the souls of the lost to Jesus, and validate the credibility of the Holy Scriptures. The worship the Devil desires was denied to him in Heaven, so he has worked diligently to steal worship from as much of God's creation as possible. To achieve this, he would need to ensnare the whole world simultaneously.

This world did not shape itself into its current form by accident. The current decayed condition of the average human mind is by intelligent design of the second most intelligent being in existence. The mental capacity of the human mind for processing truth has been eroded purposefully since the invention of the newspaper. In time, the introduction of the overload of superfluous material from the telegraph pushed the world into an addiction for the next great emotional high. The radio satisfied this need further and took away the mental exercise of reading, allowing the mind to mindlessly consume whatever was fed to it. The television then shaped the thought processes of all information through images and programs. And now, the human mind, fat and weak through a lack of mental exercise and an unbalanced diet of raw emotional content, has set the stage for the successor to television. TV is becoming more obsolete by the minute and will eventually join its progenitors as a bygone set piece from an old era.

We have entered a new phase of this social regression, and that phase is the age of the internet. The World Wide Web is now living up to its heritage. It has brought in, under its now fully fledged wings, the greatest tools of apostasy and sin that the world has ever seen. It encapsulates the most detrimental features of those that came before it and has forged new tools with which the Devil afflicts humanity. The crowning achievement is that the internet is able to do something that nothing in recorded human history ever has before. It has achieved a nigh omnipresence in both the developed and undeveloped world. While Satan has used many tools before, none have had the capability of reaching more than half of the world simultaneously. Studies show, that as of June 2016, more than 50% of the population of the world had access to the internet, and it is likely that more than 90% of the world will have access to the internet through a smartphone by 2025 (World Economic Forum, 2015-, p. 7). The internet is too large to ignore, too impactful to avoid, and most importantly, too deliberate to be an accident.

A thorough dissection of what the internet is and how it sustains itself is necessary to understand exactly what it is doing to the human mind. Exposing the lineage of this invention allows a Christian to understand what to expect from the age we live in. An understanding of how the internet sustains itself is vital to understanding how the internet operated. A further investigation into the financial drivers of this new creation will demonstrate that the system on which the internet relies in order to sustain itself is, at its core, based entirely on love. Although pure in its intentions, this love requires the decay of humanity to survive, as it thrives on a single concept. This love is corrupt. It is the love of money.

CHAPTER 2) **EATING THE HAND THAT FEEDS IT**

As the technological backbone of the modern world has fleshed out to its current form, its source of sustenance has altered greatly. These developments, such as the telegraph or telephone resulted in the formation of corporate entities that were transparent about user costs. It was visibly apparent to the users that in order to use the service in a particular manner, it would cost them a set amount that they would pay to the company. The revenue stream from user to provider was a simple transaction that was understood by all. In the case of the internet, this could not be further from the truth.

In a basic sense, the provision of access to the net by Internet Service Providers (ISPs) is a set rate that is likely delivered in a monthly bill to the user. These companies, such as Verizon or Comcast, do not create the content that the user consumes online. They are simply the messengers that deliver the content to the user. They are digital mailmen. They do not write the letters or magazines that are delivered to the users, they simply ensure that the desired content, once ordered, arrives at the house once the postage has been paid. The types of mail delivered can be broken down into three different groups, which are mimicked by the different types of online content. The three basic types of mail are personal mail, solicited items, and junk mail.

There are also two sources of mail that are significant to understanding the workings of the internet. All of the content on the internet originates from one of these two sources: User-Generated Content (UGC) and Corporate-Generated-Content (CGC). User Generated Content is created by those individuals who use the internet and add to its vast library of information purely out of their desire to create or communicate. Their motivation is entirely personal, not financial. Social media sites such as Facebook, Reddit, and Instagram are the most basic examples of platforms that host such forms of content and are represented as personal mail in the example above. These sites draw in audiences through the allure of being able to create your own content and share it. This may be simple entries, such as posting pictures of food you ate on Instagram or talking about a good time you had with friends via Facebook. The postal service gives the user the ability to communicate with others for the simple pleasure of doing so. These online services rely on people to create their own content for free, just for the enjoyment of sharing their lives with those close to them. While the motives of individuals or accounts created by companies do blur this line some, the vast majority of the content is created by the users for the sole purpose of sharing. This is like personal mail. As individual users grow their online influence, they will often seek to monetize their popularity, which is a concept that will be explored in greater detail later on.

Corporate-Generated Content is generated on all other websites, such as news outlets, online stores, or other services that have moved to online models. As humanity further entwines itself into the World Wide Web, more and more services will be made available online, as marketers will always direct their efforts where they are able to address the greatest quantity of their target audience. CGC is sponsored using either passive or active payment methods, which is where the business model begins to become highly problematic.

Content can be paid for passively, through advertising, or directly, through fees paid by the users. This can be understood through the examples of mail as solicited items and junk mail. Content that is actively paid for is a simple concept and is represented by subscribing to magazines and ordering packages delivered by the mailman. The user sends out a request correlated to a given dollar value, for which they receive the items that they have requested. In the online world, content which must be actively paid for includes sites such as Amazon and Netflix. When a person goes to Amazon.com, they go with the understanding that they are going to enter their credit card information and spend money, which will result in a package arriving at their doorstep in several days. Amazon is able to pay its employees based on taking a percentage of the money derived from these purchases. Netflix allows a user to pay a set amount of money every month for the right to watch as much of the content as is provided on their platform as they want. It like a season pass which allows the user as much access to the park as they would like. There is an understood cost and an understood service.

The opposing form taken by Corporate Generated Content is appropriately represented by junk mail. Junk mail is unsolicited and sent out in bulk at no cost to the receiver. The goal of junk mail is to provide the receiver with information about services or products in the hope that the user will decide to purchase the advertised products. This is basic marketing, and all companies, in some form or another, engage in this practice. Their ultimate goal is to get their message to as many potential buyers in their target audience as possible. This is a gamble, as marketing invests initial costs into paying designers to create the ad and paying the mailman to deliver it to each house in the neighborhood. Their hope is that enough people will decide to make a purchase that the marketing costs are outweighed by the profits of the sales.

This is the model taken on by the majority of websites, and inevitably it has begun its invasion into the two forms of content. This is the driving form of income for every website hosting content that is not either generated for free or actively paid for by the consumer. These sites do not operate for free and must make back the costs incurred from host servers, tech support agents, domain registrations, and a slew of other factors. In order to make back this money without charging the user any fees, they allow for advertisements to be posted on their pages, for which they are paid a certain rate. The sites that operate under this business model include search engines such as Google, Yahoo, MSN, and nearly every news outlet in existence. Any website that has ads for it or hosted on it uses this business model to generate their funding. While this business model is similar to that which has been employed by radio and television for years, the twenty-first century has added a very disturbing twist. This chapter will demonstrate the danger of this business model, as it is the most damaging to the general populace, but by far the most lucrative and accessible.

Much like the history of communication, the operational workings of the content provided on the internet must be understood before delving into the implications that this bears upon the user. This chapter will explore the core workings that drive this machine to demonstrate that these themes are present in virtually all content provided on the internet, and they are not good for you. If any single concept is stressed above all others in this chapter, it should be made blindingly evident to the readers that "...the love of money is the root of all evil."

SHOW ME THE MONEY!

The introduction of advertisement-based revenue stream was originally established in the newspaper. As time passed, and the business model evolved, it became apparent that more money could be made through advertisement than through user subscriptions and purchases (Tebbel, 1969, p. 125). As the potential of this market has begun to become fully realized, the amount of money spent on advertising has skyrocketed. In 2013, the global spending on advertisement was more than $500 billion per year and rising (Tungate, Adland: A Global History of Advertizing, 2013). In 2016, Facebook made more than $27.6 billion in advertising revenue (Vaidhyanathan, 2018, p. 2016).

When the telegraph was made commercially available in 1847 (Kane, 1933), communication to another individual was possible only through physical means such as letters or speaking, and the receiver would be the only person to receive the message. When the telegram came into being, customers would pay a small fee for an operator to translate the message into Morse code, which would be tapped through the wire to the destination, where another operator would translate the message back into English. This was a basic form of UGC that operated much the same as sending a letter via the postal service.

When America upgraded to the radio, it became obvious that there was no way to charge individuals for using the radio as a service. The radio waves could be transmitted over large areas and received by as many people as wanted to tune in at any point in time. There was no way to regulate the signal once it was put out there, and anybody who knew the frequency would be able to listen at their leisure. The radio broadcasting industry knew that it would have to rely on a different form of revenue to maintain its ability to fund programs. This is where advertising began to take the dominant role in media. Since the majority of the funding for the business came from the companies that were advertising on that frequency, the content creators had to be especially careful to cater their content in favor of their advertisers. This meant that information was no longer edited by a person with an idealistic goal in mind (no matter what that particular goal may be), but was edited by a person that made sure that the sponsors were never offended, downplayed, or portrayed in a negative light (Tebbel, 1969, p. 228). This is due simply to the nature of business. Any business that wished to be successful must remain true to the interests of the most financially influential parties. Since media was now ruled by marketing, the purpose of mass communications was no longer to inform the populace, but to please the shareholders. The goal of all media is still to please the largest target audience possible, but this still stems from the need to advertise. The larger the audience, the more money that commercial time can be sold for.

This principal applies directly forward to the working of the internet. Any company that has any web page has a single goal in mind: to make a profit. Some companies sell a tangible resource that you must pay money for to acquire, and their pages are designed to ensure that you spend as much money as possible while jumping through the fewest possible hoops. Some sites will offer some content for free, while other content (the more enticing material) must be paid for. Most websites, including most major news outlets and social media platforms are entirely free. The user pays no fee to access the site, and all of the features are available at no cost. The company will simply put advertisements along the sides of the page, before the video, or along the top and bottom. Just like a newspaper, the content is there, and you just have to thumb through the advertisements along the way.

This business model by nature bears with it many unpleasant implications. Revenue is driven primarily by the amount of traffic that a web page can generate. Not only that, but since all of this information is presented through computers, the data can be collected to determine the success of every single advertisement presented. As these implications are evaluated, it must always be kept in mind that this business model was not the original intent of the inventors of the internet. The original minds behind the internet never intended for it to become what it is today, but they never could have predicted that this is what it would grow into. It is because of the evil nature of corrupt men. The problem is that the most effective way to make money on the internet is the way that is also the most detrimental to mankind. It would seem that Satan has handed humanity a catalyst to its own destruction that he has disguised behind the allure of technological progress. Unfortunately, hindsight is 20/20 and the practices that will be discussed developed as a necessary evil to compete with everybody else who was doing the exact same thing.

TARGET AUDIENCE: ACQUIRED

Computers hold a distinct advantage in terms of adaptability that is unlike any other human invention before them. Computers are able to track, with perfect and immediate reporting, any action that they are programmed to track. Rather than relying on human scribes that (barring divine intervention) commit scribal errors, computers can immediately create reports on data as they provide it. This data can be instantly transmitted back to a central computer that compiles all kinds of data from every computer that feeds it. This data can be as simple as what product you have purchased from an online store. This information is recorded by the website that you purchased the product from, as well as the web browser (Google Chrome, Safari, Firefox, Internet Explorer, etc.) that you used to view the site. For the sake of example, consider only the data that is collected by the browser that is used in the online purchase. In light of the example of the internet being like the mail, web browsers are like the envelopes that mail comes in. The browser does not have any purpose in itself, it simply delivers information to the home.

The difference is that, unlike an envelope, the web browser reads all of your mail. The web browser has now recorded that a specific user has purchased a specific product. It may record that a user has visited a specific page, or that a user has been to that page multiple times. All of this data is recorded and sent to the company that produced the browser.

The difference between web browsers and envelopes is that envelopes must be purchased, while web browsers are free to download. But nothing in the world is truly free, and the companies that code browsers don't create them out of the kindness of their hearts to make the world a better place. It is key to remember that nothing on the internet is free. The developers want, and deserve, to be paid, just like anybody else who works a job. Instead of charging you to download their product, they are able to make money by selling the data they collect from you to advertisers. Internet browsers have a distinct understanding of what a person cares about based on what they spend their time on the internet doing. It is the equivalent of your envelopes reading your mail and then selling your address to companies that you might like to buy from.

If you spend your time on the internet researching used

cars, the resale value of used cars, the durability of used cars, or what used cars have the best safety ratings, your browser stores all of this data and combines it to conclude that you are looking to buy a used car. It then takes that data to companies that sell used cars and advertise online (such as CarMax) and tells them that they know of a potential customer, and they can put their ads on the browser of that *individual* if the seller will pay them a fee. All advertising in every industry intends to advertise, not to the greatest number of people, but to the greatest number of people in their target audience. Members of the target audience are much more likely to purchase a product than a person not inside it. This is why child-themed television networks advertise products geared towards children, rather than the elderly. They want the maximum return on investment. The difference between the television advertising toys on a kid's network and the internet putting ads in a browser is that the internet is a thousand times more effective at determining and reaching the target audience than the television is. Television marketers have to figure out what shows their target audience tends to watch and then put their advertisements where they think that the audience will be. Internet browsers learn about their users and then target their products based on the hard data of what a person has been doing on the internet.

This was how advertising on the internet began, and it has rapidly evolved into a much more sophisticated and disturbing advancement since then. In addition to the hard data collected from online activity, browsers also began collecting metadata. Metadata comes from the words "meta", Greek for "with" and "data", meaning "information". This is additional data that comes along peripherally with the data being intentionally supplied by the user. This is everything from the time of day that the research is being done, to the device used to access it, to the location that the device is at when the data is being collected. This is why a phone can recommend a restaurant to a user based on the fact that the phone has been in that kind of restaurant before, it is close to a restaurant, and it is close to lunch time. The metadata that a person is driving (GPS indicates movement at a high speed), they have not eaten in a while (movement has been consistent for several hours), and they like fast food hamburgers (it has been in two different McDonalds in the last week), can be compiled by the browser in a phone, sent to the company that designed the browser, and then sold to fast-food companies that have their chains set up near where the device currently is so that they can have their advertisements played on the internet radio app that is streaming through the car's Bluetooth sound system. None of this data was ever searched by the individual with the phone. None of it was ever directly typed into the browser. All of it was taken with your permission, but not your knowledge, thanks to the "Terms and Conditions" being too dense for anybody without a law degree to read. Twitter alone collects, corroborates, analyzes, and sells more than 65 points of metadata on each user (Singer/ Brooking, 2018, p. 57). This can be everything from what time of day it is posted, to where it was posted, to who is tagged in it, to who likes it or how many comments it gets. All of it was collected passively from the user and then sold to companies that can find their target audiences as individuals in exact situations.

A chilling illustration of the power of metadata at work can be seen through the practices of an adult dating website, the name of which will be withheld, but is documented in the book *Likewar* by Emerson Brooking and P. W. Singer. This particular website was founded with the direct purpose of helping individuals to connect romantically with other people who are looking to cheat on their spouses. Simply put, this is commercialized adultery. This website looks for specific markers in metadata to time their advertisements when potential clients will be the most vulnerable. Using metadata, they target people, generally businessmen, as they enter hotels and log on to hotel wifi, since it is likely that they are on business travel and away from their spouses. This company understands the nature of temptation and has leveraged it using metadata to profit from weakening marriages. This happens without the person in the hotel ever having an online history of looking to cheat on their spouse. When you add in other factors that can be tracked, such as time spent of other dating sites or the social media profiles of attractive women, the data can determine if a person is likely to cheat before they even know it themselves (Singer/Brooking, 2018).

This has changed the advertising methods from profile-based guesswork to an individualized science perfected through an algorithm. This also means that the consumer-based economy of the first world has expanded exponentially. Marketing is now more effective than it has ever been because it is now more personal than it has ever been. The unfortunate nature of marketing is that it is entirely based on covetousness. Covetousness is discontentment with what you have (Hebrews 13:5), and a desire to obtain it despite what the will of God is for you, at which point the desire becomes an idol (Colossians 3:5). The driving force behind all internet advertisement is an enhanced version of consumerism that perpetually tempts the user with the allure of happiness through more stuff.

THE MORE THE MERRIER

Since website owners now earn money based on advertisements, the question of the hour becomes "how can I make my users see as many advertisements as possible?" This is simply the result of the business model that has evolved over time. The algorithm will determine the appropriate ads to show to the individual, the website owner simply need to get the users to see the ads. Getting information or entertainment to the users is key because that is what keeps them coming back. The underside is that the more they come back, the more money the site makes. This statement cannot be emphasized enough, because this is the business model for every website that provides a service to the users at no direct cost. This includes social media websites, such as Facebook or Instagram, search engines, such as Yahoo!

or Google, and every major news website from Fox to CNN to Huffington Post to Wired. No free content or service is actually free. Even minor services, such as easybib.com or free online music converters all have to make money to support the costs of running the site. Biblically, a laborer is worthy of his hire (Luke 10:7), and a person who will work to complete a task should be paid. What must be understood is that these sites are designed around the purpose of presenting the advertisers with a target rich environment as often as possible.

The best way to ensure that a user views the most possible ads is to design your site to have a large quantity of content that is broken down across as many web pages as possible. Fortunately for these websites, quantity is a lot easier to come by than quality. Social media websites are engineered to encourage engagement. They employ addictive mechanics that draw people back time and again to check their feeds, likes, and comments. This is why websites request that you enable notifications on your phone. Each time a piece of content gets some form of feedback, the site will notify every involved party to remind them that something has happened that they should look at. Each time they return to the site to check the activity, they view more ads, and the company makes more money. On search engines, each time that a search is done, ads litter the sides of the page, luring viewers away from their original intention. By providing tantalizing bits of information, search engines can lead a user down a rabbit hole of interesting information that has nothing to do with the original source. Companies can even pay to have their sites (which may also be funded by ads) appear at the top of a search results page that is related to the original search. Each search engine strives to be the best so that people will use theirs more than the competition's, increasing the money that they can charge for their space (This makes your favorite search engine the new prime time). All news websites know that the best way to increase traffic is with attention grabbing titles, so they write as many of them as possible to beat the competition and increase their own traffic. Just like with newspapers, they have to trigger the emotional response of the readers to get them onto the site.

In the intense fight for the attention of the average internet user, the desire for quality is now negligible. As quantity increases, by default, quality must decrease. A site makes money for each time a viewer views an ad. There is no additional money generated from a person who stares at an ad versus a person who glances at it momentarily, although ads may cycle on the sides of the pages, allowing different companies to vie for attention against each other in some strange form of intellectual combat. Advertisements may pay out a small bonus if a user clicks on the ad, which also sends the browser a message that it has successfully selected a revenue-generating customer.

The bottom line is that those ads are there to sell products, and the winner is whoever can make the most money. It is simple economics. Since this electronic world is funded by human minds that are most profitable when they are frequently diverted, the goal becomes to distract the user as quickly and as many times as possible. Each site has its own method of doing this, but when it comes to the online news media, all content is guided by adhering to three main fundamentals. All articles must be short, emotional, and cheap to produce. This business model is great for making money, but as will be discussed later, is catastrophic to how the human mind perceives and processes information.

YELLOW JOURNALISM 1.0

The inundation of the modern mind with articles rooted in short, emotional, and cheap content is reminiscent of a previous era in the history of American reporting. There are several parallels from this form of journalism to the current state of affairs. It is critical to learn lessons from this dark time in order to avoid falling into the same pitfalls in the future. This bygone age was known as the age of Yellow Journalism, or the Yellow Press.

The age of Yellow Journalism was a time when newspapers began to operate purely on scandal and relied on the sordid underbelly of human nature to draw in the maximum amount of readers (Tebbel, 1969, p. 192). It peaked throughout the mid to late 1800s and ran somewhat into the 20th century. Thoroughly examining the nature of journalism at that time will demonstrate that Yellow Journalism has returned in the form of Yellow Journalism 2.0, and that it may be here to stay this time.

The key driving factor behind Yellow Journalism was the basic appeal to the darker emotional appetites of the human race. Newspapers have always appealed emotionally to readers, especially during the time of the American Revolution where the writing of some key founding fathers galvanized the populace into action by spreading rebellious, anti-British content. This cause was noble in its intentions and drew on wholesome desires to evoke dreams of a brighter future. Yellow Journalism similarly appealed to anger or frustration, but not with the intent to better society in any way. Papers, such as the Denver Post in the 1890s, operated on two main principals. They proclaimed their own self-righteousness as a betterment to the citizens of Denver, and they made sure to attack somebody or something in every printing that they issued (Tebbel, 1969, p. 159). There was no loyalty, only a constant spewing of indignant and righteous fury that allied them with readers against everyone and everything else. They appealed to the prideful nature of humanity and launched baseless attacks in order to draw in their readers as close allies that would continue to support their paper. Charles Dana, editor of the of the *Chicago Sun* and the *Herald* in the mid-to-late 1800s, was noted for giving "'what the great mass of the people' wanted – that is, murder, scandal, gossip and interviews" (Tebbel, 1969, p. 186).

By the late 1870s, the worst of society had begun to climb the social ladder as celebrities simply because they drew on the ire of the general public. In 1871, Edward Godkin wrote a scathing editorial regarding the media coverage of a man named James Fisk to address this very issue. Fisk was a professional conman and socialite whose escapades could easily be highlighted and exaggerated by newspapers for a guaranteed and easy sell. He was reported on for the sake of being reported on, and his daily activities became the fascination of Chicago. Godkin, in a desperate attempt to improve the moral bearing of the city wrote "The newspapers ought to remember that, while for some offenders against public decency and security denunciation may be a proper and effective punishment, the only way of reaching others is not to mention them" (Tebbel, 1969, p. 192). Godkin understood that harping on the poor behavior of others markets self-righteousness. People needs others to radically misbehave in order to feel better than someone. The negative press was emotionally and financially supporting Fisk's lifestyle. Fisk had to misbehave in order to feed the ego of the Chicagoans (which funded the papers), which in turn promoted the negative behavior. The system was feeding itself. Godkin knew that the only way to truly downplay his attitude was to avoid drawing attention to his life. Some people must be punished with silence. His plea fell on deaf ears and Fisk continued to thrive on public attention simply because of his brash, unconventional character and assault against public moral bearings. He lived on as a legend until he was murdered in public during a dispute about the love of a prominent actress.

In terms of format, newspaper articles must be short. While the average length of articles may have varied throughout history, the key factor is that they are much shorter than books. During the earlier ages of American history, America was a nation composed of avid book readers (Postman, 1986, p. 38). Written literature contributed heavily to the development of American culture, resulting in a population that was incredibly well-versed in the greatest literature available of the day. As a result, America began to produce literature in great quantities. Newspaper articles are a stark contrast to books, with its daily articles requiring only minutes of investment. As Yellow Journalism began to thrive, it was able to do so based partially on the length of the articles. The cheap, emotional drivel being churned out by the presses was not based on cohesive intellectual thought, but the emotional knee-jerk reaction of potential readers. In consideration of the nature of the newspapers, it would seem that Yellow Journalism was practically inevitable.

The third defining aspect of Yellow Journalism was that it was cheap to produce. The addiction to the emotional buzz generated by the newspapers began to develop cravings in the human mind. Newspapers created a need and then filled it, which they were more than happy to do. In any free market economy, as the demand increases, eventually somebody will be willing to provide the supply. The market for the news was originally filled on a weekly basis, which was largely due to the technological capabilities of the printing presses. In the late 1700s and well into the mid-1800s, the technology remained largely unchanged and it demanded a tedious and laborious process to produce the papers themselves. When the Industrial Revolution met the presses, the result enabled the editors to generate more content at a lower cost (Tebbel, 1969, p. 94). The ability to produce more addictive material inevitably resulted in the production of additional material, and as was stated before, when quantity waxes, quality must wane. Thanks to the invention of the telegraph, sensational information was available from every corner of the globe and could be obtained with minimal effort. Editors were able to fill the void of actual content by inflating the emotional hype behind each story, thus resulting in a newspaper that told the reader less information, but was much more entertaining to read.

Yellow Journalism was able to thrive due to the ability of men to exploit the developments in communication technology. Were it not for the bolstered mental capacity provided to the American people by their thirst for books, America may well have never escaped the clutches of this emotional cesspool. By roughly the 1930s, Yellow Journalism had peaked and the general public had begun to become sick of the concentrated emotional high being peddled to them. The desire for honest, simple truth began to intensify. This surge away from Yellow Journalism is largely attributed to Adolph Ochs, who believed that people were only buying the papers as they were because there was no decent alternative. He aimed to establish a reputation for quality that would enable him to compete as a better source of information. This moment of clarity brought about the business model of subscription-based newspapers. The new business model asked the citizens to pay a fee to have access to the weekly news as it was produced. Since the competition was no longer to sell each newspaper every day, but to provide the readers a reliable source of information, Yellow Journalism was brought into check. The subscription-based newspapers were now able to sustain a steady income by providing the public cohesive information that was informative, rather than inflated. At this point, the quality of the information could be brought back as the driving force behind a newspaper's marketability, and although Yellow Journalism was never quite dismantled, it did go into remission towards the mid-1900s (Holiday, p. 87).

YELLOW JOURNALISM 2.0

There are two key differences between Yellow Journalism then and now. The advancement of communication technology has given Yellow Journalism a second wind and enabled reporters to gather and disseminate information instantly to a global audience.

The first of these factors is that the printing press has been rendered largely obsolete by the ability to electronically publish information at almost no cost, pushing more and more newspapers to change to a "digital only" business model. The cost of computer memory to store one gigabyte of information in 2009 was roughly 10 cents (World Economic Forum, 2015-, p. 15). To provide perspective on the amount of information that this can contain, a 250-million-word document occupies about

1 gigabyte of storage space. Printed on 8 ½ x11 paper with an average of 700 words per page, this is the equivalent to a 350,000-page book. While there are costs to host information on servers that are accessible through the internet, the quantities of scale demonstrate that printing costs are exponentially greater than the cost of digital distribution. Based on rough printing costs at the time of publishing this book, publishing in print is roughly 56,000 times more expensive, and that is assuming that storage costs have not decreased since 2009 (which they have). At the time of this writing, Google will give you 15 GB of cloud storage for free. What this effectively proves is that the only expenses in journalism today are for people.

The other main factor is that at the time, Yellow Journalism was competing against a highly literate public that intellectually consumed both literature and the press. Modern media has had more time now to drive out the burdensome task of reading books from mainstream society to the point where reading must be enforced in the public school system, albeit relatively ineffectively. The additional inventions of the internet, radio, and television have reprogrammed the human mind to feed more effectively on short bursts of information that are emotionally charged. The modern attention span has been raised on a diet of Yellow Journalism that has completely altered the way that the human mind processes information. The modern mind has never tasted the complicated and bittersweet depths of "real food". It knows only the bloat of highly processed, freeze dried, high-fructose information. The inner working on the effect of the modern technology on the human mind will be examined in depth in a later chapter.

The three main pillars of Yellow Journalism as mentioned in the previous section can now be expressly seen in the modern reporting methods used largely today. All material must be produced quickly, emotionally, and cheaply. The subscription-based model managed to curtail the effects of Yellow Journalism in the early 1900s, but now nearly all reporting is made available on the internet at no (tangible) cost to the readers. Yellow Journalism 2.0 has a much easier audience to conquer that it did 150 years ago and is alive and well in modern society.

TIME IS MONEY

Consider the two possible methods for writing an article on the internet. Option one would be to write a short article with a trivial amount of information and divisive conclusion. Option two would be to write a long article with a large amount of information that explains the nuances of a complicated conclusion using the information provided. While there are many questions surrounding the issues of quality of writing, the reader's attention span, or the available information surrounding the issue, there is only one question that concerns the mind of the highly competitive news and entertainment industry: what makes the most money? All of these questions may peripherally apply to the issue of dollars and cents, but the biggest issue at hand is what has the highest return on investment. This is always the key issue because if a site is not willing to employ the most rewarding strategy, it will be beaten out by all of the competition that is.

If the two options described above are applied to the business model of the internet, option one will beat option two every time for the following reason. On all web pages, advertisements can be placed at the top, sides, bottom, and throughout the article, with the most attention-grabbing advertisements at the top. After all, the top of the page is what will be seen the most, and therefore it is the prime real estate of the advertising world. Advertisements can also be placed at the beginning, middle, and end of videos (which, by default, are set to automatically begin playing when you access the page), and since they include audible and visual attention arresters, are even more lucrative. With all of these advertisements generating money, if a person spends a long time reading, rereading and analyzing a thoughtful article, they are not paying attention to the advertisements on the side. Articles that maintain the attention of the reader and cause them to think begin to dull the allure of the advertisements. Keep in mind that, as was stated before, the greatest allegiance of all new outlets has been to the advertisers, as they provide a greatest portion of revenue to the sites (Tebbel, 1969, p. 125). This has been the case since the 1930s and shows no sign of declining. This means critical readers and effective writers are actually detrimental to the cash flow of a website.

Consider the concentration of the reader. A person who intently reads an article and mentally attempts to block out the ads on the side will be less likely to click on them. If a reporter writes gripping, well worded essay that makes compelling points, they are actually writing a distraction from the main source of revenue of the site. If an article is short, bouncy, and shallow, once the reader reaches the end and mentally disengages from the article, they become susceptible to the flashing, brightly colored pictures of products that surround the content. An article that concludes by leaving the reader deep in thought, considering the ramifications of the presented information on their life keeps them from generating any revenue to the author because they aren't thinking about the ads. And after all, a site with a higher click-through percentage can sell their "marketing real estate" at much more profitable rates.

Good writers being detrimental to reporting may seem counterintuitive initially, but there are many additional factors that support this claim. Good writers must have access to good information. That information must be obtained from reliable sources, which are difficult to locate and even more difficult to verify. Good reporting requires a considerable amount of time, research, scrutiny, and editing. In the age of instant communication, Proverbs 18:17 rings true. "He that is first in his own cause seemeth just", or as we like to say, "the early bird gets the worm." The first report of a scandalous, miraculous, or life-changing event will garner the most attention, and ergo the most money. This is not necessarily the most well written, the best edited, and especially not the most scrutinized report. In the world of reporting, time is always against you, and a constant supply of new information is mandatory when developing a large quantity of articles. This has remained largely intact since Acts 17:21, where it states that "For all the Athenians and strangers which were there spent their time in nothing else, but either to tell, or to hear some new thing." These concepts will be explored below.

PLAYING THE HEART STRINGS

Much like the headlines of the newspapers, the headlines of online articles must arrest the attention of the viewer well enough to cause them to make a purchase. The key difference is that newspapers require a purchase with money, while online articles only require you to view a few ads on the side. Both require the reader to want to know more, but one is much cheaper to access. The fundamental concept of making a sale through alarming the user remains fully intact. James Gordon Bennet, a newspaper mogul who thrived throughout the age of Yellow Journalism said that the purpose of the press was "not to instruct, but to startle". (Holiday, p. 84) To put it in modern context, consider the words of Tim Ferriss, a bestselling author. "Study the top stories at Digg or MSN.com and you'll notice a pattern: the top stories all polarize people. If you make it threaten people's three Bs – behavior, belief, or belongings – you get a huge virus-like dispersion" (Holiday, p. 64).

The most profitable way to advertise an article is to provide it with a title that will either scare or anger a potential reader. This can be outrage or fear in any form, but it still works. This is where the term "clickbait" comes from. It may make people mad because it is so scandalous, because it is so against what they believe, or simply because it is so obviously wrong that the reader wants to find out if the author could possibly be *that stupid*. This may seem like a good way to lose all credibility, but credibility does not build a successful online news outlet; clicks do. In the world of the physical, a person who sees an article in a newspaper that they know to be incorrect would never contribute money to that paper just to read the entire thing. There is a mental connection between spending money and supporting the vendor, and nobody want to give money to a liar or a fool. However, on the internet, where all of the reading is "free" and there is no tangible monetary connection between reading the article and supporting the author, people are much less hesitant to click on and read through the post. In the end, this is a win-win for all online newspapers because after all, a click is a click, and it doesn't matter if you are reading the article out of rage or joy. They have made the same amount of money.

To further increase the amount of time that a user spends seeing ads (and articles), all news outlets now include comments sections. The basic idea behind a comment section is that the readers can leave feedback on their opinion of the article that the author, and most importantly, other readers can see. There is no literary value added to an article by having a comments section, since anybody with an email address can leave feedback. The comment could be made by a leading expert in the subject or a monkey with a keyboard. This online business model exploits this feature massively. In order to leave a comment, a user must first click on the article. They scroll to the bottom of the page after reading it and click on a button that says "leave a comment" or something to that effect. To leave a comment, though, you must create an account on that website, which is almost always also free. To create an account, you input your personal information (on a page with ads) and then they ask you for permission to send you advertisement emails (more ads). You then create a "username," which is an alias that you will show up as on their site, on a page with more ads, and then you create a password on a page with more ads. Finally, you confirm your email account from your email provider and then go to a page with more ads. You can then access the original article that you want to comment on, reloading the page as well as the ads, and then scroll to the bottom, past all the ads, to where you can post your comments. Now that you have viewed pages and pages of ads, you can express your thoughts and feelings about the article.

This is where the polarity of the article really comes into play. The more polarizing an article is, the more likely it is to make one group of people very happy and the other group of people very angry. While fear and anger are the easiest two emotions to trigger with words, fear (usually of losing something valuable such as freedom or money) can be easily converted into anger against the party seeking to remove what they are afraid of losing. Thanks to the comments section, the readers can now directly voice their concern to the author and anybody else who may be wrongly influenced by the article. Now that they have posted their direct contradiction to the article, those who agreed with it will feel that they should run to the author's aid by defending it. Now, there is a fight, and since the entire conflict is faceless, it makes it that much simpler to be cruel, vitriolic, and petty. This feeds the ego of the people posting comments because they can feel superior to other readers while avoiding the repercussions of their words (more on that later). This is all done while advertisements stream down the sides of the page. Each reader that wishes to attack or defend any point must go through the process of setting up an account and then re-accessing it in order to express their opinion. Furthermore, comments can be directly replied to by other users, which will send a notification to the original poster that another person has responded to their response to the article. If that person disagrees with the comment, they can log back in, viewing more ads, in order to contradict the person who has contradicted them. The possibilities are now endless, and so are the potential profits for the host site. Its like two people having a brutal argument while a third person tells them they should have it in a McDonalds.

To complicate things even further, this is where the concept of "trolling" must be introduced. "Trolling," or, being an internet troll, is the idea of irritating others for the sheer enjoyment of feeling superior to a person you have angered because they are angry and you are not. Being a troll, or "trolling," has been present throughout the establishment of Internet Culture and is a fundamentally understood concept by anyone who has spent any time reading public comments. When one person is seriously concerned with an issue and another is not, the other person can, through any means they wish, irritate the concerned person. The concerned person will react aggressively because they wish to make a meaningful contribution that will draw other people to their point of view. When a troll identifies a person who is legitimately concerned, they can post personal insults, threats, outright lies, illogical arguments, fake opinions, or whatever else they feel will elicit a reaction from the concerned party. This angers the concerned party who will try more fervently to express their support for their belief system, to which the troll will post an even more irrational response. This method of personal entertainment is an incredibly immature form of communication that is only possible on a computer, since, if it was done in person, the troll would look like a fool (and probably get punched in the nose). Throughout time, these people have been known as hecklers or smart alecks, but those roles carry with them the inherent physical and psychological risks of being beaten, physically or intellectually. The remoteness of a computer enables the activity of trolling because no other media or in-person form of communication has ever made this possible. If a troll loses an argument, they can either disappear without facing any humiliation, or they can resort to personal insults that have no physical repercussions. There are no consequences on the internet, which enables and feeds trolling to the point where it has gone completely out of control. But not all of it is done so blithely.

Since an internet troll's purpose is to evoke an angry reaction from another person who feels passionately about an issue, there is no better breeding ground than comments sections of polarizing internet articles, especially when political views are expressed. This is a target rich environment for people who feed on the anger of others, and the bigger the name of the host site, the more opportunities they have to sow their discord (Proverbs 6:17). While most trolls likely just stumble upon an article they want to heckle, the publishers themselves have stumbled upon an awful truth. They can be their own trolls in order to artificially inflate the attention that their article gets. By creating fake accounts, personalities, and opinions, they can start arguments on their own articles, driving up the number of actual arguments from faithful or hateful readers. After all, a click is a click. This concept is explored in detail in Ryan Holiday's book "Trust Me, I'm Lying", and the execution of this concept is now in full swing. Any outrage can be created by any user, and if an author has to create their own fight to get attention, it is easier now than ever. The consequence of this is a subtle destruction of the emotional and intellectual capacity of the readers, which will be explored later. An additional consequence is that a person can fake their support for an illogical and unsupported opinion and thus making the proponents of the opposing point of view appear to be more foolish and less human than they actually are. This is what is called "dehumanizing the enemy," and it feeds a divisive culture. The reality of the nature of the internet is that an overindulgence in emotional reactions drives profits, and the companies willing to engage in emotional warfare will simply outpace those who are not.

MINIMIZING THE INVESTMENTS

The foundational rules of economics dictate that if two companies create an identical widget and sell if for an identical price, the company that is able to produce it with the greatest profits will eventually surpass the competition. Applied to news reporting, the news has never been mass produced as it has today. More news is available thanks to our ability to connect with new outlets around the world, and anybody can start a news outlet of their own since the operating costs of running your own blog are nonexistent. There are countless sites where you can create your own website at no cost, so long as you allow the host site to place their ads around the edges. When it comes to paying a journalist to write articles, economics dictates the quality of work that an author can provide.

Based on the economic model described previously, a massive quantity of low-quality work is required of journalists in order to provide the most lucrative return on investment. When an author is constrained by a tight deadline to create a high volume of work, the key elements of investigative journalism have to fall by the wayside. Investigative journalism is what journalism should be. It is when a journalist selects a subject, investigates to discover what the truth is, and reports it in a way that is easy for the target audience to understand. This practice is, at best, on life support, and the rest of the journalistic world is trying to unplug it so they can charge their iPhones.

Ideally, when a "newsworthy" event transpires, witnesses are present that will describe their recollection of the event. Since they have seen the event take place, they are the most reliable source of information, and should be consulted in order to portray the event accurately. Unfortunately, tracking these people down can take a great deal of time and effort. It requires that the journalist sniff out leads, find witnesses, scrutinize their testimony, and then provide an accurate record of the important facts. Furthermore, in order to validate the claims of the first source, additional witnesses should be consulted to determine the whole of the story based on the stitched-together perspectives of multiple individuals. After all, "in the mouth of two or three witnesses every word may be established" (Matthew 18:16). This is highly labor-intensive and requires a significant investment of time from the journalist. The reality is that investing a large amount of time into a story is necessary to provide the most realistic record of the event. Due to the nature of the news media on the internet, this is not a profitable use of time by journalists. Information must be gathered quickly and, most importantly, before the competition. The early bird gets the worm, and in the age of modern reporting methods, the early story gets the clicks. In the race to secure the largest portion of attention from the masses, events must be covered quickly to ensure profitability, and haste has never been the ally of quality.

The nature of the internet allows for an entirely new can of worms to be opened: internet sources. Since social media allows people to become reporters themselves on anything and everything that they see (you do, after all, read your *"news feed"*), anybody can be a source for a reporter. Traveling to a place to contact individuals who saw an event and interviewing requires personal investment. Finding people on the internet who claim to have been witnesses is much cheaper, and, importantly, much faster. What is even better than this is that a reporter who already has established somewhat of a following can post that they are looking for sources, and people will flock to them to provide quotes in order to secure their few seconds of fame. No matter what the method, the key issue is that the sources that come through the internet are free, fast, and easy to come by. They are by no means consistently reliable. While this may seem to be unlikely, Katie Couric, one of the most well-known journalists of modern times, has admitted that she uses Twitter to source some of the stories that she presents on national television (Holiday, p. 28).

To make matters worse, lying through the internet by pretending to be a person you are not is much easier than doing it in person as it requires no verification of your character or understanding of the events. Furthermore, since the author is held so tightly to their deadlines, their ability to fact check and dissect the information is greatly hindered. This opens two terrible doors for lying: one for reporters and another for the rest of the world. People who did not witness the event but wish for it to be portrayed in a way that favors their personal or political opinions can pretend that they saw the event and cast it in their own light with no fear of repercussion. Reporters can scan through profiles and comments provided to them and can pick and choose what way they want to portray an event based on their own previously established bias. After all, the more opinionated that a journalist can be, the more polarizing their article can be, and the more clicks it will get. The rabbit hole gets deeper, as they can then attack their own article using contradictory sources that may or may not be legitimate, and then drive up their readership by starting fights. And all of this can be done very cheaply, and very quickly. Ryan Holiday quotes from Kelly McBride of the Poynter Institute who says "Even though credibility is all you have to sell, it's not enough anymore. Credibility is not working as a business model. Credibility of journalism is at an all-time low anyway" (Holiday, p. 54). Accuracy doesn't pay. And so, credibility dies.

The death of credibility in the mainstream media comes at a price that is not initially apparent. When nearly every source in an industry that is built on trust habitually lies to the public, people begin to question a lot more than just the accuracy of the reporters. Trust is essential to society. As that trust is continuously exploited for personal profit, the value of truth continuously decays. Since trust is based on an assumption that the truth on a subject has been provided, when trust is eliminated, so is the belief that truth can be provided by anybody. The implications of this are world-altering and will be discussed later. It is vital to understand that as trust is sold, truth loses its value.

THE SENSATION EQUATION

Drawing back to the earlier years of the original state of Yellow Journalism, the world became enamored with life of a man named James Fisk. Fisk, as was discussed before, became famous, but not because of any great contribution to society. The man was, after all, a professional conman who thrived on pushing the moral limits of what society would let him get away with. But Fisk was more than an easy source of scandal. Fisk was the living embodiment of everything that Yellow Journalism thrived on. All of the information about Fisk appealed to emotional appetites rather than intellectual. He lived a life that was high energy, constantly on the brink of destruction but always a step ahead of the competition and police. His life, though depraved of any moral bearing, was secretly envied by the common folk. He had risen above the monotony of the rat race and lived by his own rules. He was able to do whatever he wanted and get away with which made information and gossip about him easy to come by. Fisk was known for loving attention and had no qualms about spilling his guts to the press whenever they came running his way. All of the information about him could be obtained cheaply, described succinctly, and inflamed emotionally. He was a man with nothing to lose. When the presses would attack him for committing some societal faux pas, he got more famous, and the press made more money.

The more vilified he was by the press, the more that he became their hero, and the more essential that this made him to their revenue. The presses treated him like a campfire. They allowed him to burn so that they could stay warm, but also made sure to fuel the fire so that it never went out. The problem is that in this scenario, the fire is a bad thing because the ideal outcome for the public would be for this beacon of immorality to extinguish itself to prevent anybody else from getting burned. The scandals were his fuel, and scandals beget scandals. The heightened drama created by living a life that was constantly reported on to friends and enemies alike made him a superstar. After all, there is no bad publicity when you are the media, because publicity is what pays the reporter's bills. The only crime that he could commit that would not be forgiven by the presses would be for him to become boring.

At this point, the social position of James Fisk should begin to sound familiar to a consumer of 21st century reporting. Since Yellow Journalism 2.0 follows the same general rules as its predecessor, people of similar moral character should rise to the top of the headlines like dead fish at high tide. The greatest celebrities of the modern world are those individuals that are at the forefront of pushing social boundaries and, most importantly, have nothing to lose from bad press of any kind. These individuals become famous by simply living extravagantly, in a way that the average person would want to but lacks the means and mental fortitude (and also possibly social intelligence) to do so. They become vessels that people can live vicariously through, if only they weren't constrained by money, societal expectations, or basic morality. The people that are adored by the presses are those that embody the total fulfillment of hedonistic human nature and give no regard for the impact that they have on those around them. Some such individuals that meet this quota and are the darlings of the modern news media are the Kardashian dynasty, the cast of the Jersey Shore, and, more recently, the cast of Tiger King. These people are known to be totally devoid of moral guidance, and often take pride in their deviation from biblical moral standards that used to govern society. They live extravagant lifestyles in which they do whatever they want to, whenever they want to. Their personalities are driven entirely on emotional impulses, resulting in high stakes drama. The drama begets more drama, and thanks to social media, these feuds, highs, lows, spats, makeups, love triangles, and so on can be consumed by audiences in real time. The quantity of available information available about these heathens has increased tenfold.

This introduces the concept of "reality television," the title of which is an entirely unfit description. Reality television is a genre of television that is filmed in a manner that seems to be cameramen following people around and filming their day-to-day lives. This thrives on the jealousy of average people who want to live just like the rich and famous do and escape the mundane nature of reality. These cameras follow people who are claiming to just be living their ordinary lives, doing whatever it is that that person became famous for. The problem is that, regardless of who you are, life has parts that are simply boring. To make the lives of the rich and famous more appealing to the public, the boring parts are edited out, streaming efficiently from one interesting event into the next. There is no tedium or repetition, only the appearance of constant adventure and excitement, which is entirely contrary to real life. In order to retain the audience and compete with other shows for the most viewers, reality television has to become the opposite of reality. Furthermore, all reality television is either scripted or prompted by writers, and then edited heavily. This makes all of reality television more dramatic than real life, all while playing it off as the completely normal life of people that are simply better than you.

Since the events taking place on the television are pawned off as "real," they can be reported on by celebrity news as "real" events. Since celebrities are only famous because they are loved by masses of people, the celebrities now produce as additional form of news to the general public: tabloids. Tabloids report on celebrity divorces, feuds, pregnancies, marriages, deaths, and any other emotional hook that will cause concern to whatever beloved public figure an individual mentally relates to. The problem is that all of these events are highly emotional and have, literally, no bearing on the life of the people who want to know more. The personal lives of celebrities, who are generally artists in the field of either acting or music, pertain in no way to the daily turn of events inside the daily life of the average person. The only impact that this can possibly have on a person is that they will be able to discuss it with another person who is interested in the same celebrity. Furthermore, the events that take place are often staged to the point that they have been rehearsed and stitched together across multiple takes. The fights are scripted to cause fake conflicts that generate buzz. The fact that there is a conflict forces other to take sides, which further inflates the situation, making it even more dramatic, and creating even more buzz. The system feeds itself, and the drama begets more drama.

Reality television has expanded to include much more than the lives of celebrities. While shows like "Keeping up with the

Kardashians" follow the fake-real lives of the Kardashian family (a family whose legacy is built around sex, the O.J. Simpson trial, and Kayne West), reality television has created its own stars out of non-celebrities in order to thrive off of drama. This includes television shows like "The Real Housewives of _____" (there are several versions of this show), which follows, again, the "real" lives of women who are married to very rich men. They live exorbitant lifestyles, full of fashion, expensive liquor, and exotic beauty treatments in which they feud endlessly with the other rich women. It also includes shows like "The Jersey Shore," which follows the lives of a group of young, attractive, rich friends who live in the lap of luxury and spend their time fighting, trying to improve their physical appearance, and participating in flippantly casual sexual interactions. Shows like these play heavily on the desires of mankind to live richly and without care in whatever sin besets them. Though most individuals who watch these shows will openly admit that the people on them are bad people who create an example that should not be followed, there is still a desire to be them and live freely in the whim of the moment. The modern term for this is "guilty pleasure," which adequately describes the act of sinning vicariously.

Reality television has also begun to take on additional forms, such as game shows, like "Survivor" and "Big Brother," which are nothing more than popularity contests in which the least popular person is voted off the show. It also includes cooking shows, such as "Guy's Grocery Games" or "Chopped," in which all chefs may be cooking food, but the "main course" is actually the dramatic backstories, tragic cooking mishaps followed by emotional meltdowns, and heart-wrenching motivations for competing. This is made evident through the fact that the TV's "Food Network" only hosts dramatic shows during their prime hours, rather than informative shows that would educate viewers on how to improve their abilities in a valuable life-skill.

Home renovation shows such as "The Property Brothers," "Extreme Makeover: Home Edition," "Love it or List it," and "Fixer

Upper" are all reality programs that are set in the environment of building or renovating a house. The dramatic decisions and difficulties are accentuated by supporting background music, well-edited supercuts, and well-timed commercial breaks. Commercial breaks happen right before a major decision or right after a major difficulty (but before telling the audience exactly what the disaster is) so that the audience will watch the entire commercial break to see what is going to happen next.

Careers are also the subject of reality TV and include fishing ("Wicked Tuna" and "Deadliest Catch"), owning a restaurant ("Restaurant Impossible" and "Kitchen Nightmares") and modeling ("America's Next Top Model" and "Toddlers in Tiaras"). Some shows are just based on the lives of people who provide enough interesting content to be shoved into 30 or 60 minutes a week of entertainment ("Mountain People", "Swamp People", "Life Below Zero" or "Duck Dynasty"). The sheer number of reality television shows, in which fake or highly exaggerated stories are pawned off as the real version of real life, are too numerous to count and have been thematically adapted to every subject imaginable.

Overtly dramatic television has taken the center stage as the primary form of entertainment and bleeds through into all other forms of televised media. Drama proves to be the most lucrative form of amusement since it engages an emotionally bound audience through a visual medium. If this were not the case, it would not be used across all major television networks. A dramatic drive guides news programs, informative programs, and even sports. News programs exploit and amplify dramatic events to convince viewers that the contents of their reporting are valuable to the viewers. Emotional interviews of victims, witnesses, or experts provide no intellectual benefit and serve only to elicit sympathy or outrage from the audience and prove whatever ideology the network has determined to follow before the event happened.

"Informative programs," which are aired by networks

such as The Discovery Channel, Animal Planet, or The History Channel have had to become increasingly less informative and more dramatic to keep up with the entertainment level of the rest of television. Shows now, such as "Ancient Aliens" or "Drunk History," have to overdramatize historical events or theories because it makes them so much more entertaining. While historical studies often examine fascinating events that are played out by unique individuals who are worth learning from, a substantial amount of intellectual work and study are required to develop an accurate understanding of these individuals or events. The act of study itself is a "weariness of the flesh" (Ecclesiastes 12:12) and will lose out to fun programs "which minister questions, rather than godly edifying which is in faith" in a society that is engorged on dramatic material.

Sports, one of this world's most worshipped gods, are dramatized relentlessly under the guise of "analysis" at sports desks. New recruits have their eventful upbringings drawn into the limelight so that people can emotionally connect with the new faces that are constantly monetized. Emotional investment eventually produces financial investment in memorabilia, as well as the attentiveness that drives up the value of their advertising slots. Emotional stories, comebacks, falls from grace, and unexpected upsets are all flaunted in front of an audience that consumes them without hesitation, but often with a good bit of frivolous deliberation.

This is irrefutably problematic, but that basic bit of truth is entirely eclipsed due to its sheer profitability. Reality television encompasses so many subjects and extends so deep into the culture of television that defining a boundary for the purpose of determining its total profitability is nearly impossible. What is clear is that each of these shows, as they rise and fall in popularity produce an abundant amount of emotional drama because this is simply the most profitable and efficient use of televised media. Televisions themselves are not evil pieces of destructive technology that were invented for the purpose of intentionally undermining society's emotional/intellectual balance. Unfortunately, much like the internet, the most profitable use of television just happens to do exactly that.

ALL HAIL THE ALMIGHTY DOLLAR

From a purely humanistic point of view, the modern media movement is detrimental to society's development and advancement. Some good causes can come from televising material or posting it to easily accessible websites. Unfortunately, those who control it are willing to exploit it to its full monetary value, regardless of whatever consequences may lie ahead. The impact of this will be analyzed further in the following chapters. Biblically speaking, this is to be expected. I Timothy 6:10 states that "the love of money is the root of all evil." This world is entirely aware of the effect that television, social media, and the internet have on individuals. By effect, it is not difficult to see the effects reflected and amplified in modern society. Nearly every intellectual analysis on the usage of modern digital communication technology concludes that the nature of technology is emotionally and intellectually detrimental to society and its use must be curtailed for the betterment of all. Their pleas are echoes of a sentiment that has been preached by Bible-believing men of God since the television began its invasion into the home. Ironically, the world's intellectual community is just now beginning to catch up with a slew of preachers whose only source of information is a book that was translated 400 years ago. They that have drawn their ire since the invention of "science falsely so called" (I Timothy 6:20) and will continue to do so until Jesus Christ returns to set up the Kingdom of Heaven on the Earth.

The dominant revenue stream for all modern media outlets of any kind is directly through advertisement. Advertising is, from a biblical perspective, an attempt to grow a seed of covetousness in the heart of the viewer. Viewers must be persuaded that the quality of their lives will increase if they purchase the advertised product.

Advertising is only successful if the invested cost in developing and distributing the advertisement produces a positive return on investment. Considering the ubiquity of advertising in modern society, this approach is largely successful, and covetousness now runs rampant through the streets. While the modern, civilized world may think it is above the idolatrous behaviors of lesser, superstitious heathens, Colossians 3:5 identifies covetousness as idolatry. Biblically speaking, the definition of covetousness is wanting something bad enough that you would sin to obtain it, since it will provide for you in a way that God has not. This would make the civilized world more devout in their idolatrous worship than most "underprivileged" populations. The idolatry of *things* includes items, such as clothes or gadgets, but also envelops larger concepts such as lifestyles, experiences, or attitudes that are showcased in the limelight of modern dramatic television and reporting.

Technologically developed societies now worship the false god of consumerism which preaches the tenet of destructive debt. The consumerist society in which we live places all value on the physical and the present, often including payment options as a selling point. The future should be sacrificed to benefit the present, which was the mindset of Esau that cost him his birthright in Genesis 25:32. This mindset has made debt a way of life to American society. The total amount of household debt in America was 14.27 trillion dollars in the summer of 2020 (Federal Reserve Economic Data, 2020), which equals out to about $43,500 per person. Solomon warned that debt makes you subservient to the creditor in Proverbs 22:7. God promises the Jews that when they serve him, he will bless them with money, which in turn allows them to rule other nations through debt (Deuteronomy 15:6, 28:12). Economic trends indicate that the average amount of debt is rising and has been for several years, slowed only briefly by the recession of the early 2010s (Federal Reserve Economic Data, 2020). This debt is the fruition of the desire to obtain in the present at the cost of the future. As a side note, it is rather ironic that society is blaming capitalism for its woes when it willingly funds the banking industry through credit cards, student loans, and mortgages. The transfer of wealth is not stolen, but rather given up in order to obtain items of great value before they can be afforded. Modern society not only serves the idol of consumerism, it sacrifices a great deal to it.

CONCLUSION) GUIDED BY THE UNSEEN HAND

There is no pretending that the business models sustaining modern communication technologies are in any way healthy to the world. What is largely understood is that the most profitable way to leverage the technology of the television and the internet is to ruthlessly bombard the mind with as much highly emotional content as possible in order to retain the attention, thus permitting the agencies to shoot off as many ads as possible. This, in turn, results in massive invasions of privacy and new concerns regarding the ownership of your internet traffic. The moral implications are obvious, as stalking everything that a person reads about to determine what they will buy is clearly something that most people would not be comfortable with if directly confronted. The legal aspect significantly lags behind this since the internet is a relatively new concept and mankind's inherently sinful nature makes it impossible to anticipate all the ways in which he will violate his conscience to turn a buck. Often, the law has to play catchup with issues that are technically legal because the sinful practice has not been banned in every conceivable manner. This would not even be possible. The legal aspects alone of the privacy invasions, questionable advertising choices, and ownership of metadata are far reaching, but will not be covered in this thesis as they are only tangentially relevant and would require a great deal of research to prove already-established biblical truths: mankind is naturally corrupt (Jeremiah 17:9) and all evil comes from loving money (I Timothy 6:10).

The inventors of these technologies never intended for this to happen, and it is likely that they did not anticipate that this would be the outcome when they initially filed their patents. Predicting this type of outcome would have been a stretch and would likely not have been more than an afterthought due to mankind's tendency to overestimate himself. In Kevin Kelly's book "What Technology Wants," he lists several quotes by men who were either the fathers of key modern inventions or were largely responsible for their distribution. He quotes Orville Wright, inventor of the airplane, who said "I think it (the airplane) will have a tendency to make war impossible." Jules Verne, a science fiction author, said of the submarine that it "may be the cause of bringing battle to a stoppage altogether...war will become impossible." And Hiram Maxim, inventor of the machine gun, said of his invention that rather than make war terrible, that "It will make war impossible". While the airplane, the submarine, and the machine gun are all directly associated with war, later on, Kevin Kelly quotes historian David Nye, who said "Each new form of communication, from the telegraph and the telephone to radio, film, television and the internet, has been heralded as the guarantor of free speech and the unfettered movement of ideas." He closes with a quote from author Joel Garreau who says that "Given what we know happened with television, I am astonished that computer technology is now seen as a sacrament" (Kelly, 2010, p. 192). From there, much like all humanistic futurists, he predicts that the problems that we have faced are simply challenges that will make us better and stronger in the end. This sentiment flies in the face of the fact that these inventions have degraded the average quality of life while increasing our capacity to engage in warfare. They may have increased our physical comfort but have ultimately crippled the mental health of the modern world. None of these inventions hindered man's capacity to kill other men, and have unsurprisingly now created new threats, such as disinformation campaigns, mutually assured destruction, international propaganda, and the introduction of truly global issues.

The inventions are leveraged in their most efficient manner to produce the greatest return on investment, regardless of the impact that it will have on the public. By examining the trends and progressions of communication technology, it becomes evident that there is an unseen guiding force that is uniting the world into an antibiblical mindset. The mentality of the new world system hinders the ability of the lost world to seek after spiritual fulfillment as well as the Christian's ability to know God. The following chapters will provide an in-depth analysis of the effects that modern communication technology has on human emotions and intellect. They will then be evaluated through a biblical lens, which provides an understanding of why the world is in the state that it is in. These effects all occur due to the nature of the technology that drives society, and, based on the fruits produced, it will become evident that society is on a downward spiral from which there is no recovery apart from Jesus Christ.

Section 2 ⟩ How

CHAPTER 3 ⟩ THE SCIENCE OF ADDICTION

The internet itself is an intangible resource. It can be used, but never quite runs out. Unlike physical items that are used until they break down from the wear, the internet can theoretically operate forever. Software does not require physical maintenance or the expenditure of resources to maintain. It exists much in the same way that the information in a book does. While the pages may wear out, the information can be recopied and reused in an identical book. Software is the same, only it does not require an additional book to be printed for the information to be retained. The physical storage of the software may degrade, but the program itself operates free of the constraints of physicality. For this reason, the economics of the internet can operate on an entirely different scale than traditional economics.

Modern manufacturers balance on an interesting line between high and low durability. If a product is too durable, it will never break, and the consumer will never purchase another one. Make it too flimsy, and it will be perceived as a cheap and the user will go to a competitor for a more durable version. The delicate balance of these two schools of thought is known as "planned obsolescence." Software does not work like this. Since software can be used indefinitely by a plethora of users with no need to recreate the product, software's monetization can be based on using the product as many times as humanly possible. The profit that is able to be generated is limited only by the interest of the available users and the website's ability to host internet traffic. Increased traffic brings additional users, which generate additional profits. Therefore, the primary goal when attempting to maximize profits, must be to maximize the amount of traffic.

Maximizing traffic can be done through one of two ways: either a large number of people can use the site a few times, or a smaller group of people can use the site a large number of times. The literal million-dollar question then becomes, how do internet based for-profit companies ensure that their users stay on the site as much as possible? Whether their target audience is large or small, they must use the site as much as possible in order to maximize profits, so the answer is to make them become addicted.

The exploration of this topic has ranges across all internet usage. Attention has become the currency of the 21st century. In the online world, addictions feed the shareholders of all platforms, be they social media, shopping, entertainment, or information. Each of these fields have implemented addictive features of some sort to maximize their profits, but the field that most visually demonstrates each of these addictive qualities is social media. The remainder of this chapter will show how these qualities are intentionally programmed into the system to increase profitability for the creators, but the principals presented can be applied across all internet-based markets.

The science of fabricating addiction in the human mind began with trial and error, but it has long since evolved into an exact, repeatable formula that can be used to manipulate the passive working of the human brain and induce a technological addiction. The subject of addiction has long been debated in its nature as to if it is genetic, environmental, or a combination of these factors. In reality, addiction can be induced into a person by implementing basic concepts to any activity. The recipe for technological addiction has six ingredients that can be intermingled to varying degrees and vary in their efficacy for each individual. They are laid out by Adam Alter in his book on technological addiction entitled "Irresistible: The Rise of Addictive Technology and the Business of Keeping us Hooked". In his words, the ingredients are "compelling goals that are just beyond reach; irresistible and unpredictable positive feedback; a sense of incremental progress and improvement; tasks that become slowly more difficult over time; unresolved tensions that demand resolution; and strong social connections" (Alter, 2017, p. 9). These six items as described by Adam Alter are leveraged against the inner workings of the human mind and have been scientifically proven when applied heavily to technology to reproduce the neurological patterns associated with substance abuse addiction (Alter, 2017, p. 71). Each one of these is prevalent throughout television, internet surfing, and social media because they produce the greatest results. By forming a mental association of addiction similar to heroin, LSD, or ketamine, web and entertainment developers are able to keep an audience hooked, much to the pleasure of their advertisers. In examining these ingredients, the extent to which they are used becomes more evident. Each one will be examined through its practical applications.

COMPELLING GOALS

Setting goals is beneficial to personal achievement, and setting small ones are critical to breaking down large goals into manageable milestones. When a person sets small goals, they can achieve great feats by gaining momentum and measuring success. The issue with modern communication technology, especially in the field of social media, is that the goals prey off of human insecurities. Social media has no set goal that it provides to the user as a measure of completion, and largely depends on the mentality of the user. Social media is able to prey on the human mind in a way that has never been possible before.

Until recently, social success, aka popularity, was defined by achieving a favorable standing among the people that an individual wished to be associated with. Other people may have been envied for their perceived success or apparent prominence, but it was impossible to quantify a social position among others in meaningful, tangible terms. Thanks to the tracking mechanisms implemented in social media, the individual popularity is numerically tracked and available for the whole world to see. Likes, comments, favorites, shares, retweets, and so on are hard datapoints that are visible on each social media post, regardless of the site. This is a key feature that defines what social media is. Every user has a profile, containing the personal information of the user, and always hosts key metrics that numerically define populatiry within that site. Achieving popularity is no longer a nebulous concept: it has a scoreboard. And that information is available to anybody who wants to play. The issue now is that as people create content, they are informed how well their content was received by the peers that they value with exact numbers and timings, creating social issues that could never have existed before. The innate human goal to be respected and accepted by those held in high regard is now quantifiable and public knowledge. This allows for people to set goals and reach for their own definitions of personal success.

While this may seem somewhat beneficial, social media companies have made that all data in these sites is public, and rather than setting personal goals, the understanding of the success of others places a competitive drive into the situation. By making the successes and failures of others on social media public, users are compelled through pride to surpass the achievements of their fellow users. This also introduces the *Popularity Principal*, a phrase coined by Jose van Dijck. This principal states that a person who gains more popularity becomes more important because they have achieved more popularity (Dijck, 2013, p. 2013). The size of their following dictates their online value, thus connecting self-worth to a person's online presence. Where popularity was once simply an idea that was pursued until personal contentment was attainted, it is now a numbers game that labels personal success with unfeeling statistics that define that success.

The extent to which this affects a person is largely contingent upon the user. Some people are more prone to care about the opinions of others, while some people could not care less. The issue is that for people who do care about their social position, they now have to consider the factor that all of their social media postings will be judged based on not only the content, but also the quantity and quality of reactions that it receives. Paul warned against this behavior in II Corinthians 10:12 when he said, "For we dare not make ourselves of the number, or compare ourselves with some that commend themselves: but they measuring themselves by themselves, and comparing themselves among themselves, are not wise." The numerical measures of popularity make it impossible to not understand your exact position within the social media pecking order, and the only natural reaction is to set higher goals to reach a better position, which can be done by spending more time on the sites.

The sites, after all, want the best content. When users post good content in high quantities, it drives more traffic, meaning more peripheral ads are viewed. When good content is created, it is consumed and shared with others to consume as well. By establishing a dogmatic measure of popularity, social media websites are able to drive individuals to dedicate more time and effort into improving their numbers. It is vital to understand that the technological and social architecture of these sites is to drive up as much user interaction as possible in order to generate the most money. The stats are not posted to profiles by accident, and there is a reason that all social media websites make a point to let you know exactly how much interaction you are generating. Your success is their success, and they are very interested in their success.

INCONSISTENT POSITIVE FEEDBACK

Solomon commanded the sluggard to go to the ants to learn how to work. To learn how to create an addictive feature, neuroscience directs you to the pigeons and the rats. Both of these creatures have been experimented on extensively to determine how the human brain works, and both of them predict human behaviors quite well, especially in the realm of receiving feedback.

Psychologist Michael Zeiler placed pigeons in a cage with a button in it that would drop a pellet of food every time the button was pushed. When the button produced a pellet perfectly consistently, the pigeons would press the button some and eat some. When the button produced pellets 10% of the time, the pigeons lost interest. But when the button produced a pellet 50-70% of the time, the pigeons pressed it about twice as much, resulting in a net gain in the number of pellets produced (Alter, 2017, p. 127). Now consider the rats. Psychologist B.F. Skinner discovered that if you put rats in a cage with a button that deployed food each time the button was pressed, they would press the button until they were full and then use it whenever they were hungry. If the button delivered food inconsistently, they would push it more than they needed to in order to try to figure it out (Vaidhyanathan, 2018, p. 36).

These two studies explain the psychology of why gambling is such an addictive vice. Gamblers wager money for the opportunity to gain more money, and they do so through a variety of different games. The unifying factor behind all of these games is that between the investment (money is put down, the cards are dealt, the bets are made, the coin is in the slot or on the table) and the outcome (the cards are revealed, the tumblers stop turning, etc) there is a waiting period where the player has to wait to see if they will win or not. The high that gamblers chase is not the high of winning money, but the high of having a chance to win. (Vaidhyanathan, 2018, p. 38) This explains why when gamblers win at machines, most of them will immediately put the money that they won back into the machine until it is all gone. Gambling is not an addiction to winning money, but an addiction to being able to win money.

All of this information is provided about rats, pigeons, and online gambling to make a simple point. Any pleasurable response that is delivered inconsistently through a small effort is psychologically addicting. The small investment downplays the actual investment, such as the sum of investments or the moral breakdown that had to take place to arrive in that position. The inconsistent win baits the addict into trying one more time until there are no more tries to give.

This is exactly why all social media is highly addictive to most people. Each piece of content generated by a user is placed on display for the entire world to view and judge. A passing judgement will be rewarded with a like, retweet, share, comment, follow, or subscriptions. A failing judgement is rewarded with criticism or, even worse, silence. When we receive a notification of online interaction, our brain produces a small shot of dopamine, which is a chemical responsible for making us feel happy (Turkle, 2011, p. 227). This tiny hint of happiness is a scientifically documented biochemical reaction that is based on the investment in a post on social media. And since it is impossible to predict the public reaction to any single media event, each post is the mental equivalent to pulling a lever on a slot machine to see if a win will register. Some posts will receive a lot of positive feedback, some will receive some, some will be totally ignored, but you never know how much interaction you are going to receive until you post, which is exactly why people post and check for status updates obsessively. Some people are less socially dependent and consciously resist this pull to an extent. Some people are less drawn to social media. But the truth is, regardless of your level of susceptibility to the addiction, social media is hard coded to addict.

INCREMENTAL IMPROVEMENT

Humanity has, since its creation in Eden, consistently sought to improve. Many of these steps have actually diminished our quality of life, such as humanity's first attempted step forward, taken by Eve when she ate the fruit of the tree of the knowledge of good and evil. Even though all of the results were negative, the intent was purely positive. The drive to improve fosters invention, and each new creation promises to alleviate some previous woe and ensure a better quality of life for the user. This drive is part of human nature.

This progression exists in our social desires as well. Each person desires to be held in high regard by those that they respect and hold in high regard. Similar to the concepts presented in the section on compelling goals, incremental social improvement now can be numerically quantified and compared. The tracking metrics made available to all social media users dogmatically state how popular each user is, and with whom they are associated.

This issue is that, in a day, people will only encounter a limited number of people within their physical sphere of social interaction. Social events where you may meet a new person well enough to want to permanently connect with them on social media are rare, and our personal, mental network of peers is limited by the constraints of the human mind and body. Social media websites are fully aware of this fact, as well as the fact that stagnant interactions tend to drive people away. To combat this, social media websites have taken several direct measures. Suggested friends or topics line the sides of media feeds. Events are hosted to find individuals of like passions and draw them into interaction with each other. Profiles of individuals are made public by default, so anybody who you may pass on the information superhighway can be analyzed for interest and easily pursued. The sites know that in order to keep content fresh and engaging (engaging content results in greater ad revenue), they have to keep 'stirring the pot.' Likeminded individuals will become invested in each other's lives, and thus spend more time on the sites interacting with them and viewing ads. And much like how metadata can be used to predict the shopping practices of consumers, social media sites use metadata and well-guarded algorithms to suggest friends that a user is likely to connect with. The internet can predict who and what you like, just as much as what you will buy. The algorithm created by Facebook reads more than 100,000 different signals from users and contains more than 60 million lines of code (Foer, 2017, p. 73).

All of this is precisely done so that a user can see how many people they can please on their site. As was explained in the previous section, inconsistent positive feedback drives addictive behavior. Only getting a few likes may upset some users, since everybody can see the posts and the number of likes that popular people gain. It is much easier to gain a large amount of interaction from a large audience than a small audience, so people follow the bait given to them of suggested friends, groups, communities, and clubs to artificially inflate their sense of importance. Pride, after all, is naturally a driving force in the human psyche (I John 2:16). As the numbers continually grow from an ever-increasing group of technologically connected individuals, mental milestones are achieved. Even if they are not intentionally striven for, there is a conscious awareness of one's status relative to those you are associated with. This takes the eternal struggle of continuously striving to improve oneself and makes the goals much more measurable and visible.

But psychological addiction goes beyond the desire to gain more impressive numbers. It also roots itself in the fear of failure. While a post with lots of interaction will make a person feel great (from a large number of dopamine hits), a post with no interaction is an online showcase in failure, akin to having a dish at the potluck that nobody eats. This fear of having low interaction and therefore an unimportant social position amplifies the need to discover others online to interact with. Psychologists have proven that this can drive people continue doing behaviors that they dislike because they feel that it would be worse to abandon it. They may want to keep climbing the social ladder, but that doesn't mean that they like it anymore (Alter, 2017, p. 152).

PROGRESSIVE DIFFICULTY

Progressive difficulty plays largely into the hand of Incremental Improvement and builds on the concepts already established. As a person climbs higher among the social pecking order and gains a greater following, a higher quality of content is expected of the user. A basic user of social media will generally post the highlights of their very average life. This is due to the inconsistent feedback that will eventually, consciously or not, condition the user to post only those things that will garner the most attention. Thanks to the marvels of modern technology, they may take many amateur photos and post a few of the best. This will receive some attention and produce some interaction but will be limited to the small audience of the media novice. When this is posted online, it will end up in the news feeds of other users that will be littered with other interesting events from the lives of the people that they associate with.

This is where the truly competitive nature of social media comes into play. While liking, commenting, or sharing may not cost the user monetarily, they will pay a fee in terms of their own social standing. Liking too many things cheapens the value of the like. Not liking a post when you tend to like most things that are posted will indicate that this user dislikes something, simply because they didn't explicitly indicate that they did like it. Tagging (when a person posts something with another user in it in a way that notifies the tagged individual) merits some form of interaction but tagging too frequently can produce annoyance. There is a delicate balance of ensuring that one's social currency is spent, without cheapening its value. Ultimately, in a system very similar to that of money, the goal of social media is to gain the greatest amount of social currency.

The only way to do this is to rise above the average social media user in order to gain more attention than everybody else. The way to do this is to lead a more exciting life, become more visually appealing, post more often, and appeal to the largest percentage of your followers. All of this takes work, and the more effort that is put into it, the greater the results that are produced. The increased investment produces incremental improvement, but also introduces progressive difficulty. In order to be better than everybody else, you have to try harder and be willing to invest more.

Because the goals set by social media users are set

personally, there is no way for social media to be considered "completed." There is also no way to ignore the competition. A friend who was once unpopular may go to college, gain many friends, and skyrocket their social media popularity. Now, a person that the user once looked down on is looming over them indirectly with their success, posing questions of adequacy and true contentment. The array of possibilities on social media are endless, and every user is subjected to all of these factors and more when they engage in it. This is because social media has no *stopping rule*, as described by psychologist Paco Underhill. Paco discovered that people who have the flow of a task interrupted are less likely to finish the task because they have been prompted to end it prematurely (Alter, 2017, p. 184). Social media has no definable measures of success or completion, and the news feed provided to the user will continue endlessly until all the content that has been posted by all the users has been viewed in a single session, which, practically, is impossible. Social media removes all measures which would consider it "completed" in both the short-term and long-term scale. By removing barriers and enabling an unlimited capacity for interaction, progressive difficulty hits a sweet spot that drives interaction. This effect was dubbed as flow by Hungarian Psychologist Mihaly Csikszentmihalyi who proved that people who enter flow will continue to work towards a goal obsessively if they are uninterrupted (Alter, 2017, p. 176). This is why it is so easy to spend hours on social media scrolling through the news feed and various profiles, only to suddenly realize how much time has passed unintentionally. Progressive difficulty is imprinted on the user while eliminating any stopping rules that may hinder progress, generating an addictive habit that is fed from an addicted lifestyle.

UNRESOLVED TENSIONS

Alfred Hitchcock once said, "What is drama, after all, but life with all the boring bits cut out" (Truffaut, 1966). The same could be said of social media. All social media postings are designed to elicit some form of emotional reaction. Emotions are far easier and quicker to stimulate than intellect, and as social media only exists virtually in the internet where quick bursts of information reign supreme, there isn't much of a market for posting intelligent content on social media. Solomon said that "much studying is a weariness of the flesh" (Ecclesiastes 12:12) and the nature of social media is not conducive to "much studying." The best way to gain the elusive inconsistent positive feedback is to make a post that makes people feel something. A political post, for example, can draw all forms of emotional responses, especially given the highly polarized and volatile nature of American politics. An edgy, politically-charged accusation can draw joy from supporters, anger from dissenters, anxiety from passivists, or distrust from skeptics. Photos of a party can draw positivity from other attendees, jealousy from those uninvited, sadness from those unable to attend, concern from those worried about the content of the photos, or irritation from those who live next door and enjoyed the party in the same way that many people enjoy second-hand smoke. All of these reactions are emotional, and all of them are displayed through comments, likes, additional posts, tags, not liking photos, negative comments, and passive-aggressive postings that vaguely refer to the original event in ways that are not totally clear. Each post, designed to gain the most interaction, may play heavily toward or against any of these emotions from anybody who encounters them online. When describing his experience with Facebook, Siva Vaidhyanathan described it by saying "Nothing prompted me to think deeply. Everything made me feel something" (Vaidhyanathan, 2018, p. 43). The ultimate result of social media is inevitable: drama.

Social media produces drama, drama produces tensions, and tensions produce social media interaction. And so, the circle of internet life goes on. Each post brings with it the potential to cause tension between the poster and literally any other individual on that platform. The spread of the content is limited only by the number of people who choose to share it. The reaction to the post is what creates the drama. Since social media is available at the press of a button or two on any computer, phone, or tablet with internet access, people are able to observe and immediately react to everything that they see.

The ability of the users to react immediately hinders the quality of the response because users are not forced to wait to respond. There is no time for self-control or empathy to kick in. The temptation to react in a way that is self-gratifying or shortsighted becomes much more tempting when the availability of that reaction is introduced. Adam Alter explains this in great detail by analyzing the psycho/sociological experiments that made this a firm principal in the scientific world (Alter, 2017, p. 275). The massive effort expended in the research and experimentation of this principal could have been avoided by simply believing and applying a few Bible verses. Jesus told people to ask God to "lead us not into temptation" in the Sermon on the Mount (Matthew 6:16), because after all, it is easy to avoid temptation when it is not present. I Corinthians 10:13 states "There hath no temptation taken you but such as is common to man: but God is faithful, who will not suffer you to be tempted above that ye are able; but will with the temptation also make a way to escape, that ye may be able to bear it." The second half of this verse make it clear that the way to avoid falling to temptation is to try to find a way to escape it.

Social media enables people to make bad decisions on a stage unlike any other. In this theatre, stupid decisions are made with a larger audience than ever before, and these mistakes are archived forever. The goal of social media users is to gain social standing, so all content must be inherently public. All content created in social media is "Public by default, private through effort" (boyd, 2014, p. 61)(note: the author's name is intentionally lower case as she had it legally changed to not contain upper case letters.) The naturally public and available state of social media for the immediate reaction of every user that is a friend or follower of the original poster can only mean one thing: bad decisions are inevitable.

The result of these bad decisions is drama, and one of the biggest side effects of drama is tension. Social media is a hotpot of emotional turmoil that invariably seethes with tensions being continually generated, irritated, exposed and agitated. Bad decisions can range in variety from poorly chosen verbiage in a lack of context to "liking" too much of another person's content, to not "liking" enough of another person's content, to responding to content that is too old, to not responding fast enough to new content. The list goes on. Socializing used to be only between people physically present in a single space, in which cases context and body language were readily available. People would speak as needed in order to portray the appropriate information to those people specifically who they knew were listening. Content could be modified based on the known audience, and the delivery could be adjusted in real time based on the reactions of the people around them. None of these principals exist on social media. In fact, social media not only lacks these key aspects of beneficial social interaction, it also encourages the negative possible outcomes. Hilarie Cash, a clinical psychologist, explained that the neurological effects of being in the same room with the person that you are communicating with enhances the quality of the interaction (Alter, 2017, p. 229). This is a concept that will be commented on in greater detail in the next chapter. What is key to understand is that due to the nature of social media, tensions will inevitably mount that require resolution.

The issues created on social media require resolution of some kind. If a fight breaks out in the public realm of social media, both parties are now mired with the ugly outcomes of ugly words. A fight held privately between two can be resolved personally, and apologies are much easier to give when not presented in front of an audience. When the fight or drama or dilemma is experienced where both are in full view of everybody that they value, it becomes much more complicated and much more difficult to resolve. This creates a permanent quagmire of dramatic interaction that grabs users and won't let go. The chaos created must be continually managed while simultaneously growing one's own reputation. To leave the fight would allow the other person free reign to reshape the narrative into one that puts them in the best light. Leaving the fight is social media suicide, so users are now tied to the trouble they have created. The end result is an addiction to the site because leaving it would worsen a person's social standing. It would mean abandoning the effort that they had exerted to reach the goals they had achieved, and, by quitting, they render all of their previous self-set accomplishments on the site as meaningless. Addictions, after all, are rarely enjoyed by their victims. They are simply emotionally demanded (Alter, 2017, pp. 79, 89).

The unresolved tensions of social media go beyond the emotional turmoil that it generated. The rise of Social Media Influencers makes every user a candidate for immediate fame. Any content that has been posted to the internet immediately becomes public property. That post can be shared by anybody with anybody else, and every piece of content has the possibility of going viral. "Going viral" is a phrase used to describe any piece of content that is shared widely beyond its initial target audience and is seen by a large number of people. The etymology of the word comes from the idea of a virus which replicates and spreads exponentially from person to person. On the internet, it describes content that is spread by lots of people sharing it on the internet. There is no formula for what goes viral and what does not. Virality is impossible to predict and depends on so many factors that it cannot be accurately reduced to a science. Virality is also relative. Some content can be considered viral if it spreads to most of the people in a school. Other content becomes an internet sensation and can attract literally billions of views. Each post has the potential to be entirely ignored or to enshroud the user in the limelight of popularity

In a way, each post plays a little bit like a lottery ticket. Most of the time, it will not generate anything special, but will generate enough feedback occasionally in order to keep somebody hooked.

There is a tiny chance though that one ticket could result in a life changing flurry of positive responses through an arbitrary chance that the user has basically no control over. This makes each post, in a way, a tense interaction that dangles the potential of success just barely out of the control of the user. Each post creates some tension in not knowing what the response will be.

SOCIAL INTERACTIONS

Social interactions are inherent to social media. The extent of these social interactions is also largely dependent on the nature of the individual experiencing them. Some people are content with only a few friends or very limited interaction, while others live for the approval and acceptance of others. This is why some people experience a life-altering addiction to social media and others are able to try it and quit it after not enjoying it. It depends entirely on the person experiencing it. Based on the cultural trends seen across the world, it seems that those who wish to use social media vastly outweigh those who don't.

Since social media is based on the concept of interacting virtually with other people in bulk, people who choose to use it have the most influence in society. People who use social media interact more with other people than those who do not, and their thoughts, ideas, and opinions will reach a greater number of people. Each post created by a user has the potential to be seen by every single follower, friend, subscriber, etc. which means that they can potentially create content that is seen by hundreds, thousands, or even millions in a day. A person who only speaks to people in person can never match those numbers. While the interactions with them may be more meaningful and personal, the quantity provided through the potential of social media simply overruns the impacts of these interactions. Social media and the type of interpersonal relationships that it evokes are a key aspect of our culture now, with that culture rapidly growing across the entire world. On June 27, 2017, Facebook reached two billion personal accounts (Vaidhyanathan, 2018, p. 1). Two billion people is roughly a quarter of the total population of the planet Earth, or about six times the population of the United States. Of those two billion, very few currently reside in the world's most populous country, China. China's interned service is largely self-contained within its borders and access to the outside world is limited. In China however, an app called WeChat fulfills a similar function to Facebook as well as several other services. It reports all of its data and metadata directly to the communist government and hosted nearly one billion users as of 2018 (Singer/Brooking, 2018, p. 51). With these numbers in mind, having a social media account may be the single most unifying social commonality within the entire human race. Specifically having a Facebook comes in a close second.

When God saw that it was not good for a man to be alone, he made a companion for him (Genesis 2:18-25). Ever since then, man has sought the companionship of others, and the first man, Adam, was willing to sacrifice his life, a perfect world, and his relationship with God in order to maintain a relationship with another human being. Since social media is now the premier method for interacting socially, it makes sense that people are flocking to it and staying on it. We enjoy social interaction on a neurological (Alter, 2017, p. 299) and spiritual (Proverbs 27:17, Ecclesiastes 4:9-12) level. Social media allows us to know what other people think about our lives. In the constant climb to the top of the social ladder, the responses of other people to your actions are key, as it will dictate to you if you are acting like the person you want to be or not. While this introduces a massive degree of hypocrisy, it does fulfill the basic social desire to be accepted. Thanks to social media, people can now know exactly what everybody they know thinks about everything they do. The desire to be accepted directed the initial downfall of man, and the desire has retained its position as one of the leading motivational factors in decision-making. Since social media relieves the anxiety of wondering what others think of us, the social interactions on these sites have become highly addictive. The satisfaction of soothing the psychological stress of not knowing is a key factor in developing an addiction (Alter, 2017, p. 79) and social media aptly alleviates that desire.

CONCLUSION) TEMPERANCE, THE FORBIDDEN FRUIT

Temperance is a biblical topic that tends to receive little attention in modern preaching, except when it is used to justify social drinking. Nonetheless, temperance occupies a prestigious position as one of the nine fruits of the spirit, right along with love, joy, and faith. God lists this as a trait of a person who is being actively used by the Holy Spirit to produce good fruit in this life. Temperance, or moderation as it is sometimes referred to in the Bible, is being able to maintain a consistent control over one's internal desires and emotions so that feelings do not override the will of God. A person who wishes to become a master in following the will of God must be temperate, according to I Corinthians 9:25. A person with no temperance is subject to being attacked by the devil (Proverbs 25:27) and God will not give them wisdom (James 1:5-8). This fruit of the Spirit is therefore counteractive to the nature of Internet Culture and smartphone use.

Developing a biblical understanding of temperance is critical when considering the impact of social media on the human brain. So much of social media is designed to addict the users, and addiction is the opposite of temperance. An addict is not temperate in their desire to fulfill their addiction and will often sacrifice a great deal of more important things to satisfy it. The problem with social media is that the people who design it are driven to make it as profitable as possible. Maximizing internet traffic on the site maximizes profits, so the developers make it their goat to attract as much traffic as possible. I Timothy 6:10 identifies the *love of money*, as the root of all evil. The developers know that they are creating a generation of addicted individuals but are more concerned with their own profits than the potential intellectual impact that a lifetime of addiction will have on the fully connected world.

Addiction to a physical substance such as heroin or LSD will have a considerably more adverse effect on the user, which is why so many people tend to dismiss their technological addictions as habits, or just something that they do for fun. Extreme cases of internet addiction that result in massive life-changing decisions do exist, but they exist in proportionally fewer cases than that of drug addicts. The unfortunate reality is that although the apparent effects are much less severe, the passive effects are still incredibly detrimental to how society thinks.

A generally acknowledged but rarely quantified detriment of social media addiction is the amount of time spent on it. One of the key indicators of a person's severity of addiction is a simple measure of how much time is spent attempting to satiate their addiction. The dubious nature of social media is amplified by its continual availability through the use of smartphones. Social media can be accessed at anytime, anywhere. As of 2015, the average American spends two hours and 48 minutes on their phone each day, which has been part of an upward trend since 2008 (Alter, 2017, p. 28). The amount of time spent can be easily tracked using various applications designed to present this data to users. They are freely available on app stores and range from simple trackers to limiters that prevent use of individual apps beyond specified time constraints. Often, an addiction does not become apparent until the person realizes the real amount of time they spend feeding their addiction. When this time is extrapolated across a lifetime of seventy years, it equals out to looking at your phone for twenty-four hours a day, every day, for more than eight years. Since this time is broken up into tens or even hundreds of short uses each day, it is commonplace to underestimate the amount of time spent on the phone. A developer for one of the tracking apps reported that people tend to estimate that their actual use is 50% less than what it really is (Alter, 2017, p. 14).

This imbalance of time, carried out through the life of individuals across society, begins to alter the general workings of the human mind. The fundamental impacts are on the intellectual and emotional centers in the brain. Both of these centers are key to healthy mental development, and ultimately lead to a desire for spiritual fulfillment. The beauty of nature appeals to the intellect to educate the lost man that there is a God (Psalm 19). The conscious given by God to every man appeals to the emotional understanding of the nature of sin (Romans 2:15). These work in tandem to draw each man and woman toward a desire to know God and possesses his favor. In the heart of a Christian, the intellect is required to learn the fundamental content of the Bible and to begin to ask spiritual questions that can only be answered by God (I Corinthians 2:14). The heart of a Christian must be continually fixed on God in order to begin to see things from a spiritual perspective and emotionally relate to situations in the same way that God does. Temperance works to produce a productive Christian who emulates a perfectly balanced God to a lost world.

CHAPTER 4 ⟩ **BRAIN GAMES**

Modern scholars like to cite the fluidity of language as a justification for the continuous stream of modern bible versions entering the market. Historical works in English read nothing like the street language (or "koine") spoken today in England or America. Neil Postman goes as far as to say that "The Gettysburg Address would probably have been largely incomprehensible to a 1985 audience" (Postman, 1986, p. 46). Slang terms override traditional definitions, words phase out of usage, and associations are continually formed and lost.

The fascinating truth behind the linguistic power of the King James Bible is that despite the great divide between Elizabethan and Modern English, the individual words remain highly accurate in the world of today. One key word that should be studied out by the modern Bible believer in the King's English is the use of the word device. In the Bible, this word and its variation, devices, is used 26 times. Interestingly enough, this word appears to fly in the face of homiletical analysis, as the first use of it initially appears to have a positive connotation, with every single use afterwards being in an exclusively negative context, less a single neutral use in Ecclesiastes. Its first use describes the man who builds all of the devices to be used in Solomon's temple (II Chronicles 2:14-15). While the initial understanding of the passage is that the devices in the temple are good things, a deeper analysis of the passage reveals some rather disturbing spiritual implications. The devices are being constructed by a man who is half Jewish (his mother being from Dan [Revelation 4:8], his father being from *Tyre* [Ezekiel 28:1-19]) who is skilled in *graving* (Exodus 20:4), is paid in *wheat, barley, oil and wine* (Revelation 6:6) and *helps the Jews build a temple in Jerusalem* (II Thessalonians 2:6). These verses are fully immersed in contextual references to the antichrist and the tribulation, and it centers around his ability to create devices.

Throughout the rest of the Bible, the usage of the words *device* and *devices* follows suit. It is used twice in references to

Haman, a strong type of the antichrist in that he masterminds a plot from Babylon to destroy the Jews. Job, a type of a Jew in the tribulation uses it to describe the arguments used by his accusers to falsely incriminate him. David, Solomon, and the major prophets use device as a reference to ideas that the wicked use to attack them, and most of their writing have a double prophetical application to the Jewish captivities, as well as to the Tribulation. Luke uses the word in relation to the making of false gods in Acts 17. The word is used for the last time by Paul in II Corinthians 2:11 when instructing Christians to not let Satan get an advantage over them with his devices. Based on this evidence, the word *device* is irrefutably negative throughout the Bible and has strong connections to Satan and the Tribulation.

A word study on device is pertinent to modern society, as the word *device* is most commonly connected with all internet-connected communication technologies. The phrase "smart enabled device" or some such derivation inhabits nearly every commercial for Internet Service Providers, cell phone/tablet manufacturers, and personal assistants, such as Alexa, Echo or Siri. Our modern world uses the term "device" to refer to any piece of electronic equipment that connects to the internet to better suit the purposes of the user. The inundation of devices into society should raise a warning flag to any biblically literate Christian that believes in the literal interpretation of the living word of God. If for no other reason than biblical context, the arrival of devices into every corner of society should be, at the very least, an indication of the soon-coming end of the Church Age.

The significance of devices in our time does not simply begin and end with the biblical context. There is no such thing as a spiritual coincidence, and the Bible does not label concepts as sinful or evil simply because God chose some things to be bad and others to be good. Deuteronomy 6:24 clearly states that the entirety of the Levitical law was implemented for the benefit of the nation of Israel. God created man to be in fellowship with him. The only way for Adam to break the fellowship was to do the one thing that God told him not to do, and two cannot walk together unless they agree (Amos 3:3). Sin is therefore anything that draws a person away from their fellowship with God. When God gave the Levitical law, all of the laws that seemed trivial, pointless, or tedious were implemented for the good of the Jews in relation to their walk with God.

TO TOUCH THE HEART AND MIND

This analysis of the word "device" comes into play as the focus of this thesis from what the internet and its various extensions are to what the internet actually does to us. Addiction has been established as an obvious fruit of this creation, but the addiction is only a bad thing if the effects diminish mankind's ability to please God. After all, the only biblical use of the word addiction is in relation to men that addicted themselves to the ministry of serving God (I Corinthians 16:15), and the Corinthians are directed that they submit to people who have developed that addiction. If the internet enhances an individual's Christianity, an addiction to it would be admirable and worthy of emulation.

Upon examination of the intellectual effects that modern devices have on the mind, a fair analysis would begin with the preclusion that if a practice inhibits a person's ability to draw near to and walk with God, then that practice would be sinful. Oddly enough, there is not much scientific research on the cognitive effects of technology on the human mind. While the introduction of smart devices is fairly new in our society, it is surprising that more people are not looking into their effects to see if this technology that we have embraced wholeheartedly is actually good for us. To an extent, it is not possible to conduct conclusive studies in this field because it is so new that enough time has not passed to conduct extensive research. Furthermore, it would be highly unethical to conduct experiments on human beings to determine if technology is good or bad for them. Some authors and researchers have begun to breach this subject, and their studies will be examined thoroughly. The ultimate goal is to determine the effect that these new communication technologies have on a Christian's walk with God, as well as a lost person's desire for spiritual fulfillment.

This analysis will be broken down into two separate studies. The first will discuss the intellectual impact, and the second will discuss the emotional impact. Both the intellect and emotion are vital to a balanced Christian life, as both will draw an honest man towards God for redemption and near to God in service. Proverbs 1:7 says that "the fear of the LORD is the beginning of knowledge" to show that a healthy emotion (fear) generates a knowledge of who God is. No sinner can come to salvation unless they have a healthy fear of a righteous God who will cast them into Hell if they do not repent. The heart and mind are both essential.

This does bring to light the argument that a person does not need scholarship or a formal Bible education in order to be a good Christian. This is true, and in line with the concept presented above. I Corinthians 1:26-27 states "For ye see your calling, brethren, how that not many wise men after the flesh, not man mighty, not many noble, are called: But God hath chosen the foolish things of the world to confound the wise; and God hath chosen the weak things of the world to confound the things which are mighty." God truly does use the foolish things to confound the brilliant minds of the world, but it is here that God makes a distinction between spiritual intelligence and carnal intelligence. James 3:14-18 indicates that there is an earthly wisdom and a heavenly wisdom. Satan himself was marked for being full of wisdom in Ezekiel 28:12, and yet it caused his downfall. This is because pleasing God comes from knowing God personally. The knowledge of who God is, drawn from learning his character as presented in the Bible, is essential in developing the relationship between you and him. *Some* head knowledge of God is necessary (although effectively inevitable since learning about God comes from reading his words). God will provide this knowledge to a person who pleases him. He promises in John 7:17 that "If any man will do his will, he shall know of the doctrine." Anybody who follows God will eventually learn the doctrines of God, especially since reading the Bible is essential to a healthy Christian walk. Reading through the word of God will eventually produce, to an extent, an intellectual understanding of who God Almighty is.

The emotional side of the coin is equally important, although generally less contentious. There is a heavy emotional element to salvation (generally fear, shame, or guilt), as well as to the growth of a Christian (such as love, compassion, and gratitude). The fruits of the spirit given in Galatians 5:22-24 give nine traits that come from a heart that is fixed on God. As a Christian grows in the grace and knowledge of Jesus Christ (II Peter 3:18), they will become more like him. A healthy emotional condition and well-rounded knowledge of God are paramount in developing a fruitful Christian life.

The issue therefore lies in the effects of what would happen if these core elements of humanity were significantly altered in some way. This chapter will focus mainly on the effects that Internet Culture has on the typical human mind. The following chapter will discuss the effects that it has on emotions. Since both of these thoughts come from the brain, some overlap is to be expected and drawing definite lines between an intellectual and emotional impact is impossible, especially given that all human minds are unique. If modern communication technology and Internet Culture are beneficial to developing a healthy intellectual and emotional state, then it can be assumed to be a boon to the spiritual condition of this world and will bring about good fruit.

MOLDING MINDS

The human mind adapts remarkably well to the environment in which it must function. Throughout history, it was largely accepted that the brain was hard-wired (so to speak), and that once something had been learned it was a permanent structure in the brain. In April of 1972, three scientists named Paul, Goodman, and Merzenich published an academic paper proving the law of neuroplasticity (R. L. Paul, 1972). They had experimented on monkeys to prove that the brain could constantly adapt to external stimuli and that their mental structures could be rewritten (Carr, 2010, p. 26). This revolutionized the way that science looked at the development of the human brain, and continued experimentation has served to prove this to be true.

The practical application behind this is that an old dog can learn new tricks. And when an old dog is exposed to nothing but a new trick, it forgets the old ones. Nicholas Carr states this eloquently when he says "It seemed ludicrous to think that fiddling with a computer, a mere tool, could alter in any deep or lasting way what was going on inside my head. But I was wrong. As neuroscientists have discovered, the brain – and the mind to which it gives rise – is forever a work in progress. That's true not just for each of us as individuals. It's true for us as a species" (Carr, 2010, p. 38). As was stated earlier, it is estimated that 90% of the world's population will have access to a smartphone by 2025 (World Economic Forum, 2015-, p. 7). This means that any impact that Internet Culture and cell phone use have on the human brain, it will likely have on 9 out of 10 people in the next few years. Whatever impacts this is having on the collective human consciousness, it will be firmly established as a universal human behavior in the all-too-near future. Since the developed world is the most technologically dependent, these impacts are already metastasizing in the dominant cultures of the world.

MONEY ANSWERETH ALL THINGS

The internet has had an indelible impact on our culture, and, in turn, our culture has impacted how we use the internet. This is an endless loop that sociologists, anthropologists, and the like will debate until the end of time if God lets them. Until now, the examination of the nature of technology has determined the manner in which it will be used. All communication technologies that have had major impacts in the course of human history have been optimized for maximum profits by the free market. The blame for this does not lie in the free market, as the modern socialistic drive would have you to believe. Peter endorsed capitalistic beliefs (Acts 5:4) and only promoted "socialistic" ideas in terms of Christians voluntarily taking care of those in need (Acts 2:44-46, 4:32-35. This is also known as *charity*. It is voluntary, and the government is never involved.) The blame for the monetary optimization lies in the human nature's tendency to love of money at the expense of itself and others, which is not specific to any economic system, be it capitalist, communist, socialist, etc. The brokenness does not come from the *oppressiveness that is inherent in the system, but rather the oppressiveness that is inherent in human nature* (Jeremiah 17:9). The sin nature of mankind has always been the problem, and it will dominate any governmental or economic system that we enact.

The idea of optimizing invention for maximized profits has already been explored in depth, but it should be remembered in light of how the internet operates. As a communications platform, the internet is able to transport unfathomably large amounts of data in absurdly short amounts of time. Data storage costs have been plummeting for the las 30 years with no sign of slowing down. Since communication technology has proven to trend towards optimization, it would seem that the internet would be primarily used to transport large works of information and would specialize as an educational tool that would enhance the quality of life for the entire world.

If the internet had been invented a few years after the printing press, or during the Age of Enlightenment, this outcome would be a much more plausible prediction. At those times, there was a much greater appetite for conglomerated information presented through a logical progression. But why have appetites changed so much? If an intelligent population was presented with an unhealthy alternative, it seems apparent that they would reject it in light of the greater benefit. This is true, but the Devil, master of subtlety, knew that in order to fully enrapture the human mind in the overly dynamic nature of the internet, it would have to be implemented in stages. Chapter two explains the degradation of the human mind in correlation with the increased capacities of communication technology. Once Internet Culture was introduced to the developed world, it had already been tenderized to a pulp by television culture, which only gained momentum through radio culture. As humanity progresses with its technological development, it regresses in its intellectual appetite.

There are three main facets of informational content on the internet, and all of them operate on a single principle. These facets are social media sites, search engines, and informational websites (most commonly news sources). Since websites generate the most money when their users click on multiple links (causing them to view the most ads), the user must be distracted with alluring content as much as possible. The more you click, the longer you are on the site, and the more money they make. This concept has already been explored, but there is a universal trait which all of them share that is integral to the business model and is only possible thanks to humanity's regressive habits.

SOCIAL MEDIA

Social media is designed to addict, as was explained in chapter three. It is meticulously crafted to engage the user and eventually produce a dependence on stoking the emotional turmoil that it creates. In a way, it is like smoking a cigarette. By using nicotine, people develop a craving for nicotine that makes them uneasy until they can get their nicotine fix, which only strengthens their addiction to it. While social media provides an emotional stimulus, the intellectual impact is also key, in that a one unifying factor in all social media is that the posts are always short. Facebook prompts users to post their thoughts and experiences for the day, to share stories, or provoke discussions. In all of these cases, short posts are the norm. Novels are not written on Facebook, and some sites, such as Twitter, have character limits that prevent the users from writing or responding with more than a set number of characters. The existence of comments sections under posts prompt even less thought, as the cultural understanding of a comment is a short statement expressing a thought related to the presented subject.

Social media also promotes the sharing of pictures. In 2015, it was estimated that across all social media platforms, 1.8 billion photos were being uploaded on a daily basis, which would equal out to about 657 billion photos shared in a year (Vaidhyanathan, 2018, p. 47). Photos do prompt a good bit more thought than short posts but ultimately are cheapened through the quantity available. Photography and art can provoke some deep thought in the viewer, but ultimately lack the necessary context to promote the growth of the viewer. All photos posted to social media sites request comments or likes, which devalue the potential analysis of the work to a level that to a reaction that must be set in a limited amount of space. Any thoughtful prose would soon be lost in the deluge of additional postings, or anonymously stolen and reposed elsewhere, rendering any meaningful discussion to a mere frivolity. This mindset in turn reciprocates to the content creators an effort to produce a large quantity of low-quality work in rapid succession that is devoid of any true benefit.

SEARCH ENGINES

Search engines generate profits through advertisements that line the sides of the page and promoted content, which are sites that pay to be at the top of the list when a relevant term is searched. They also use the searches done on their engines to create consumer profiles and sell this information to marketers. This is how search engines makes money. The issue in terms of intellectualism lies partially in the presentation of ads, and partially in the presentation of information.

Advertisements and promoted content provide an apparent shortcut to the users, allowing them to immediately access a store or site that promises to offer a solution to their quandary. These promoted sites do not always offer the best solution or the right answer. They offer the best *paying* solution to the problem. This means that there is always a website or two that is given top billing based on their ability to pay Google, not their ability to help the user. This provides a distraction that diverts the attention of the user from their original intention to whatever is being advertised, causing a mental break in their search for knowledge.

The second issue lies in the presentation of the knowledge. Since the internet would be nigh unnavigable without search engines, the format in which they present the information that is out there is key to their continued business (this effectually makes search engines the intellectual gatekeeper of our time, since they make a point to present only information that they deem to be correct, and in the order in which they choose). They are able to undercut the profits of all other websites through their presentation of the sites are that are searched. When any search engine delivers the search results to a user, it presents key phrases, article titles, and a short quote of text that is related to the search query. While convenient to use, this decontextualizes any information presented (in the already truncated online articles) and presents a quick quip of information that the user can read without analyzing the entire article. Search engines give short answers to questions and make it simple to read a large number of decontextualized statements from different sources, creating the illusion of research while presenting nothing more than a glorified comments section. The results presented are kept short, sweet and to the point, but at the cost of depth. This calls back to Neil Postman's comments on the telegraph, in which he states that the immediate availability of knowledge redefines intelligence as "knowing lots of things, not knowing about them" (Postman, 1986, p. 70), bringing back into focus the consideration of depth. Adam Alter, when speaking about search engines says

"We don't see the forest when we search the Web. We don't even see the trees. We see twigs and leaves." (Alter, 2017, p. 91)

INFORMATIONAL SITES

Websites that are marketed as reliable sources of information present this information after a universal pattern. Be they sites for news (the primary offender, generally because it touts the most self-importance), recipes, do-it-yourself projects or blogs, all will present the viewer with as many distractions as possible. These distractions can come in the form of advertisements for outside products that have purchased space on that page, or advertisements for other pages within that website. Readers have to be kept on the site as much as possible to ensure that they view the maximum number of articles. Viewing more articles means viewing more ads, and that means more money. There is a delicate balance that occurs in which the owners must determine the maximum amount of abuse their readers are willing to endure and then to stop as close to that line as possible. Ultimately, the end result is a greater quantity of shorter articles or posts. The key here is that the length is driven down to a minimum because once a reader has accessed the page, web editors put a greater focus on distracting the reader into clicking on another article than they do on providing beneficial information to the readers. Distraction must be maximized and information must be minimized, since after all, information and analysis are expensive to generate.

NOTIFICATIONS

Another great tool in the intentional war on the human attention span is the notification, which is always cleverly disguised as a helpful tool. All websites that encourage the creation of an account, be it for posting, purchasing, or prime viewing will ask users if they would like to receive notifications. Some sites will have notification settings on the user's personal profile page. Others will request permission to send emails to your account with promotions, sale notifications, or product information. These notifications can range greatly in variety, but all serve the same purpose of notifying a person whenever a certain trigger is met. This means that at any point, a user can receive an email, phone buzz, or pop-up stating that they should return to that site and see whatever new content has been created or become available. Notifications are so common that most cell phones reserve the top portion of the screen to display all of the notifications that the user has received across their entire online presence, granting easy access to any site at any time.

While this is a helpful tool if you wish to be kept up to date on a developing or time-sensitive situation, it should also be taken into consideration that these notifications are designed to interrupt whatever else the user is doing to get them to return to that site. All websites on the internet compete for a limited amount of human attention and time, so notifications serve as the perfect offense against every other competitor for that limited resource. This produces a constant stream of interruption to whatever the user is concentrating on. When on the site, these notifications tend to appear as either red bubbles with numbers in them, indicating the quantity of newly available distractions. They can only be removed by viewing them, thus creating a mental conflict that must be resolved. Emails appear with subject lines that are designed to catch the attention of the user but are in a constant evolving competition for the attention of the receiver. The end result is advertisement via emotional sensationalism, which was discussed earlier in the analysis of Yellow Journalism 2.0.

The end result is that that website developers know that people must be constantly interrupted in order to keep their attention of their own site as much as possible. With the advent of the personal smartphone, notifications are no longer limited to emails and popup ads on desktop computers, but now have alluring and unique tones, symbols, and vibrations to notify a person to return to the site anytime, anywhere. Since these distractions are perpetually available, they demand attention individually, rather than in bulk, which is the least efficient method of addressing any problem. The efficiency of the user's time is not the concern of any site that wants to maximize their profits, so this actually works against the user's best interests. The underlying theme is that all sites that want to maximize their profits must attempt to maximize the distraction that they create.

MUCH STUDY IS A WEARINESS OF THE FLESH

The universal theme across all of the major types of websites is that in order for profits to be maximized, the user must be distracted constantly. The effect of this is that all internet surfing produces a passive consumption of short material that keeps the mind perpetually moving. Since the neuroplasticity of the brain mandates that it constantly rebuild its cognitive architecture to adapt to the surrounding environment, the brain is constantly attempting to make its thought processes more efficient. When humanity moved into a culture of surfing the internet, the human mind of each person in that culture began to adapt to what it was presented with. While this does occur to a lesser extent in the elderly (thus the more widespread rejection of Internet Culture by the elderly), neuroplasticity never ceases in the human brain (Carr, 2010, p. 26). The inevitable conclusion based on these facts is that the internet is passively programming the human mind to reduce its ability to focus. Catherine Steiner-Adair, a clinical psychologist with a specialty in children and clinical instructor at the Department of Psychiatry at Harvard Medical School, notes in her book "The Big Disconnect" that there is a strong correlation between the internet use of children and the rise in ADD/ADHD diagnosis. In the context of this assertion, she discusses a case study in which a child who was diagnosed with an attention disorder was able to improve to a level of normal functionality after the child *and their mother* both reduced their dependency on screens (Steiner-Adair, 2013, pp. 116-123). An increased acceptance of Internet Culture is correlated directly with our decrease in attention and our decreased consumption of printed words (Carr, 2010, pp. 87-88).

Decreasing ones' ability to focus has many lasting and unpleasant effects on the human mind, but one of the most detrimental plagues lies in a general decrease in the interest and reading of the Bible. Composed of 66 books, most of which are not directly written to a person living in the Dispensation of Grace, reading the Word of God is a trying task to all who approach it, regardless of their spiritual condition. No word of the Bible is without consequence (Proverbs 30:5, Luke 4:4), and the Bible contains many words, stories, and descriptions that require concentrated study, service, and prayer to begin to comprehend (I Corinthians 2:14, II Timothy 2:15, John 7:17). All of these take time and dedication to reading and studying a book that tends to run about 1500 pages, contingent on the size of the print. This book is full of words and phrases that require additional study and references in order to define using *Sola Scriptora* (Scripture only), and there are several portions of the Scriptures that provide a great deal of detail about subjects that, at surface level, have no impact on life of any living human today (i.e., the composition of the tabernacle, the priestly courses, or the dimensions of the millennial temple). When these passages are presented to those who are serious enough to display a modicum of interest in beginning to study the word of God, it becomes exponentially more difficult for their brain to maintain an intellectual investment. Human nature has always protested to the reading of the word of God, but thanks to the tangible impact that the internet has on the human brain, it now requires a reader to think in a manner that is presented in a manner contrary to everything else that they consume to begin to grow spiritually.

This effect is present regardless of the content that is presented through the web. Any frequent user will reduce their attention span passively by consuming information presented in Internet Culture. The content consumed may have an impact on a Christian's walk with God if it is sinful, but the method of consumption inevitably produces a negative impact on the human brain. Bible readers are warned time and time again against the subtlety of the devil, and this passive detriment aligns with his method of operation. Much study has always been a weariness to the flesh, but now, from an intellectual perspective, it is more difficult than it has ever been.

SCREEN TIME

The internet, appropriately enough, does not exist in a tangible form. All of the information that has even been stored on the internet is recorded as a collection of ones and zeroes that are assembled in very specific patterns. These patterns are called binary, and every bit of data and code can be ultimately broken down into this format. It is like an alphabet for computers but contains only two letters. To the human eye, it is completely illegible and must be processed (or, in terms of language, translated) into programs, images, videos, sites, etc. that people can use. Since it is stored in this manner, the only way to view this information is through a computer screen of some kind.

This draws into question the issue of if screens affect individuals differently than physical objects or written words. Based on a study in 2009, most Americans spend at least eight and a half hours a day looking at a screen of some kind, be it a television, smartphone, or computer monitor. A large number of people reported that they use multiple devices at the same time (Carr, 2010, p. 87). Each day has in it a limited, consistent amount of time. As screens have begun to encroach on more and more of it, time spent doing other things must by necessity be decreasing. The US Bureau of Labor Statistics reported in 2008 that the average American spends 143 minutes a week reading print media (about 20 minutes a day), which represents a decline of 11% since 2004 (Carr, 2010, p. 87). Screen time now dominates print reading by a factor of over 25:1. If the brain does process virtually presented information in a different manner than physical materials, then based on the precepts of neuroplasticity, it must be altering the brain functions of the human race.

FROM THE GROUND UP

Although screens have been a part of the American lifestyle since the advent of the movie theatre in 1902 (Kane, 1933, p. 299), the impacts of screen learning have not been explored in depth. This is partly because in order to test hypothesis, experiments would need to be run on humans that could potentially impair them for their entire lives. All experiments involving human subjects must first be approved by the American Psychological Association or they will not be recognized by the scientific community. This means that all data regarding how the mind processes screen information must be derived in terms of correlation rather than causation, making it difficult to isolate variables and validate theories.

The results of excessive smartphone usage seem to begin at an early age, but the first effects begin to take place before the child has their first electronic device. Barbara Morrongiello, who is a psychology professor at the University of Guelph in Canada has spent a significant portion of her career specifically researching the impact that smartphone use has on childhood injuries. The injuries that she has studied however, are not caused by children using smartphones, but the parents. She states that the usage of smartphones by the parents provides a distraction that hinders their conscious protection of their children. In correlation with this hypothesis, the CDC reported that injuries to children rose 12% between 2007 and 2010 after decreasing in the previous years (Steiner-Adair, 2013, p. 12). In the same study, 14% of adults admitted to accidentally causing physical harm to themselves due to the distraction caused by their screens. These years correlate directly with the release of the iPhone (2007) and the iPad (2010). This was the same portion of time in which the number of clients at the Oregon-based rehab for tech users reported a dramatic uptick in business. The majority of their clients at the time were users who played games on their mobile phones (Alter, 2017, p. 256). This indicates only a correlation, and while it cannot scientifically be established that there is a causational link between the advent of the smartphone and these unfortunate statistics, the relationship is undeniable.

Moving past the infant stages of life, studies have been conducted on babies to determine the most effective method for teaching language skills. Neurobiologist Maryanne Wolf concluded through multiple studies that children under the age of two developed linguistics skills best when completely unaided by any technological devices or programs (Steiner-Adair, 2013, p. 81). In fact, research by Patricia Kuhl indicates that when children view screens, even when presented with material designed to educate them in language skills, it only stimulates the visual part of the brain, not the areas related language or cognitive development. She goes as far as to say that it may negatively affect language skills and attention span based on how the brain reacts to it (Steiner-Adair, 2013, p. 80). Another study conducted in 1973 concluded that educational programs on television negatively affected the language development of children younger than two years old (Chapman & Pellicane, 2014, p. 15). The television show used in the study was Sesame Street, so the issue cannot be blamed on the quality of modern educational programs for children. In 2007, a study concluded that 90% of parents who had children younger than two years old allowed them to use some form of electronic media (Chapman & Pellicane, 2014, p. 15). The conclusion that must be reached based on this information alone is that the majority of children living in America today have cognitively deficient language skills in comparison to children born before screens invaded the home.

The studies indicate that the problem is not in the content presented, but in the method in which it is presented. It is a scientific fact that screen-based learning in children is inferior to in-person learning. Screen time is nearly universal for children in the developed world, and children raised on more screens than just a television are well on their way to becoming active members of society. On an even more alarming note, the global reaction to COVID-19 has converted the majority of public educational systems to a "virtual learning environment," in which instruction is done mostly or entirely through computer screens. Universities that once offered "hybrid learning" or "remote sessions" are now operating with fully virtual classroom environments. As of the writing of this thesis, there is no reasonably estimated date for the elimination of the coronavirus and return to the traditional classroom environment. While the efficacy of the modern public educational and collegiate systems has been hotly debated, the scientific analysis of "virtual learning" seems to unanimously agree that it is inferior to classes taken in person.

MISSED CONNECTIONS

Beyond implicitly educational material, screens also have a jarring effect on human communication. God has blessed humanity with the gift of language, and we have learned how to communicate with each other through one of two main avenues. Words can either be spoken or written down, and technology cannot communicate either of these two avenues with the same efficacy as traditional methods.

Verbal communication requires people to be in the same place at the same time, and carries with it vital contextual clues such as tone and body language. Eye contact is actually one of the most effective communication tools that people have and can often convey an entire conversation of its own between two people. According to clinical psychologist Hilarie Cash, in-person communication releases several neurological chemicals that result in biological reactions in your body that do not occur when communicating through text over the internet (Alter, 2017, p. 229). While webcams attempt to emulate in-person communication, the brain does not process conversations held between two people the same way that it does in person. This is because of the cognitive association that your brain has with the screen, as well as the fact that when using a webcam, eye contact does not work the way that it does in real life. While eye contact is nearly attainable, there is distance between the camera and the display on a screen. When engaged in webcam chatting, the users are faced with one of two options. Their first option is to look at the camera to create the illusion of eye contact on the other person's screen while not being able to receive contact from the other person. The other option is that they can look at the eyes of the other person on their screen but appear on the other person's screen to be looking slightly below their eyes. In short, real-time eye-to-eye contact through a webcam is impossible. Furthermore, factors such as the positioning of a person's body, their movements off-camera, and the reality of their surroundings are all not truly displayed. These context clues simply cannot be conveyed. This is not to say that webcam communications are entirely without merit, or that it should never be used. It is simply inferior to talking in real life. When presented with the options of webcam communication or phone communication, webcam communication is far superior. But it will never be equivalent to going "belly to belly" with another human being. Far too much is lost on a screen.

Since text-based communication is rooted in the interpretation of words as they are written, it would seem that the brain would process information printed in a book in the same manner as information presented on a screen. Unfortunately, recent studies have proven that this is not the case. Anne Mangen, a literary studies professor, discussed in an article published in the Journal in Research in *Reading* that there is a strong motor connection between a physical book and the cognitive stimulus that it provides, which greatly affects the immersion of the reading experience (Mangen, 2008, pp. 406-419).

There are two factors that could contribute to this. The first is that in order to create a physical book, something must be permanently sacrificed. Paper is made out of trees and once it has been stained with ink, it cannot be undone. The sacrifice of tangible materials gives weight to the item, which helps to prove to the audience that the author personally was personally invested in their own creation. Money and effort were expended in its creation. This does not of itself prove that the work is of any merit or truthfulness, but it does show that effort was invested to produce something of value. In stark contrast to that, screen-based communication tangibly costs nothing to produce because no physical materials are used in the creation. All technological communications are based on the rearrangement of electrons on various pieces of hardware and sent through either imperceptibly small low voltage communications or invisible light signals, transmitted via light spectrums not visible to the human eye. Since they exist in electronic form only, there is no effective cost in their creation or destruction. There is no investment by an author to prove their personal dedication to the value of the words. Electronic communication is physically valueless.

The second factor largely builds on the foundation laid by the first. Since all electronic communication exists only in a virtual world, it can be continuously altered with no consequence or notification. Written works, once created, cannot be modified to ever read in a different way. Additional editions of scientific books may be released, but the physically written first edition does not become a second edition once the second edition is released. This means that the author had better get it right the first time. Webpages, such as Wikipedia, are crowdsourced, meaning that all of the information on that site is voluntarily uploaded, modified, and cited by users in real time. There are thousands of unnamed editions of all of their pages. Each page is continuously in flux and can be modified at any time, by anyone, to read anything. Social media sites all use proprietary algorithms to determine what posts are presented to what users in what order. Heraclitus said that "No man ever steps in the same river twice, for it is not the same river, and he is not the same man." (Hagopian Institute, 2008). Adapted to modern day, it would read, "No man ever surfs the same web twice, for it is not the same web, and he is not the same man." This statement does not apply to written works. A man may change, but words written in books never do. Physical materials have been forever marked to bear the words of an author, and a man can return to them across his entire life to glean information or enjoyment from something that never changes. Books provide a singular viewpoint through which a person can examine themselves to determine how they have changes based on a constant. While some aspects of the internet are forever archived and do not change, they are often buried or overwritten without a second thought. Hackers or moderators can modify content to change it to read how they wish, and forgery of online identities results in untold losses due to theft each year. While it may be unlikely that information stored on a computer will change, thanks to the potential of the internet, this subconscious possibility permeates the permanence of all electronic material. This is simply an impossibility with printed works.

To further elaborate on this point, there is a fundamental difference in the way that the mind frames a book and a screen. A book contains the intellectual property of the author and can only ever display the information that was written in it. A cookbook is always a cookbook. It can never display content about cars, biology, or your favorite sports team. It is limited to display the same content perpetually, and that physical object will permanently become associated in a person's mind as directly related to cooking and only cooking. It can only ever serve one purpose. A screen is entirely different. As a physical object, the screen is either a small rectangle the size of a post card on your phone, a medium sized rectangle sitting on a desk for a computer, or a large rectangle sitting on a shelf as a television. The single item of a screen is capable of displaying any electronically stored content that it has access to. It can be used to do good things (like write messages to friends,) bad things (like view pornography,) boring things (like pay bills,) entertaining things (like watch videos,) and so on. The possibilities are endless on a screen. This means that screens have no specific association with any singular thing. They are actually associated with everything. The reach of technology will only continue to extend as more and more daily activities are moved to screen/internet-based platforms. This means that it is not possible to mentally frame a device to focus on a singular task or thought process. The same screen that may be used to read books on is used to text, watch videos, and play games. This prevents the brain from associating the device with a single task that it can focus on, thus reducing the depth of content that can be drawn from any multipurpose electronic device.

BIBLES: HARDBACK OR SOFTWARE?

An important tangent must be taken at this point to discuss the new debate among Christians as to if reading an e-Bible is as good for you spiritually as reading a physical Bible. This is a hotly contested and fairly new topic of conversation in churches struggling to adapt to the modern world. In churches across America, it is a common sight to see a congregation where, when the preacher tells the members to open their Bibles, some open books and others pull out their phones. Since the focus of this thesis is to delve into the effects of modern communication technology on Christians and the lost world, this subject cannot be avoided.

The Bible does make a great emphasis directly on the importance of the words of God. This can be seen clearly in passages such as Psalms 12:6-7, Matthew 5:18, II Peter 1:16-21 and countless others, with Psalms 138:2 potentially being the most important, as God stated in this verse that He has placed His word above His name. This is a remarkable statement in light of Philippians 2:10-11 in which Paul states "That at the name of Jesus every knee should bow of things in heaven and things in earth, and things under the earth. And that every tongue should confess that Jesus Christ is Lord, to the glory of God the Father." Per Revelation 4:11, this is the purpose of creation. An investigation on the name and word of God would require a vast investment of study, the depths of which have never been fully plumbed by man. The information stated above will have to suffice for the purpose of investigating the potential differences in the printed and electronic words of God. It is essential to understand that the power comes from the words themselves, and there is a great deal of power in them.

The Bible also spends a great deal of time discussing the importance of the Bible as the "book" of the Lord. This can be seen in Isaiah 34:16, Exodus 17:14, Revelation 1:11, and the entirety of Jeremiah 36. God makes a specific point to emphasize the importance of the written book. Obviously, electronics of any kind did not exist when the words of the Bible were written, so it would be a flawed argument to say that God does not approve of the use of electronic Scriptures, since he never directly mentions them. If this argument is to be used, it should also be noted that the Scriptures do not mention Sunday School, Bible colleges, bus ministries, indoor plumbing, HVAC, or buildings created to hold church services in. So, in order to fully determine the potential of the electronic Scriptures in contrast to the written words of God, a different approach will have to be taken.

In both print Bibles and e-Bibles, the words are presented identically, and this digression will only consider the implications of reading identical King James Versions in these two formats (although many e-Bibles do not indicate which words are italicized in the Bible). Based on the analysis presented in the previous section, text-based communications between two parties are interpreted differently when presented through different mediums. In terms of the physicality of one form over the other, electronic communications lack the physicality to create the essential mind-body connection between reader and written work. Data exists as electrons stored on silicon, and although their existence and behavior are scientifically sound, electronic storage can only exist as a concept to the human mind since it cannot actually be observed or interpreted with the naked human eye. Books are able to provide the physicality that links a physical human to a physical object. This passively gives a written Bible more intellectual weight than an e-Bible, simply because the brain understands the two objects, the book and the screen, differently.

This is emphasized through the impermanence of screens. Screens change constantly, even if only used for a singular purpose. The small box that is a phone is able to display the entirety of the Bible on an area smaller than an index card by constantly changing to display the continuance of the text. This causes the brain to retain this information as passively less reliable due to the lack of investment in its creation. This is not to say that the Scriptures were preserved without a great deal of sacrifice, as the preservation of the words of God across time have cost the lives and livelihoods of countless believers over thousands of years. This is simply stating that the presentation of the Scriptures through a screen brings with it no indication of investment by the one making it available. Developers must invest time, money, hard drives, and servers into the electronic preservation of the Bible, but none of this is directly tangible to the readers.

Furthermore, screens serve a great diversity of purposes to the users. If a person uses their phone for purposes other than reading the Bible, which is not a stretch by any means of the imagination, then their brain associates the reading of the Scriptures as an activity that is equivalent to all other activities done on that phone. The key here is that it impacts the ability of the reader to say, definitively, that the reading of the Bible is a special activity that should be given emotional precedence over other forms of reading. By reading electronically, the brain processes this information as an activity akin to that of reading the news, readings texts, or checking social media. There is no separation in the activity. This greatly reduces the reader's ability to prioritize the importance of reading the words of God.

In terms of simply reading books written by men, all of the above stated arguments apply, and it has been extensively documented that the brain is stimulated intellectually to a greater extent when reading a physical book instead of an electronic book. The Bible, however, does not follow the rules of books written by men. I Corinthians 2:14 and II Peter 1:20 explicitly show that the Scriptures are interpreted through the Holy Spirit and not the intelligence of mankind. The Bible is a spiritual book and requires its author, God, who is a spirit (John 4:24,) to interpret it through the Holy Spirit (I Corinthians 2:13), who is also a spirit. So, in terms of spiritual understanding of the Scriptures, it would seem that even through a more difficult medium of concentration, the words of God still retain their original power. To an extent, this is true. The power of God is not manifested to the world during the church age through icons, artifacts, or other physical items, but through the power of his God's words. God is able to use electronic devices to convey these words with power, but that power is greatly resisted to a greater degree when considering the importance of studying the Scripture. II Timothy 2:15 delivers a direct command to the Christian to "Study to shew thyself approved unto God, a workman that needeth not to be ashamed, rightly dividing the word of truth." God puts the onus on the Christian to commit themselves to reading the word of God (Acts 6:4). As a Christian continues to read and submit themselves to the Bible, God will begin to open their understanding of the Scriptures (Isaiah 66:2). That person must commit themselves to their own study first and then allow God to open the Bible to them. Without the study, the Scriptures will remain closed, since it is impossible to learn something from a book without first reading it. Since the brain processes a screen as a less deep source of information, it will passively erode the reader's ability to comprehend the Scriptures exactly as they stand. The King James Bible is written in Elizabethan English, which requires study to understand in terms of basic concepts such as sentence structure. Without this study, God is not able to open the spiritual interpretation of the words to the readers. This is still undoubtedly possible through a screen, as the words do bear the same power from God. The simple truth of the matter is that screens subconsciously push against that power due to their effect on the brain.

The stories of the Bible document several underlying themes. One theme that is universal across all Bible characters with an admirable walk with God is their personal communion and individualized relationship with God. God created man to be pleasing to him, and man understands God better via communication with him through prayer, and God communicating back through the Scriptures. The Christian life is essentially a long conversation between God and man, and two cannot walk together unless they are in agreement (Amos 3:3). While individuals in other dispensations were able to know God through dreams, visions, incarnate visits, and messages from prophets, these are not the methods that God has approved for his church. II Peter 1:19 makes this abundantly clear as he places the words of God as having a greater authority than hearing a voice from Heaven, which is exceedingly important in light of II Thessalonians 2:9. The personal relationship with God is possible through the reading of the words, but, as with all relationships, it grows much stronger when it is established in private. Matthew 10:34-39 states this directly, as Jesus says that in order for a man to be worthy of serving Jesus, he must be willing to deny his entire family. In order to understand and know God, it is required that a man spend time alone with Him. This is shown through the lives of Enoch (Genesis 5:22), Noah (Genesis 6:9), Abraham (Genesis 12:1-2), Jacob (Genesis 32:24-29), Moses (Exodus 3:1-4:23, 19:20-25), Gideon (Judges 6:11-23), and Samuel (I Samuel 3:1-10). God speaking to His chosen men when they are alone is persistent and universal throughout the Bible, and the given list is far from complete. God chooses to speak with men when they are alone because it is more personal.

In considering this principle, a problem arises when reading the word of God specifically on a phone or computer. All internet enabled electronic devices bear with them an understood connection with the entire civilized world. Adam Alter's book "Irresistible" discusses a study in which people were asked to introduce themselves to strangers and converse for a short period of time. Some people did this in a room where a book was sitting on the table next to them, and others in an identical room where the book was replaced with a phone. The individuals in the room with the cell phone described their relationships as "lower in quality and their partners as less empathetic and trustworthy" (Alter, 2017, p. 16). Relationships built in the presence of the phone tend to contain fewer of the building blocks that create long-lasting, meaningful relationships. While the screen of a computer or phone may contain the same words as a Bible, the mental association that the phone brings with it hinders the ability of the mind to focus on God. It also has tendency to, at any time, ring, buzz, or pop up a notification from one of the various communication tools that a phone has in it. When a person is trying to read the Bible, the phone and computer offer a plethora of available tools to the devil to break the concentration of the reader, ultimately cheapening the experience. If the Bible is a tool for God to speak to man through, the internet allows for God to be interrupted constantly. No individual who is seeking to deepen their relationship with another wants to be distracted from getting to know the other person. Distractions from the web are essentially the same as bringing along all of your friends and family on a date and hoping none of them interrupt. The internet is ultimately a tool for connecting humans with other humans. It allows for the communication of ideas and conversations between individuals that are ultimately, still people. When a person wishes to know God better, they must be willing to shut out the rest of the world and the opinions of everybody else, regardless of their relationship. Jesus makes a direct point of this in Luke 14:26. The end of the matter is that, while a screen connected to the internet can be used to connect with God by reading His word, the purpose of the tool is to connect with man. The internet constantly reminds man that other people exist who may have disagree with a person's desire to conform to the old, socially unacceptable and politically incorrect paths (Jeremiah 6:16).

Ultimately, screen-based Bibles have too many negative

passive effects on the human mind to be considered a functional equivalent to a physical Bible. Each of the issues stated above cheapen the experience of reading the word of God and offer limitless possibilities for distraction. The Bible teaches the believer not to fight temptation, but to flee from it (I Corinthians 10:13, Matthew 6:13). This is because it takes more willpower to resist something that is nearby than it does to resist something that is distant. Adam Alter states this in in the portion of his book dedicated to resisting addictions: "The first principle of behavioral architecture, then, is very simple: whatever's nearby will have a bigger impact on your mental life than whatever is farther away. Surround yourself with temptation and you'll be tempted; remove temptation and you'll find hidden reserves of willpower." (Alter, 2017, p. 275) Adam Alter, conscious of it or not, is stating exactly what the Bible has said since the New Testament was penned nearly 2000 years ago. Look for the "way to escape" in I Corinthians 10:13, "that ye may be able to bear it." Resistance is the last line of defense. The best way to avoid the potential distractions, the passive associations, and the fickle nature of a Bible on a screen is simply to avoid all of these issues by using a physical Bible. In the end, books and screens are tools that can do the same job. But the screen is a tool designed for a different purpose, and it is simply more difficult to get the job done when you have the wrong tool. In the modern world of distraction, open sin, and perpetual noise, the last thing that a Christian should be doing is adding an additional roadblock to a successful relationship with God.

One final point must be made when considering the choice between a printed and electronic Bible. This is not a consideration for the user's own good, but for the sake of those around them. Physical copies of the Bible tend to have very specific characteristics. They usually have black fronts and backs, and are the only books that people put in special cases to carry around. They tend to be larger than most other books, have covers made to resemble leather, and made with thin pages so that the 1500-odd-page book is easily transportable, unlike history volumes of a similar word count. The point is that the Bible, as a physical object, is easily identifiable from a distance *as a Bible*. To a person unfamiliar with the defining features of the Bible, it is still obvious that this book is not a typical book. When a person is reading a Bible, it is obvious to everybody around them that they are reading, since there is nothing else that they could be doing.

When a person reads from a phone or computer, the nature of their activity is not evident to those around them, and there can be no guarantee that reading the Bible is the only thing that they will be using it for. In a church service, a person who reads the Bible on their phone only appears to be using a phone. From a distance, it is impossible to tell if they are texting, playing Candy Crush, making notes in their Bible, checking cross references, or liking photos on Instagram. Even if they are reading their Bible, the phone does not confirm that they are paying attention to the preacher to those around them. When using a computer screen to read at home or in the office, it is simple to flip from tab to tab and go from the Bible to whatever else may be open. While the reader may focus all of their available attention to the screen, anybody who cannot see the screen does not know that the reader is doing. This can be discouraging to a preacher who has no guarantee that his congregation is paying attention to a word he is saying if they are all using their phone Bibles. Preachers constantly have to combat wandering minds during their sermons, so adding the worlds greatest distracting device to the laps of all the listeners doesn't help at all. Anybody who does see the screen knows how easy it is to fake doing one thing on a computer and then switch tabs when you are alone, even if the other item is not something sinful or wrong. This has nothing to do with the appearance of evil, because a Christian of good reputation will not be assumed to be doing evil on a screen. This has to do with being seen doing something that is good. This does not mean that reading the Bible should be a show, the way that the prayer of the Pharisee is in Luke 18: 9-14. This has to do with the perception that other people have of you as a Christian. The purpose of reading the Bible is not to be seen reading the Bible, but being seen reading the Bible has an indelible impact on those around you, especially children. The Bible says in I Corinthians 8:3, "But if any man love God, the same is known of him." You show your love for a person by spending time with them.

This section will conclude two personal accounts from the author that show the importance of a physical Bible above an electronic one. I have two, personal friends that were both raised in Christian homes and have experienced considerable family difficulties directly related to their parents' walks with God. The first of these individuals recounted to me how, when she was growing up, she has imprinted on their mind the image of her mother, sitting in a chair, every morning, reading her Bible and doing her personal daily devotion. It showed to her the importance of reading the Bible and, as she grew older, that if it was important for her mother to do, then she should do it as well. Her personal Bible reading helped her to establish her own walk with God, and then to establish this custom on her own as an example to her children. She directly told me that it was important to her, as a mother, to show her children the importance of reading the Bible, and that they had no way of knowing that she was doing that if they just saw her on her phone every day. The phone is not special to her children the way that the Bible is.

The second friend has had considerable trouble with technology in her home growing up and has witnessed a great deal of confrontation between her parents based on how much one of them uses a computer in private during the mornings. Nobody was certain what that parent was doing, and it may very well be possible that they are reading the word of God and doing a daily devotion the same way that the mother of my other friend is doing. But it was impossible to be certain. The privacy provided by the screen in the corner gave way for roots of distrust to grow deeply into the house and divisions and accusations to flourish. Sin began to take root and private usage of screens introduced a great deal of sin into a family apparently secluded from the world. It could have been used to do something good. It could have been being used to do literally anything. A screen can display anything that the user wants. The Bible cannot. And children see a great deal more than they are given credit for.

NO, NEVER ALONE...

Subconscious associations are the most influential factors when considering the difference in reading a physical versus a digital book. The light in which the brain interprets the information provides an overarching theme that subconsciously affects the way it is interpreted, stored, and recalled. While information presented on a screen is passively determined to be less trustworthy and significant, there are many other factors to consider. The most significant of these associations is the connection between screens and interaction with other people.

Since the mainstream acceptance of the internet into the home through the computer, one of the main functionalities of computers has been the ability to connect with anybody at any time via email or a chat service. Phones have always represented a connection to other people, and up until the birth of texting, this was their only function. Once touch screens became mainstream and internet connection dawned in the world of smartphones with the iPhone in 2007, connection became ubiquitous. As other companies raced to keep up with Apple, smartphones surged in popularity. Since smartphones could do things like access Facebook or Myspace, play games, and take high quality photos, the flip phone, which could basically only text or call, was condemned to obsolescence. The connectivity provided by calling with a landline phone or sending a text via a chat service on the computer was now accessible anywhere, anytime.

Given that proximity to temptation is the greatest factor in determining how much willpower you have to resist it, the ability to connect constantly brought with it the tendency to connect constantly. Data collected from a smartphone app in 2014 monitored how much the phone is used on a daily basis. The data collected was concerning. Users tended to check their phones, on average, 39 times a day. The total time spent on the phone averaged just under three hours a day, and the average user *underestimated* their actual usage by about 50% (Alter, 2017, pp. 14-16). Since then, the tech industry has only broadened the scope of what phones are capable of, further increasing our actual and perceived dependence on them, and further embedding their influence on our culture.

The reality of the situation is that the exponential rise of the culture of connectivity has an unmistakable impact on the psyche of its constituents. Thanks to smartphones, the opinions of the rest of the world can be solicited for any subject. True independence from others and the risks associated with isolation have been effectively eliminated. When a person becomes perpetually aware of the opinions of the world around them and their ability to connect constantly, it drastically changes how they make decisions and what they value. The focus of this next section will be on how the culture of perpetually connectivity alters the human through process.

IT TAKES A VILLAGE

A key driving factor in our use of the internet to connect to others is that the value of connectivity is ingrained in our culture. In his critique of the culture of perpetual connectivity entitled *"Hamlet's Blackberry,"* William Powers summarized the philosophy of the day in a single sentence: "It's good to be connected, and it's bad to be disconnected" (Powers, 2010, p. 35). He goes about the rest of his book explaining the value of time spent alone, physically and emotionally. The time alone is key to personal growth and helps people to consider the more important questions of life. These questions, unlike those posed to Google, have no easy conclusions and can take years to answer. The answer itself often does not lie in a simple phrase or quip, but in the application and dedication to living out a successful personal philosophy. A common theme in Christian testimonies of salvation is that there was a considerable amount of time and personal development between when they began asking questions about God and when they finally called on Him for salvation. There is also an overwhelming discontentment that builds when evaluating the consequences of their own personal sins on their present and future. This is spiritual growth worked on the heart of a sinner prior to salvation and is explained fully in the biblical analogy of a seed eventually producing fruit, but only after being sowed, watered, and being grown by God (I Corinthians 3:7). That seed must be planted in the heart and given time to grow. It will not grow unless there is some attention paid to it by the person it is planted in. There must be time given to the consideration of their own mortality, their sinful conduct, the existence of God, and the nature of his personality. When these are contemplated, God grows the seed in their hearts and eventually an honest person will come to the conclusion that they must come to God on His terms alone to seek forgiveness. The seed of the gospel may be planted by another person (Romans 10:14), but the growth must take place alone. This is because in order for a person to understand God, they must go directly to Him through His word.

Part of the issue with perpetual connectivity is that questions that should be answered alone, or by somebody who is qualified to provide a quality response, are diverted onto the internet. Growing up is an inherently difficult task, and children inevitably will begin to ask the questions of life in their hearts. Since connection to friends is a few taps on a smartphone away, it makes it easy for them to revert to a method known as *crowdsourcing*. Crowdsourcing is the act of diverting the power of the few to many (Singer/Brooking, 2018, p. 64). In basic terminology, it is the act of providing a large problem to a large group of people and allowing each member of the group to contribute a small amount. While this does have some useful applications, the easy access to the internet has allowed children to crowdsource their difficult questions to those on the "broad way" of Matthew 7:13. According to Catherine Steiner-Adair, the internet is causing children to "rely on their peers at a much earlier age…tech allows them to hide more from us…and turn instead to strangers online" (Steiner-Adair, 2013, pp. 230-231). This means while children used to confide in their parents to help them grow up, they can now go online where the questions are easier to ask (this will be explored in the next chapter), and they can choose the answer that seems the most correct to them. Advice gathered online through social media, message boards, or comments sections pales in comparison to that provided by a parent. Proverbs 29:15 says that "…a child left to himself bringeth his mother to shame." In time, the more easily-gathered advice, counsel, and direction will lead to the child developing philosophies for life that they got online.

This idea, on its own, is bad enough. When children are able to get advice from people who do not know them as well as their parents, or are not as experienced in life, terrible decisions follow (see Rehoboam in I Kings 12). The problem goes much deeper though than children learning from other children. The greater issue lies in that any questions asked online can easily solicit the opinions of the entire world. When somebody makes a post online, the post is viewed by everybody in the poster's friends/ followers list. This means that before any question is asked, the question is mentally vetted out by the person asking. A question about sinful behaviors may be seen by parents or teachers and get them in trouble. It could also reveal that they are not as "cool" or "mature" as their friends, who may already be experienced in that sin. A question exposing a personal vulnerability could be seen by a bully who would use it to attack them, or it may make them seem like they are being dramatic to gather attention. They must either compartmentalize their questions to groups of people that they trust (again, see Rehoboam), or phrase it in a way that is acceptable to the rest of the world. The result is that the questions are all self-policed before they are even asked.

Part of the reasoning behind this is that all of their questions must be asked inside of the concept known as the "Overton Window." The "Overton Window" is a concept that states that all political opinions must reside within a certain range of extremes (Conceptually, n.d.). Opinions within the Overton Window may be expressed without fear of rejection by the general public. While other people may hold differing opinions, there is an understanding that it is socially acceptable to have that opinion. Opinions that are outside of the Overton Window are not socially acceptable and are frequently denounced by the political right and left, even if the opinion extends in their direction. The issue is that as the Age of Grace progresses towards its inevitable conclusion with the Laodicean Church, that window will move further and further away from biblical principles (II Timothy 3:13). One key example of this is shown in the shift of the Overton Window in America is the public opinion on the legalization of homosexual marriage. Based on a Gallup poll, in 1996, roughly 33% of Democrats and 16% of Republicans thought that same-sex marriages should be considered legally valid. As of 2019, that number had risen to 49% of Republicans and 83% of Democrats (McCarthy, 2020). The general public opinion had switched from most people being against it to most people being in favor of it. As the window has shifted more toward the general public being in favor of legally recognizing it, "fringe opinions," such as the biblical perspective that it is an abomination in the eyes of God and should not be recognized at all (Romans 1:18-32, Leviticus 18:22), go from being acceptable to being unacceptable. Hence, when children begin to question how the world works and why, they must do so in a way that conforms to the limits set by their perception of the Overton Window, or risk social ostracization. Furthermore, the responses that they receive will also be inside this window (baring the interaction of a political extremist, which will be addressed later on). This will become a continually growing problem as the world shifts and narrows the Overton Window on all issues closer to the worship of the antichrist. As the Overton Window movers further from the biblical position social topics, children online will receive more answers in contrast to the word of God.

NO PAIN, NO GAIN

Internet counseling also removes the parental expertise from the equation. When parents deal with children, they are often able to understand what their children really need and identify underlying issues that the child may not be willing to ask. They can also pull information from their children that needs to be brought to light. When children are able to ask their questions online, all of this is lost, and they are able to look for answers on their own terms. The discomfort that comes in the physical conversation with the parents is part of the growth and strengthens the bond between parent and child, and the pain is necessary for personal growth (Steiner-Adair, 2013, p. 183). By avoiding this pain, children are emotionally coddled in a way that actually prevents growth. This concept is demonstrated throughout the Bible and is explicitly stated in Romans 5:3-5 where it states, "knowing that tribulation worketh patience; and patience experience; and experience, hope: and hope maketh not ashamed." Biblically speaking, tribulation is the only way to avoid shame, gain experience and become patient.

The ease of asking a deeply personal question online and immediately receiving a human response also teaches children, and adults for that matter, another principal. If a question can be asked online and receive a quick response, then quick responses become the expected resolution for every question, or at least, most questions. Since the feedback for the query is usually immediate, the standard expected response should come within a few minutes, possibly a few hours, and most likely within a few days. Keep in mind that the deluge of posted content on social media sites quickly buries all "old" content, much like the way that news sites continuously bury old articles with new ones. This will kill even the most compelling posts in less than a week. As was stated before, the brain will begin to adapt to whatever it is exposed to, so by continuously associating conflict resolution with social media postings, the brain begins to rewire itself to think reflexively, rather than deeply. This is shown in Donna Freitas' book *"The Happiness Effect,"* in which interviewed students felt that they needed to use their smartphones continuously in order to block of the fear that they felt when considering important questions regarding "life, relationships, love, work, school, family, friends, choices, their futures" (Frietas, 2017, p. xiv). She explicitly notes that the word *fear* was the word used by students to express the feelings they felt when contemplating the questions of life. The perpetual exposure to their smartphones had absorbed all of their time and attention, relegating anything that could not be solved using one to be an intimidating question. They were lacking the tribulation necessary to build hope.

Even when difficult issues are addressed online, the fact that all responses are hidden behind a screen allows for the development of unhealthy coping mechanisms. Sherry Turkle noted that some people use online message boards anonymously as confessionals to alleviate themselves of guilt that they may feel. Online confessions, even made anonymously, are made on the terms of the confessor, not the wronged. The environment allows them to remove as much pain from themselves as possible when dealing with the trouble they have caused. There is no eye contact, there is no need to see the visual reaction of the person you have wronged, and with the boards being anonymous, there is no closure for the victim. Online confessions allow people "to confess, not apologize" as one woman she interviewed put it (Turkle, 2011, p. 233). This means that people can find closure for their sins without providing closure to others or revealing who the really are to the people who care. This is selfish and hypocritical. It is the equivalent of walking up to a stranger on the street and telling them your sins and waiting to see how they respond. It is cowardly and done only to relieve the burdened conscious of the offender. Apologizing, while uncomfortable, promotes the personal maturity of the offending party and helps to decrease their propensity to wrong somebody again in a similar manner.

Emotional pain is a powerful deterrent that makes people less prone to wronging each other, and the anonymity of the internet deletes most of that nurturing pain.

Smartphones also have provided an alleviation from a sense of isolation that has been a part of human nature since its creation. Up until phones became commonplace, when a person left from one place to be in another, they could only have an influence in the place that they physically were at that time. Should an event occur somewhere else that was pertinent to them, that information would have to be sent by letter, telegram, or messenger, at which point they would be unable to have an impact on what was happening, only a reaction to it. With this came an acceptance that the distance created a mental isolation. If nothing could be done to change what may happen, then it would be senseless to constantly be concerned with other people in other places. This is not to say that people never used to care what other people thought, said, or did in relation to them, but that there was an understanding that a person could only be at one place at one time, doing one thing. Mentally, people were constantly aware of and interacting with what was physically surrounding them. This isolation creates an empowerment that forced people to only work with what was physically around them. It inspired independence, creativity, and personal interaction.

Smartphones psychologically annihilate the growth derived from physical isolation. Sherry Turkle summarizes this in an illustration about her daughter being constantly on her phone when she states "Emotionally, socially, wherever she goes, she never leaves home" (Turkle, 2011, p. 156). At any point, because her daughter has a cell phone, she is immediately able to contact anybody close to her to solicit their assistance, opinion, or company. There is no "thrill of disconnection." There is no need to learn to adapt to life as it was because the concept of isolation no longer exists in the developed world. Where there once was a learned independence, there is now a learned dependence. In describing this, Turkle states "This is a new nonnegotiable: to feel safe, you have to be connected" (Turkle, 2011, p. 247). She blames this on the ubiquity of cell phones in modern culture, and partially blamed the 9/11 attacks on the World Trade Center and Pentagon as the catalyst. Parents of children suddenly felt that they needed the ability to immediately connect with their children in case of emergency. While this is simply her speculation, the news media does monger fear to the world at every marketable disaster, which can be alleviated with the immediate connection capabilities of a phone.

Think for a moment about cigarettes. The human body is not naturally born with an addiction to nicotine. But when people start smoking cigarettes, they begin to crave the nicotine that they previously didn't need. It creates a craving that only it can fulfill. The only way to alleviate this nagging desire is to stimulate the brain with the chemicals absorbed by a drag on a cigarette. This is exactly what perpetual connectivity does. Unlike cigarettes, connectivity certainly does provide peace of mind to parents, but the unfortunate reality is that the comfort provided by phones nurtures an underlying anxiety. The ability to connect constantly creates a fear of disconnection. Humanity used to be required to develop an internal understanding that physical isolation was also mental isolation. Personal judgement, adaptation, and improvisation were simply standard because it was impossible to function without them. People had to think for themselves, and they had to trust that others were able to do this as well. The smartphone with its connection to the internet, ironically, is the perfect tool that inversely enslaves its users (Carr, 2010, p. 4). The ability to connect with another person at any time creates a level around anxiety on any failure to connect. Unanswered texts and calls seem to indicate that the receiver is unable to respond. It could also mean that the other person has no desire to connect to you, or that you are not important enough to merit an immediate response. A lack of connection inspires doubts in the mind of the sender, which creates the nicotine withdraw of our generation: anxiety. Where people once had confidence in their ability to be separated from others, there now is a whole social etiquette that revolves around the methods and timing of communications. Because communication is so easily available to the majority of the population, any deviation from the norm indicates some form of distress. The ability to connect instantly is now subconsciously accepted as the norm, so when disconnection occurs, it is the outlier. Disconnection must be adapted to, rather than connection. Smartphones have been commonplace for the last 15 years, and the most recent generation does not know life without the ability to connect electronically. If this ability is ever removed, people are exposed to the world that they have forgotten how to function in, or in a growing number of cases, have never needed to function in. Smartphones have created a culture of connectivity which we now depend on. Connection is our nicotine, and we are hooked.

ALWAYS ON

This addictive sense of connectivity creates a strong sense of social codependence. It extends far beyond the need to simply connect in times of emergency and into every facet of our lives. It creates a world in which personal identity must be crafted from public opinion. Social media creates an addictive rating system by which people can quantitatively observe their social standing. By being perpetually available to users, it essentially forces people to live their lives on stage, in which they are simultaneously both the star of the show and the center of judgmental attention. As was shown earlier, the availability of a vice directly correlates to the tendency of a person to use it. Combining a platform designed to hook people with perpetual access is the perfect recipe for addiction. Statistics have already been presented on the overuse of smartphones and internet activities, as well as the exponential growth of the social media industry.

Dr. Jean Twenge has rather impressively documented the change in generations across time in her book "*iGen: Why Today's Kids are Growing Up Super-Connected, Less Rebellious,*

More Tolerant, Less Happy – and Completely Unprepared for Adulthood." As a rule, she only cites data that has been collected in an identical fashion across generations. She does this to prove that the statistics of today's children, and adults, are different than they were in the past, allowing her to analyze the trends rather than to make assumptions. Much of her data is surprising and counterintuitive but is ultimately backed by empirical research. Her findings on social media use of high schoolers shows that the average percentage of high schoolers who use social media almost every day has increased annually from 2008, when it was used by 53% of twelfth graders, to 82% in 2015. As of 2015, 98% of twelfth grade girls reported using social media sites at least sometimes. Another study indicates that the number of twelfth graders who spend 10 or more hours a week on the internet has increased from 20% in 2006 to 44% in 2015 (Twenge, 2017, pp. 54, 55, 75). With Facebook boasting more than 2 billion accounts as of 2015 (Vaidhyanathan, 2018, p. 1) and WeChat boasting roughly 1 billion additional accounts (Singer/Brooking, 2018, p. 51), social media is undoubtedly rooted in the culture of modern society and, based on the data, is continuously expanding its reach.

As social media continues its dramatic rise in popularity, it simultaneously continues to impede upon human thought processes. Nicholas Carr, when commenting on social commentaries by Joseph Weizenbaum and Marshall McLuhan notes "Our intellectual and social life may, like our industrial routines, come to reflect the form that the computer imposes on them…Every tool imposes limitations even as it opens possibilities. The more we use it, the more we mold ourselves to its form and function" (Carr, 2010, pp. 207, 209). Overuse of social media has taken root in modern society to the point where social media is becoming, and likely already has become, the primary method of socializing. This has been given an incomprehensibly massive boost due to the spread of the coronavirus in 2020. As governments have closed down social functions, bars, restaurants, malls, parks, schools, churches and more, the only way to socialize "safely" is via technology. Social media has gone from being a method of socializing to the only method of socializing for some people.

When the internet was still a fledgling invention and "instant messaging" services were at their peak, certain slang terms came into being. Typing "lol" meant "laughing out loud", "rofl" meant "rolling on the floor laughing", and "g2g" meant "got to go." Most of these abbreviations became commonly used during that time and have stayed in circulation to this day. One term, however, has not survived the transition from solely computer-based chat functions. That term is "brb", meaning "be right back." The reason that this term has fallen out of use in modern society is simply because nobody is ever coming back to the internet because they *never leave*. When the internet was only accessible through a desktop computer and a modem, people could power the computer up, work, socialize, shop, and then leave and shut it down. Thanks to smartphones, 5G service, and unlimited data plans, nobody ever has to leave. There is no "being back," there is simply "being here." Anytime somebody has "got to go", they take the internet with them in their pocket. While people do not use their phones or tablets or computers perpetually, they are always able to respond to a notification, check an email, or send a comment to a friend. The great problem does not lie in the ability to connect, but the loss of the ability to disconnect.

Disconnecting from others is essential to personal growth. William Powers discussed this in his book *"Hamlet's Blackberry."* He wrote about how his family would disconnect from the internet on the weekends as an experiment. This was before smartphones were invented and he could simply unplug the modem. He stated that as they began to adapt to the lack of internet, they began to realize that "We could just be in one place, doing one particular thing, and enjoy it." The perpetual connectivity of the Internet Culture in which we live demands that we always be able to reach out and connect with another person. As this demand has become unrestricted by technological advances or infrastructure, connection has replaced the natural standard of disconnection. Psychologically, people never leave the internet because they know they can get back on whenever and wherever they choose.

This means that every decision is made with the subconscious understanding that the decisions will be made in public. There is a continual awareness of what the world *could* think if they were made aware of this decision, even if it is not shared for all to see. A study cited earlier demonstrated that people had a greater difficulty forming lasting bonds when they were in a room with a cell phone. The visual presence of a cell phone diminished the quality of the bond that they felt with the stranger (Alter, 2017, p. 16). This would seem to indicate that a subconscious awareness of the existence of the rest of the world impedes on social interactions. This is to be expected, given the permanence of data and rise of "Cancel Culture," in our society.

THERE'S NO "I" IN "WE"

It may be said that an elephant never forgets, but the internet never forgets and also never forgives. All information posted to social media is "public by default, private through effort" (boyd, 2014, p. 61). Once information has been posted to the internet, it can be copied, saved, reshared, reposted, or saved in a screenshot forever by another person. There is nothing that prevents the thoughts, posts, or comments from being saved forever by others. This is not the case outside of the internet. In person verbal conversations are not recorded, and once they have concluded, they exist only in the memories of the people that were present for them. Written works are explicitly protected by copywrite laws and cannot be reproduced without citation or legal permissions. Modern communication technology conveys thought by digitally encoding it and saving it, exactly as it occurred, on a hard drive. It can be reproduced and redistributed by anybody who can get their hands on it. It also does not decay like memories do and can be re-accessed at any time to provide a perfect recollection of the conversation. This means that any mistake that is made on the internet can last forever. Off-color humor, embarrassing photos, rude comments, and personal disputes are permanently cataloged and archived in the digital world.

This can cause a great deal of trouble in our connected society. For some college students, the fear of recruiters finding their social media accounts is a reality. In recent years, it has become standard practice for colleges, recruiters, and employers, to scroll through the social media profiles of applicants to determine if this is the kind of person that they want associated with their organization. Students are becoming increasingly nervous that posts that made them appear less than perfect are detrimental to their careers. This introduces social media scrubbing, which is the act of removing any posts from your social media accounts that could be viewed as negative, or show you as a mean, boring, immature, or unimportant person (Frietas, 2017, p. 48). This is done out of fear that a single poorly-worded post could keep them out of their dream college or job. The fear that this could damage their career prospects is common among college students. Some universities will offer advice to students in their "introduction to university life" or career-oriented classes as to how to become more marketable through their social media accounts. And while it is possible to scrub your own posts of any content which may not be perceived in the best light, posts created or reshared by others cannot be deleted, even though they may be of you. Real-life experiences can be forgotten or kept secret, but experiences posted to the internet retain their efficacy forever.

This brings to light the ugly truth of "Cancel Culture." In recent years, the dark side of connectivity has begun to raise its head. When people are connected, it allows individuals with specific world views to validate their opinions by garnering the support of other like-minded thinkers. This is touted as a near-universally beneficial outcome, as it allows the voice of the minority to gain social traction and strength in numbers. The unfortunate reality of this is that the social viewpoints of left-leaning, socialistic, one-world, anti-biblical humanists are able to push biblical principles out of the Overton Window. These "Judeo-Christian Values," which were once the backbone of western society, are now being driven into obscurity through the effective use of Cancel Culture. Cancel Culture is effectively an online lynch mob. When a person commits the crime of having an opinion outside of the Overton Window, their social media accounts and personal information are publicized by social activists for the purpose publicly destroying the life they have built. The ultimate goal is to cancel their life as it is by making them unemployable and friendless so that they change their opinions to appease the mob. Any attempts to side with that individual will also subject you to the wrath of the social activists, who commonly refer to themselves as *Social Justice Warriors*, or SJWs. Their online presence enables them to force people to only espouse opinions that are acceptable to their humanistic world view. As the lynch mob grows, which can be composed of anybody from anywhere who agrees with any cause, it suppresses more victims, and gains more notoriety. It has the support of the liberal agenda of the news media, which only bolsters its numbers further. Since all participation is online, it is nearly impossible to police these mobs, especially since the majority of those involved do not commit any actions that are technically illegal. Harassment is a crime if one person insults another person 1000 times. It is not if 1,000 different people only do it once. The effect is the same, but no crime is committed, and the internet makes it easy for anybody to find 999 people that agree with them. Even if it means finding 999 other village idiots.

The effect that this has on people is that it causes people to police themselves for fear of the potential mob. In one interview, Sherry Turkle discusses this theme with a girl who states "It's like somebody is about to find a horrible secret that I didn't know I left someplace" (Turkle, 2011, p. 259). As culture changes and the Overton Window shifts its view, things posted years ago that may not have been offensive at the time (for example, blackface, insensitive jokes, racist terminology, or biblical viewpoints) are becoming more and more taboo. This opens people up to be socially assassinated through Cancel Culture by using the permanence of data on the internet to target undesirables by shaming them with posts that have since become unacceptable. The means that social media accounts and internet activity must be continuously scrubbed to keep up with modern social trends. The threat, then, is not that big brother is watching you, but that there are two billion little brothers potentially watching you. Andrew Keen states, "Web 2.0 is the democratization of that Orwellian nightmare; instead of a single, all-seeing, all-knowing Orwellian leader, now anyone can be Big Brother. All you need is an internet connection" (Keen, 2008, p. 177). To avoid meeting the same fate as those cancelled, all online activity must conform to the progressive mindset of the world today, and any deviation from this must be removed due to fear of the mob.

The reality of quite literally a billion little brothers is fully realized in China. The Chinese internet is sequestered behind what is known as "The Great Firewall," meaning that China has its own private internet that is largely cut off from the rest of the world. Singer and Brooking write extensively on this. Inside the great firewall of China is a social media site that is a fierce, government-owned, *mandatory* social media platform that is essentially a combination of the Chinese versions of Facebook, Uber, Twitter, Yelp, and eBay. This platform assigns a Social Credit Score to each user. This social credit score can go up by buying essentials for your child (supporting the next generation), praising the government, or *reporting others for breaking the government-enforced "Harmony."* Your social credit score can go down by buying too many video games, or by being associated with somebody who has a low social credit score. People with higher scores are eligible for certain government-sponsored perks like free phone charging at coffee shops, preferred placement on China's dating websites, and *welfare benefits.* This is the full realization of what social media is capable of. It has the potential to support a one-world government that fully controls everything that is done on the internet and polices itself with its own users by rewarding them with real social benefits. This is beyond Orwell or any dystopian science fiction reality. This is everyday life for the single most populous and second-most powerful country in the world (Singer/Brooking, 2018, pp. 50-51, 100-101).

Many of the authors who have written or lectured on the crippling effects of the threat of an internet mob have referenced a man from the 1800s names Jeremy Bentham. Jeremey Bentham was an eccentric man who was an architect, inventor and philosopher. The work for which he is most well-known is the creation of the Panopticon. The Panopticon is part prison, part philosophy. He postulated the idea that if prisoners could be convinced, not that they were always watched, but that they always could be watched, then they would be less prone to troublesome behaviors. The design for his ideal prison would be to place the guard's watchtower in the very middle and arrange the cells in an outward pattern than made it possible for a guard to look at any prisoner that they chose (like a snowflake). Prisoners would know that even though they weren't always being watched, they could never be sure that they weren't being watched at that very moment. Sherry Turkle notes that this is incredibly similar to the social architecture of the internet, and the fear that the wrong person could see the wrong thing is "very common in the technology community, and gaining popularity..." (Turkle, 2011, p. 262). Donna Freitas, in discussing both Bentham and another philosopher named Foucault (Author of *Discipline and Punish*), says "College students (and young adults in general) are highly aware that because of social media, they can be 'spied upon' at any and all moments by people they've never met, can't see, and who may hail from far-flung locations, all of whom may have power over their lives" (Frietas, 2017, p. 47). The result is that social media, while being continuously praised for encouraging diversity, eliminates any diversity of thought beyond the limits of the Overton Window while it *is still inside the minds of the users.*

A great deal of privacy is sold for the emotional stimulation of popularity on social media. The immediate emotional effects of this will be explored in greater detail later, but the long-term psychological effect will be discussed here. The internet never forgets, and moments of indiscretion are no longer viewed and forgotten by those who witness them in person. The internet, though fickle in nature, does claim ownership of everything that it is given by its users, and that ownership is distributed to anybody who wants to know. Some have predicted that this would create a more tolerant society, since everybody would have flaws available for the rest of the world to see (this is effectively communism). The reality of this is anything but that. The opinion of the cancel culture mob is that anybody, even their own, who has at any time created any content that disagrees with the current position of the mob should be cancelled. These cancellations are supported by the liberal news media, which creates a culture of fear across the internet. Sherry Turkle summarized this by saying "We see a first generation going through adolescence knowing that their every misstep, all the awkward gestures of their youth, are being frozen in a computer's memory. Some put this out of mind, but some cannot, do not-and I think, should not" (Turkle, 2011, p. 259). Children are learning that every posted thought will be scrutinized by those who would try to tear them down if they disagree with the ways of the world, both current and future. Some of them are learning the hard way. Steiner-Adair says "Teenagers have always been drawn to the romance of the risk and in many ways what these kids did reflected the age-old developmental psychological processes at work. But tech has given them a new set of keys to the car, a new kind of substance to use and abuse, a new form of independence, and the illusion of both fame and anonymity. And as is always the case, good kids are getting into bad trouble" (Steiner-Adair, 2013, p. 225).

PRIVACY? WHAT PRIVACY?

One of the main concerns about internet use is that its use is expanding faster than can be understood. The internet brings with it many moral and legal issues that often are not prepared for until they have caused a great deal of harm. One such issue is the case of Joshua Evans and Megan Meier. Back when Myspace was the dominant social media site, a mother, Lori Drew, was concerned that her daughter might be being bullied by a girl named Megan Meier, whom she disliked. To get the truth herself, she created a fake Myspace profile with the name Joshua Evans, which she and her family then used to befriend and spy on Megan with. She then began to use the account to bully Megan and eventually drove her to *suicide*. Lori Drew was then taken to court to be tried for something that was obviously immoral, but not technically illegal. The charges were dropped because no laws existed in 2006 to punish bullying on the internet, also known as *cyberbullying* (Singer/Brooking, 2018, p. 227). The key takeaway from this lesson is that the internet is creating problems faster than the government can prevent them from happening. It is a sandbox of creativity and many people have realized that they can get away with sins, simply because it isn't illegal yet.

There is no governing authority on the internet other than its users. It is not owned by any one company, organization or government. Quite frankly, it is too large to be managed by any single group because it is so effortless to create and share content. The internet is a conglomeration of all who choose to participate, and ultimately each site is a service provided by a company or organization. This means that the greatest amount of power is held by the companies that host the most amount of traffic, since they are the primary providers of the services. They are privately owned and therefore can decide what they allow and what they do not. Governments are able to impose some regulations on what content can be hosted on a site, and the organizations can be held accountable for problematic content such as anything that promotes terrorism or child pornography (Singer/Brooking, 2018, p. 237), but for the large part, the discretion is left entirely up to the users to report problems as they arise. Unless the content crosses the criteria set by the government (which can only use blanket statements to stop the worst crimes a person can commit), the companies are able to set their own *Terms of Service*. This means that they can create their own standards on what users can do, and also on how they will choose to judge the content on their platform.

The continued growth of tech companies creates a significant issue regarding privacy that is built on the symbiosis of empowered companies and the inability of the government to predict the future. All internet-based services have a checkbox titled "Terms of Service" that every user must agree to in order to create an account. This is often many pages of legal language that few people understand and even fewer read. Applications will sometimes request permission to access other services on cell phones, such as the camera or contacts list before they can be fully utilized. The ugly truth behind this is that this is where metadata comes back into play. As companies make their services continuously more addictive and culturally relevant, their terms of service change to request a little bit more invasion into your privacy in order to serve you better. After all, the more that a website knows about you, the better it can tailor itself to suite your desires. Since there is little government regulation on what a site can ask you to give up, sites have continuously invaded the privacy of the users to greater extents simply because it makes them more money and the users have allowed them to. What most people have failed to realize is how much they have given away. Franklin Foer, in his conclusion, states "Privacy cannot survive the recent trajectory of technology" (Foer, 2017, p. 231). Sherry Turkle quotes Scott McNealy, a co-founder of Sun Microsystems, who said, when speaking about the internet, "You have zero privacy anyway; get over it" (Turkle, 2011, p. 256). Instagram, as was already explored, collects 65 points of metadata from each user to best market products to them and further engage people in the use of their system. The outrage against this may be well warranted, until it is considered that permission to access, collect, and sell each of these 65 points of data was given away one user at a time. Since metadata is such a hot commodity on the open market, it seems that the exponential growth of this market is inevitable.

UNLIMITED VOICES, UNLIMITED CHOICES

There is one additional concept to be explored before closing out this section on the intellectual effects of the internet on the human mind, and that is the overabundance of information. The ability to create and store information digitally at little to no cost has brought about the creation of an unfathomably large amount of data. Thousands of years of video, millions of photos and trillions of written words are uploaded every year, and they can be shared on a whim with no physical constraints such as time or distance. Any one person can access more information now through a computer than some people could in a lifetime of collecting materials only a few hundred years ago. The mass sharing of information has brought about a technological revolution of sorts, and people are beginning to understand what humanity is capable of when they are unbound by time and space.

Earlier, it was demonstrated that the financial market behind providing a high quantity of information to a captive audience is more lucrative than providing high quality of information. Basically, it is more lucrative to lie, cheat, and exaggerate than it is to tell people the honest truth. With the physical limitations of printing and selling papers removed, articles can now be published at an astounding rate, and with this comes a troublesome issue concerning the human mind and how it processes information. That issue is information overload. Ultimately, the Internet has made creating and sharing so easy that it is happening faster than the information can be understood or analyzed for accuracy.

This stems from a limitless poll of resources that are all competing for the attention of the viewer. On the internet, the news media is not the only entity vying for as much attention as possible. But information also comes informally from other people. Bloggers try to gain attention so that they can get famous. One viral story could skyrocket their market value and land them a position in a prestigious company. Social media users post status updates that express their beliefs and garner the greatest number of coveted "likes." But social media is used for more than just sharing your own stories. In 2017, 67% of Americans reported that they got their news from Facebook (Vaidhyanathan, 2018, p. 97). This means that two out of every three Americans made decisions that were arrived at using information that they got from social media.

When information is shared through social media, especially news events, the information presented is framed, not by the author or media outlet, but by the person who decided to share it. The article is initially determined to be trustworthy or not based on how the user views the person who posted it. People build reputations with those around them based on their actions, and as such, they are perceived by others to be smart, ignorant, funny, aggressive, or any other adjective. Their reputation often varies from person to person, and nobody, not even Hitler, is universally disliked. When a person shares an article, it is essentially an endorsement of the presented information based on the knowledge that this person believes and is in agreement with what is written in the attached article. If that person is viewed as gullible, the article becomes unreliable based on the person who believes it, not the sources who authored and edited it. If the person is viewed as bigoted, the information they post is viewed as prejudiced against some group. Even if the article cites empirical, scientific data with sources authored by reliable, modern scientists, this information is tainted by the person who shared the article in the first place. This is an incredibly difficult mental obstacle to overcome because, as was cited earlier, people tend to believe the first bit of information given to them about any subject and will rarely change that point of view due to what is known as confirmation bias (Reifler). This is because humanity's pride, derived from its sin nature, makes it much more difficult for people to admit that they are wrong once they have an opinion. Pride in the heart of man has been an issue since Eden's garden, and it isn't a problem that is going away any time soon.

This new frame of reference combined with the ability to read any news article from any provider around the globe introduces a term known colloquially as "analysis paralysis." In layman's terms, this is when a person is presented with so many choices that they become unable to determine which would be the best for them and it causes them to mentally freeze up. Barry Schwartz, in his book "The Paradox of Choice," argues that "As the number of choices grows further, the negatives escalate until we become overloaded. At this point, choice no longer liberates, but debilitates. It might even be said to tyrannize" (Schwartz, 2004). His argument is that if you are presented with two choices, it is easy to determine which one you want. If you are given 1000, you are almost certain to pick one that isn't the best for you, and this can lead to negative psychological effects. More is not always better, even if it means that you are given better options. Alexis de Tocqueville observed "It is an axiom of political science in the United States that the only way to neutralize the influence of newspapers is to multiply their number" (Singer/Brooking, 2018, p. 121). The press today is more powerful than ever before, but it has lost its influence to convince people that it is delivering the truth to them.

This comes into play with the sheer volume of informational "news" available on the market today. News on a single subject can come from hundreds of sources, from Facebook posts, to nightly news updates, to blogs, to online articles. Since information flows so freely across the web, unhindered by physicality, information can be found from any of these sources, all with their own spin, bias, and list of "credible" sources. With all of this information out there, it has now become incredibly difficult to find the truth about anything. When it is also considered that each news source is after your attention and will do whatever it takes to get it, the legitimacy and credibility of the system must be called into question. So, if everybody is lying, and motivated by money, what really is the truth?

This method of eliminating the concept of truth, rather than the truth itself, is a theme that has been at work in the world of Bible translations since the release of the Revised Version in 1885. God made sure to be clear in his words that he would preserve them perfectly, forever, and without error in Psalms 12:6-7, Matthew 24:35, and Isaiah 30:8. Since the word of God cannot be destroyed, the Devil has chosen a different method to remove the words of God from humanity: by diluting them with as many versions as he can produce. By creating a vast array of authorities, all of which claim imperfection, the idea that any one version could be perfect becomes ludicrous. This is "by far, the best method to deceive the public and give them a 'who cares' attitude about the word of God" (Ruckman P. , 1960, p. 29). Once this attitude has been applied to the only book that claims to be a timeless, perfect standard, truth in all its other forms begins to decay as well. If the ultimate authority cannot be trusted, nothing can.

This gets exaggerated to a greater extent with the ever-growing concept of "fake news". The term was fully brought into the limelight by Donald Trump during the 2016 American presidential election and it has since been used by every major American news outlet in existence to describe other news outlets that don't agree with them. The big takeaway here is not that some news media outlets (realistically all of them) spew out fake stories, fake witnesses, fake experts, or fake emotions to emphasize their point of view, but that it is now easy to do so. In 2016, it was discovered that Pope Francis' endorsement for the highly controversial American presidential candidate Donald Trump had been entirely fabricated by a *Macedonian teenager*. He had come up with the story all on his own and created a fake news outlet to publish it online. He and his friends quickly realized that they could make, literally, millions of dollars by creating stories about America, a place they had never been, that would be clicked on by concerned American voters and make them considerable advertising revenue. This was not spin. This was not bias. This was not grasping at straws. This was pure fabrication for the point of making money, and it was pulled off by a group of people who had no political opinions regarding the future leader of the United States. They fabricated the entire story simply because they were able to turn a quick buck for free, and it ended up making them more money than they would have made in a lifetime (Singer/ Brooking, 2018, p. 119). While they certainly didn't invent lying online, they did bring it into international attention, and the legitimacy of online information has been a serious debate ever since. This spilled over into the conflict in Ukraine (both of them in the last 5 years), Israel's conflicts with the Gaza strip, China's incendiary relationship with Hong Kong, the condition of the Mexican-American Border, and so on. Propaganda for any cause is now easier to create and distribute than ever before and is still has power over the mind of the readers. According to Singer and Brooking, news that is proven to be undoubtedly fake actually spreads better than real news (Singer/Brooking, 2018, p. 119). Since these articles are written specifically to grab the attention of people and are unhindered by boring things, like, for example, reality, this should not come as a surprise. Now every major political, social, or religious event is being covered by dishonest reporters and, even worse, people who know nothing other than that they want to make money.

In line with fake information comes the additional reality of "deepfake" technology. While old in concept, it has in recent years made leaps and bounds in its advancement and is now becoming more powerful than the ability of the human mind to debunk it. For years, the legitimacy of black-and-white photographs of UFOs have been debated. Is it an alien spacecraft from another planet or a hat that has been thrown at an ideal angle and photographed under controlled conditions? The arguments will likely go on indefinitely. Some people have admitted that their photographs are fake and were set up to look like something that they are not.

STRANGELY DIM

155

With computers, the level of complexity of fake photos, audio recording, and videos is growing out of control. While clever lookalikes and makeup artists may have been able to create some grainy fakes in the past, computers are learning through deepfake technology to create imitations that are continuously more and more realistic. The technology is so advanced that, with only a few minutes of video of a person giving a speech, a computer can analyze, modify, and reproduce their likeness digitally to show video and audio of them saying something that they never said *in real time*. The development of machine-learned conversational tools (generally called chatbots) has allowed computers to pick up on speck patterns of people, learn them, and then say, with a great deal of accuracy, things that they might say. The technology has developed to the point where computers that create deepfakes are pitted against computers that detect them so that each one can learn from the other (Singer/Brooking, 2018, pp. 253-257). It used to be true that you couldn't trust everything you read online. Now, outside of the Bible, you can't trust anything you read, hear, or see. Anywhere.

This is where the information overload truly comes into view. As was discussed in the earlier portion on the yellow press, the yellow press eventually died out to subscription-based media because it was inherently more trustworthy. This was solely because the readers were still concerned with understanding the truth about current events. This desire is being rapidly killed off in the minds of internet users because the truth is simply too hard to find. Every source puts a different spin with different facts, and those facts are heatedly denied by other news sources that contradict them. While some sources are able to claim a fair amount of legitimacy, news agencies are perpetually plagued by scandals where they are caught faking the news themselves. Considering also that news stories are frequently "broken" to the public and then edited continuously as new information comes to light, one can never be certain that the information is correct. This has put the world in a state of continual distrust, even though it continuously absorbs and funds the news given to them. It is easier than ever to enter this realm, with social media users becoming reporters in their own way by reporting on whatever is going on in their lives around them. The news can be invented and then shared on a whim, and the burden then lies on the readers to debunk the claims rather than the poster to prove them. Innocent until proven guilty has turned out to have a rather dark side in a society where morality is in rapid decline. The final end of this explosion of dishonest material is the death of the belief in an absolute truth, which will be explored later.

CONCLUSION) A MIND IS A TERRIBLE THING TO WASTE

In the book of Ecclesiastes, King Solomon made a prophetic statement that did not come to fruition for roughly three thousand years. In Ecclesiastes 7:29, he says "Lo, this only have I found, that God hath made man upright; but they have sought out many inventions." Here, the son of the psalmist makes a remarkable comment on the human condition. God created man with a degree of natural goodness. This fact is then immediately put into conflict with the next statement with the word "but," and the following statement indicates that man has "sought out" inventions. The structure of the verse shows that when mankind seeks out inventions, it diminishes his innate goodness. Necessity may be the mother of invention, but decay is the child. As man recedes further and further into his own creations, he loses sight of the Creator. The best way for a man to deny God's existence and the inevitability of his eventual judgement of hi, is to repurpose His creations into his own. He can replace God with himself by creating a world after his own liking and in his own image. Thus, the technological explosion of the modern world correlated directly to the decay of the Laodicean Church.

It would be scientifically impossible to fully determine the effects of the internet on the intellect of the human mind. The only way to understand the direction of the world from a tangible point of view is to consider uniformly collected data over time. This is where the data collected by Dr. Jean Twenge becomes invaluable. Based on surveys collected in a uniform manner, she has been able to present the following data. The average SAT scores of writing and critical reading have been trending continuously downward. The average critical reading score has fallen from 530 in 1972 to 495 in 2016, for an average decrease of about 0.8 points per year. This is not adjusted for the change in difficulty of the SAT. Writing was introduced to the SAT in 2006 and has declined from 497 to 485 in 10 years, for an average decline of 1.2 points per year. Math has experienced increases and decreases between 1972 and 2016, and it has actually gained a net of two points, increasing from an average of 508 to 510. The number of students who reported that they read a book or magazine nearly every day has decreased steadily from about 60% in 1976 to about 16% in 2016 (Twenge, 2017, pp. 61, 64).

What is clearly seen here is that in America, since at least the seventies, the reading comprehension of the average child has continuously decreased. This is obviously not entirely the fault of Internet Culture, since it did not come into vogue until the mid-2000s. Given the ubiquity of communication technology in our society and its unparalleled impact on our culture, to say that it does not affect the human brain would be utterly foolish. Furthermore, it would be impossible to scientifically denote a direct correlation using this data since no control group can be established in cultural studies. What can be understood though is that the science of the leading sociolegal minds of our time has noted a strong correlation between the rise of communication technology and the decay of the human mind's tendency and ability to comprehend written works. This is in *total agreement* with the biblical position that an increase of *inventions* and *devices* will damage the ability of humanity to know God.

God put His word in His books. He wrote sixty-six of them and then put them in a specific order so that man could know Him better. While entirely a spiritual transaction, God requires that those who would seek to know Him better read his words (John 5:39), study them (II Timothy 2:15) and meditate on them (I Timothy 4:15). The intellect is nearly irrelevant in light of I Corinthians 1 & 2, but by crippling the human mind, simply doing the basics becomes a much more difficult process to begin. A society that tends to not read is simply less able to read something that is convicting and seemingly archaic. Satan is acutely aware that he is unable to destroy the word of God on this earth. He also knows that attempting to crush or pervert the words of God is only effective to a certain extent. He has set in motion a greater plan, which is simply to get people to not read. This prevents the lost world from exercising its curiosity and finding a Bible. It also prevents the Christian from growing, pleasing God, and reproducing.

Consistently distracting the human mind has reprogrammed it to struggle with deep thinking, which is associated with good decision making, comprehension, and empathy. The continual movement and impermanence of all things presented on a screen devalues the importance and legitimacy of the presented information. This has allowed an overabundance of unreliable information to saturate the human mind and wear away at the desire to seek out the full truth in any scenario. Any attempts to do so are policed by the passive association of perpetual connectivity to the progressive world system, so that the truth is relegated to a "relativity" in light of "current social trends." Donna Freitas concludes that social media is a "pressure-cooker version of life itself" (Frietas, 2017, p. 248). She is speaking directly about the social media, but the concept applies to Internet Culture as a whole.

The end result is that Internet Culture, due to the nature of how the internet operates, has a subtle, detrimental impact on the cognitive functions of the human mind. It has lowered the general ability of the population to disconnect and think for itself by being perpetually on and aggressively hunting for attention. Since connection is the theme of the internet, mankind is now spending a lot more time looking at his own devices and connecting with the rest of the world, which is under the control of Satan (II Corinthians 4:4). All of this is done specifically to keep man in touch with other people and out of touch with God and His words. This will continue to increase until the world is ready to openly accept the antichrist as its king in a one-world government system. This internet is not technically the cause of this. The internet is simply the tool that will bring mankind to its knees in front of the wrong throne.

CHAPTER 5) MATTERS OF THE HEART

The mind and the heart go hand in hand in the decision-making processes of the human brain. Emotion and intellect are often counter to each other and keeping both healthy is critical to living a mentally balanced life. God did not create humans to be utterly emotionless robots, designed to make only the most logical of choices. The purpose of His creation is to be pleasing to Him (Revelation 4:11), and He chose an emotional creature as the focus of His own love to the extent that He would be willing to die for it. He loved us first (I John 4:10) and we are created in His image (Genesis 1:26). Therefore, it must be concluded that there is a love that should exist mutually between creator and creation. This love is what draws a sinner to God, in that God would forgive somebody of their sins against him if they simply ask in the name of His Son Jesus.

This love is also critical to the growth of those who have already asked for his forgiveness. It should come naturally through accepting Jesus Christ as the payment for the sins of an individual and grow continuously as that person begins to know God on a deeper, more personal level. It should be based in gratitude, but loving God is also the "first commandment of all" (Mark 12:28-30). Love must also be demonstrated between those who are in Christ (I John 4:7) and for His words (Psalms 119:140). The key takeaway here is that love is critical to lost sinners and saved sinners because God is love (I John 4:8, 4:16). If something were to inhibit or pervert the capability of man to love God, it would therefore not be of God.

Keeping this thought in mind, the effects of Internet Culture on the human mind must now be probed. The internet is quickly becoming engrained into a unified global culture, and it is clearly impacting the intellectual thought processes of all who reside within it. The question becomes then: how does it impact emotion? The internet has fundamentally altered the mediums through which we communicate, and altering the media will, in time, alter the message.

This analysis will be based on the back of a single conclusion that was established in the previous chapter. This is a biblical concept that is further reinforced through the scientific advancements and discoveries regarding the human mind. While any biblical concept does not require scientific backing, the Bible is a scientific book and modern science, when conducted honestly, bolsters the conclusions set forth in the Scriptures. The concept to be used as the grounding for the conclusions made in this chapter is the Law of Neuroplasticity, which is validated by Lamentations 3:51, I Timothy 4:2, I Corinthians 15:33 and I Corinthians 10:12. God, with His perfect understanding of the human mind that He created, knew that at all points in life, man would be affected by his surroundings and that no man is truly unaffected by his being surrounded by sin, regardless of their age or spirituality. Science has further explored this concept to conclude that the surrounding environment will always change the thought process of the human mind. We are never truly free from our surroundings and our mind will continuously adapt to the surrounding environment. Established routines, thought processes and habits are much more difficult to break, but no mind is truly invulnerable to the world around it.

Keeping this in mind, it must be understood that the state of the human mind is continuously in flux based on the cultural climate in which it exists. This would indicate that if the internet has an emotional impact on the human brain, it is a lasting impact that can theoretically change how we experience emotion, what emotions we react to, and how we process these emotions in time. The following chapter will explore these concepts.

I SEE, THEREFORE I FEEL

The internet is a conveyor of data. Through this, it presents images, videos and audio. Sharing this media has seen an exponential uptick, along with text-based communications. Pictures are uploaded to Facebook by the billions every year, despite the fact that the site is based more on text than images. Entire social media websites have exploded into mainstream culture that are based solely on the sharing of pictures, with words being augments to the visuals. Tiktok and Vine are two platforms that only allow(ed) the posting of videos, with text used exclusively as labels or hashes. Picture-based websites, such as Instagram and Snapchat are designed to stimulate visually. Prior to the invention of woodcut pressings, images could only be recreated by an artist, and were entirely unique creations representing a massive personal investment of time and dedication to the craft. When the printing press was first invented, text was able to explode in its reproductive capabilities while reproducing images lagged significantly behind. Even with the introduction of photography and printers, images could still only be reproduced using analog mediums and were bound to the laws of physicality. Text could be transmitted electronically with the invention of the telegraph, but pictures did not ascend to the digital plane until the creation of the internet. Although photos and videos could be transmitted through the airwaves and digital cassettes prior to this, they were confined to primitive storage methods and costly signal transmission technology.

When visual sharing was fully enabled by the internet, it began to change how people chose to communicate, with visuals taking a place alongside text as mainstream communication methods. This is because the human brain prefers the viewing of images to the reading of words. A recent study showed that Tweets (posts on the social media platform Twitter are called Tweets) are nearly 200% more likely to be reshared when they included a visual (Miller, 2019, p. 92). Natchi Lazarus, a social media consultant who has written several books on the subject states in his book on how to increase your church's social media impact says, "Visuals are vital for social media" (Lazarus, 2017, p. 119). The increased online interaction based on visuals shows that humanity has grown its appetite for visual stimulation over intellectual.

Humanity has always craved the visual over the textual. This is why God chose to present himself to the Jewish nation through written law, rather than a visual image. This concept is explored by Neil Postman in his book *"Amusing Ourselves to Death"*. In the beginning of his scathing diatribe on the negative outcome of television on America's religious and political system, he makes a rather profound statement. He says, when commenting on the command given in Exodus 20:3 not to create any graven images for worship, "...the God of these people would have included instructions on how they were to symbolize, or not symbolize their experience. It is a strange injunction to include as part of an ethical system *unless its author assumed a connection between forms of human communication and the quality of a culture*. We may hazard a guess that a people who are being asked to embrace an abstract, universal deity would be rendered unfit to do so by the habit of drawing pictures or making statues or depicting their ideas in any concrete, iconographic forms. The God of the Jews was to exist in the Word and through the Word, an unprecedented conception requiring the highest order of abstract thinking." (emphasis by author) (Postman, 1986, p. 10). Neil Postman's comments indicate that the God of the Bible is unique beyond any idol or false god brought about by man's creation or demonic inspiration. The God of Exodus 20 wishes to be known by His people strictly through the words He has inspired, and the interpretation provided by the Holy Spirit.

God's revelation of Himself through words, rather than any form of visual recreation, indicates that He places a higher priority on words than pictures. This is further manifested through Psalms 138:2 and II Peter 1: 16-21. Throughout the Bible, God provides continuous warnings against images, since they drew His people towards idolatry, as demonstrated in Exodus 23:24, 34:13, Numbers 33:52, Deuteronomy 7:5, 7:25, and 12:3. Jesus Christ was created in the image of God (II Corinthians

4:4), and Christians are to show God in their lives, not through pictures or statues, but by living according to the words provided to them by God (Romans 12:2). God has always desired to be worshipped by people living according to the concepts that He has presented him with, and not by paying homage towards any visual representation of himself. The "image" of God is a man, Jesus Christ, not a statue.

Worshipping a God with no visual representation is contrary to human nature as it is essentially more difficult to develop an understanding of a concept than it is to dwell on something that you can see. This forces anybody who want to know God to understand him through a personal relationship. This is why God prefers for man to work through the spiritual rather than the physical. This is best shown through Jesus's rebuke in Matthew 9: 13 when he says, "But go ye and learn what this meaneth, I Will have mercy and not sacrifice: for I am not come to call the righteous, but sinners to repentance". In his response to a lawyer's temptation about the greatest commandments, Jesus responds by telling him in Matthew 22:37-40, "Thou shalt love the Lord thy God with all the heart, and with all thy soul, and with all thy mind. This is the first and great commandment. And the second is like unto it, thou shalt love thy neighbor as thyself. On these two commandments hang all the law and the prophets." This response shows that the entirety of the Old Testament theological, dietary, agricultural, sociological, and medical laws hung directly on a person loving God and loving others. This surpassed the laborious efforts of the pharisees, scribes and lawyers to demonstrate their holiness through extreme dedication to the letter of the law. God is, and always has been, more concerned with a correct understanding of the intent. God wrote the laws that He did so that man would understand the heart of God. It is easy to forget that God is a sentient being with a personality, and there are no people on this earth who you befriend based on following a set of rules. Most religions base their standing with their God on how well they follow an explicit set of rules.

Christians must remember that God is a *living* God, not just in the sense of him being alive, but also in that he is a conscious being. This is not to discredit the rules, since breaking the rules he has put in place goes against the will of God. It is only to show that the rules provide the framework, but the relationship filly in the details.

This is why he chose to ban the creation of religious icons. He further emphasizes the greater power held in words through Proverbs 25:11 where Solomon states, "A word fitly spoken Is like apples of gold in pictures of silver." Apparently, a single word is worth many pictures, rather than the other way around. God wants to be known personally through a relationship rather than studied by experts.

This is because words are intellectual, and pictures are emotional. Factual information can only be transmitted through text because of the ability of text to communicate specific detail and necessary context. Any attempt to visually recreate a scenario, be it through camera, portrait, or an artists' rendition, can only display a visual recreation of the event. This is why paintings require titles, photos require albums, and selfies require hashtags. All visual recreations must be contextualized through words. Without words, the picture can only evoke a reaction to the viewer's perception of an event. Gavriel Solomon says, "Pictures need to be recognized, words need to be understood." (Postman, 1986, p. 72). A picture cannot convey dates or names. A picture cannot establish if a motivation for an action is just or unjust. A picture or statue can only convey a single moment in time. It cannot bring with the context to show the progression leading up to that moment, nor can it show the moments following. Siva Vaidhyanathan sums this up by saying "Photography collapses any ambiguity of fact claims, questions of context, or helpful framing of a dispute. Every photograph is necessarily and almost by definition out of context." (Vaidhyanathan, 2018, p. 45)What pictures are able to do is to make a person *feel*. Pictures can stimulate pity, anger, or love in a matter of seconds. Words can create these feelings as well, but it requires a greater deal of investment into reading, understanding, and contemplating text. While an artist and an author may both invest the same amount of time into their works, the artist's work creates a reaction immediately while an author's work requires a considerable amount of time and effort to begin to create the same effect. Pictures need words to be able to convey facts, but words do not need pictures.

This also brings about the point that pictures cause reactions while words cause contemplation. This is why advertisements always appeal to the heart rather than the mind. It is easier to solicit an impulse buy from a consumer than it is to persuade them that they should spend money on something that they need. Neil Postman discusses the transition from intellectual to emotional advertising around the year 1900. He says "…advertisers no longer assumed rationality on the part of their potential customers. Advertising became one part depth psychology, one part aesthetic theory. Reason had to move itself to other arenas." (Postman, 1986, p. 60) The rise of the power of an emotional appeal came from two distinct forces at work. The first key component of this change was the nature of how images are emotionally perceived in the human mind. The second was the continuous saturation of society with emotional material. The rise of the emotional thought process facilitated the smothering of the intellect.

ANGRY WORDS

A great deal of modern decision-making is done emotionally. For years, Disney, Hollywood and the music recording industry have been pushing the ideas that we should all listen to our hearts and do what our hearts say. This message is universally adopted by artists who have succeeded in turning their passion into millions of dollars, so it does seem counterintuitive that these messages would also apply to the common man that works a job for a living. Despite the disconnect from artist to audience, the message rings clear: think with your heart, not your head. This mantra is repeated every time Hollywood gives someone an

Oscar, an album goes platinum, or Disney crowns a new princess. The heart should not be excluded from the decision-making process, but it also must not be the singular deciding factor. This should be obvious given the biblical stance on the heart which has already been elaborated on multiple times.

Since the thoughts of the heart now hold the majority of the power in the worldly mind, a rather unfortunate conclusion must be made: if emotions can be manipulated, then the best emotional manipulator holds the greatest power. With this comes another unpleasant question, being, what is the easiest emotion to manipulate?

Provoking an emotional reaction from a person requires a decent understanding of how they have experienced the world. Depending on what that person has been through, different reactions may be elicited via the same stimuli. For example, giving a person chocolate may make them happy. Most people like chocolate, so this is a fairly easy way to make somebody happy. However, if the person has become lactose intolerant or recently went through a hard breakup, chocolate may make them depressed or angry. Chocolate may hold key emotional value due to a correlation with a lost loved one, or it may have been the catalyst for unhealthy and life altering weight gain. This is unlikely but demonstrates that a single stimulus can be interpreted in different ways, and there is no universal way to provoke happiness. The same can be said of sadness. Describing stories of animals being destroyed at an animal shelter may move some people to tears, while others have no regard for animals and would remain largely unaffected by it. Often, traumatic life experiences can make people highly susceptible or highly resistant to various stimuli. In order to cause another person to feel grief, guilt, happiness, fear, or love, it often requires a good bit of knowledge of that person's experiences and perspectives.

Of all the emotions, there is one that is universally the simplest to evoke. That emotion is anger. Physical violence, derision towards a loved one, or emotional abuse are simple methods that anybody can use to make another person angry. Threats trigger the *fight or flight* response in our brain, and it does not take a deep understanding of another person's personality and life experiences to make them mad.

This concept of anger spreading easily is biblical. In Acts 7:1-58 Stephen preaches a message that is poignant enough to cause the pharisees to stone him to death. In Acts 14, Paul's words convince the people of Athens that he is the god Mercurius, and in less than three verses, the words of angry Jews cause the people to stone the man who they had just tried to offer sacrifices to. In Acts 21, the Jews, in only a few short sentences convince the people of Jerusalem to riot against Paul, and in Acts 22:21, Paul using the word *Gentiles* causes such a reaction from the Jewish hierarchy that he must be rescued by Roman soldiers while one the castle steps. Words can cause people to be angry enough to commit murder. The Bible offers many warnings against unchecked anger and how it can cause you to sin (see Proverbs 14:17, 22:24, 29:22, Ecclesiastes 7:9, Matthew 5:22 and Colossians 3:8). While anger is a perfectly natural human emotion, and in some cases beneficial to a walk with God when directed towards sin (see Ephesians 4:26) because this is what makes God angry. Anger in the Christian life must always be controlled and properly directed. This is not natural to a lost man or simple for the saved one.

The scientific community also asserts that anger is not only easy to spread, but the *easiest* emotion to spread. Internet virality is fickle in nature, but there are some common trends among what generates the most attention. Ryan Holiday, a marketing guru of the internet age, quotes an early research article on virality by The Wharton School, as well as his own experience when asserting that anger is the most viral emotion. The research article states, "the most powerful predictor of virality is how much anger an article evokes". Holiday then goes on himself to say, "The most powerful predictor of what spreads online is anger." (Holiday, p. 68) Ryan Holiday built a career out of using anger on the internet to generate virality for free marketing campaigns. Using sex, scandal and lies, he could artificially create a conflict, anonymously play both sides of the battle, intentionally enrage key "superspreaders", and let the online rage mob do the rest without him having to pay for advertising. After all, there is no bad publicity, especially when your product is sex (the clients he found the most success with were American Apparel, a company whose ads intentionally fringe on pornographic, and the movie "*I Hope They Serve Beer in Hell*", which is about the debaucheries of a bachelor party gone wrong). (Holiday, pp. 11, 29-31, 56). His book, "*Trust Me I'm Lying*" is literally his confession of the worst of his shady marketing practices which he used to get famous that started to keep him up at night. Singer and Brooking in their book Likewar pull from a Chinese study of the social media platform Weibo when they say, "Analyzing 70 million messages from 200,000 users, they discovered that anger was the emotion that traveled the fastest and farthest through the social network – and the competition wasn't even close". (Singer/Brooking, 2018, p. 162). The quick and easy spread of anger is what fuels the majority of online reporting, since the data has concluded that it sells the best, and this is the world we live in. Franklin Foer, in his commentary on modern, online journalism woefully concludes that "Once journalists come to know what works, which stories yield traffic, they will pursue what works. This is the definition of pandering and it has horrific consequences." (Foer, 2017, p. 149). This is what they do en masse, which is why Ryan Holiday quotes Tim Ferris, a New York Times bestselling author who says, "Study the top stories at Digg or MSN.com and you'll notice a pattern: the top stories all polarize people. If you make it threaten people's 3 Bs – behavior, belief, or belongings – you get a huge virus-like dispersion." (Holiday, p. 64)

CREATING DESTRUCTION

The online rage mob has been discussed in length in terms of their fostering of cancel culture. But in other parts of the world that are under governments that are actually oppressive, social media allows cancel culture to ramp up to something greater, with results that are much more visible. Sin, when it is conceived, bringeth forth death (James 1:15), but cancel culture, when it is finished, bringeth for revolution. This is not a theory. At this point, it is history. Social media has allowed the spread of emotional outrage to the point that it can be sited as the key method of gathering support for revolutions in Egypt, Syria and Czechoslovakia, stopping a coup in Turkey (and kickstarting the Muslim Spring), spreading terrorism in Israel and Mosul, and stopping it in India (Singer/Brooking, 2018, pp. 4-7,62-67, 85-87, 194) (Vaidhyanathan, 2018, pp. 131, 145). Social media has become more than just an enjoyable way to share baby photos. It has entwined itself with every aspect of human culture, including war, and it is quite good at starting them.

A revolution must be built on the back of those who are willing to die for a cause. Any revolution against a power-hungry dictator, should it succeed or fail, will inevitably include some violence and death. Hopefully, the violence is on your side and the death is on the other guy's. As was discussed earlier, anger is an incredibly viral emotion in the online world. Now that so many people have smartphones with cameras that can send photos and videos to people across the globe in real time, governments and revolutions alike must be careful when determining who sees what. Leaving no survivors is no longer a safe way to hide your atrocities. Now you have to make sure they aren't tweeting. The line between the press and the civilian has blurred completely out of existence and social media allows for anybody to capture and share everything they see or feel, frame it for their personal benefit, and release it into an emotional hotbed where it becomes public information (Foer, 2017, p. 97).

This can be used to stoke the fires of Revolution, as it was in used in Egypt, rally the people to stop a military coup, as it was in Turkey, or instill terror in the heart of a city and conquer it before stepping foot inside, the way ISIS blazed onto the global stage and conquered Mosul. To quote Singer and Brooking, "All thanks, essentially, to the fact that ISIS was very good at social media." (Singer/Brooking, 2018) Since terrorist organizations threaten the beliefs, behaviors and belongings of those around them through fear while bolstering their own numbers through anger and self-righteousness, it only makes sense that social media would revolutionize terrorism. Propaganda can now be spread directly from one side to the other without having to drop leaflets from a plane or staging a daring espionage mission on a printing press behind enemy lines. It can be done from the comfort of a bed as long as there is good wi-fi and the user has a decent knowledge of how to navigate Twitter. Radicalization and recruitment can now take place across the globe and pull in likeminded individuals who were once isolated by physical distance. Sympathy for a cause can be generated on an international platform by displaying humanity in between the bloodbaths. Money can even be crowdsourced to support whatever side of the revolution you want to. At Christmastime, charitable organizations will ask people to sponsor agricultural necessities for poor children in Africa or Asia. Now, in wartime, you can choose to fund your preferred side of a revolution. In the case of the Syrian Civil war, you could purchase an RPG for a Syrian rebel for $800, and Muslim imams began to preach that this counted as tithing, which according to Islam, is a requirement for getting into Heaven (Singer/Brooking, 2018, p. 65) Thanks to social media, anger can be leveraged to support anyone, anywhere, so long as they can ask for help online.

The cruel reality of social media is that it creates and fuels anger. Once this flame war begins, it continues as long as somebody in the world believes in a different cause than you. It is no longer sufficient to win the war on the ground. You must win the war on the internet in order to solidify your control, otherwise you will be continually buffeted by outside entities that disagree with you and have no skin in the game, literally or figuratively. And that war is not winnable. The ability to communicate publicly with the rest of the world means that anybody can support any cause for any reason, real or not, with no consequence. And quite frankly, impossible to completely push one side into obscurity. Even though Twitter has devoted countless resources to locating ISIS on their platform and instantly deleting all of their content and profiles, they are still largely unsuccessful because it is so easy to start over again (Singer/Brooking, 2018, p. 236). It is a never-ending game of cat and mouse where Twitter writes code to eliminate terrorist accounts, and the terrorists write better code to make different profiles. Social media unintentionally created a platform that enables rebellion in a way that was never before possible.

From a humanistic standpoint, there are some rebellions against established governments that have been largely in favor of the will of the public and common decency. There are many times that governments have become tyrannical and began to take advantage of the people that they ruled, only for the people to rebel and establish a new government that better met the needs of the masses. But starting a revolution has always had risks, and it has always required that the revolution hit a "critical mass" of committed supporters before going public. Going public prior to this moment would result in the rebellion being squashed before it could begin. Social media helps rebellions to gain steam due simply to how they function. As the internet is best at spreading rage, all it takes is a few viral posts about the government mishandling situations, some videos out of context, a sad looking child or two to provoke some self-righteous indignation, and at that point, protests basically organize themselves. Since protests inevitably involve clashes with law enforcement (aka the strong arm of the government) and everybody involved is likely to have a smartphone with a camera, every misstep can be documented and used to fuel the online rage. Even situations handled properly in accordance with law and order can be used as fuel for the detractors if they are documented from the correct angles and captured at the ideal moments. Editing software, the inability of pictures to display factual information in context, and a plethora of crowdsourced content make generating propaganda a walk in the park. Online influences spread beyond borders or countries, so garnering international support is now easier than ever. People can support revolutions with money, hacking skills, or by petitioning their own government for causes of countries that they have never been to, will never go to, and know nothing about.

Siva Vaidhyanathan writes about how Facebook enabled the Egyptian Revolution of 2011 through viral videos of the abuse of citizens and protests organized online. He proves that the viral rage that was created by citizens and egged on by international support *online* overthrew Mubarak. But this kind of revolution, rooted in social media, became too caustic to survive past the initial chaos. The revolution, when sparked by social media created a new kind of a revolution. "Coordination without clear leaders, without hierarchy, could emerge." In other words, Facebook created a mob, not a revolution. He says further "…communication is not conversation. Social media, and Facebook in particular, do not foster conversation. They favor declaration. They do not allow for deep deliberation. They spark shallow reaction. There is political power in declaration and reaction. But they are not enough to pursue anything more than stronger declaration, fiercer reaction, and strong blowback." (Vaidhyanathan, 2018, pp. 131, 144) Social media is great for causing unrest, but it can only cause unrest. He concludes the chapter by continuing the story of the revolution in Egypt. The revolution was successful in overthrowing Mubarak, but it immediately crumbled and was eventually quashed by the Muslim Brotherhood in a military takeover, which was the opposite of the intent of the liberal uprising. He ends the chapter with a quote by a man named Ghonim, who was a key player in the revolution and escaped before the military takeover. He says "We failed to build consensus and the political struggle led to intense polarization…Social media only amplified that state by amplifying the spread of misinformation, rumors, echo chambers, and hate speech. The environment was purely toxic." (Vaidhyanathan, 2018, p. 145) Since no social experiment can truly exist in a vacuum, it is impossible to say that the revolution would have succeeded in establishing a peaceful government had Facebook not existed. It is impossible to turn back time and try again in an alternate reality where the revolution was coordinated via email, text, or word of mouth. What can be stated empirically is social media enhanced the chaos of the revolution in ways that were both beneficial and detrimental to the original cause. Social media cultivates rage. The winner is determined by who can harness it the best.

WHOSOEVER WILL, LET HIM COMMENT

Part of the reason that polarization can occur so simply online is that the internet makes it possible to represent an extreme with no consequence. When the Founding Fathers of the American Revolution signed the Declaration of Independence, most of the signees knew that their signatures could cost them their lives. They also knew that it could cost them the lives of their families, their wealth, and their property. For many of them, it did. In modern times, putting support behind a cause can be done with no personal investment whatsoever. A great deal of the support for the liberal uprising in Egypt was from liberal people living in countries that are not even on the same continent as Egypt. While botnets and trolls certainly played their part, as they do in all major online movements, the support by real people across the seas came at no cost of their own. They simply "liked" some Facebook posts, read and commented on some news articles, and retweeted something that resonated with them on Twitter. When the revolution was overthrown by the new Islamic government that was backed by the full support of the military, there was no need for anybody in American or Europe to worry about scrubbing their online presence for fear of arrest and imprisonment. The international community can simply go on as they always have and throw their verbal support behind whatever cause makes them angry today.

This is because the internet eliminates both the time and

space constraints of communication, as was discussed earlier. Governments can only enforce their laws on their own citizens, and they can only do this by deploying armed forces. Online, the laws of cause and effect are now largely disconnected, and this is true all the way down from enforcing Federal Laws to suffering the consequences of social indecency. The end result of this is clearly defined in Ecclesiastes 8:11. "Because sentence against an evil work is not executed speedily, therefore the heart of the sons of men is fully set in them to do evil." When there is no immediate correlation between offense and repercussion, the human heart begins to believe that it can act without consequence. This newfound freedom sets evil in the human heart. The Bible, being accurate, describes human nature as more inherently sinful than good. When all consequence for action is removed, humanity tends toward evil deeds rather than good ones. To quote Sherry Turkle, "We cannot blame technology for this state of affairs. It is people who are disappointing each other. Technology merely enables us to create a mythology in which this does not matter." (Turkle, 2011, p. 237) Singer and Brooking quote a foreign official who described social media by saying "The germs are ours, but Facebook is the wind." (Singer/Brooking, 2018, p. 136)

Some might say that being online allows them to be their true selves. People can be whoever they wish to be when they are protected through the anonymity created by the internet and technology. This means that negativity towards other people can be expressed with no consequence towards the speaker. The internet is the perfect vehicle for anonymous hate mail. Trolling has been discussed previously in that it enables people to irritate other people without fear of physical harm. Trolling is easy to do and is easy to get away with. Dealing with trolls is nearly impossible since you can only respond with words, which do not affect trolls since they are there to spread chaos for personal enjoyment rather than to participate in legitimate dialogue. This is where the internet phrase "Don't feed the troll" comes from. The only way to win the argument is not to participate, and let the troll do as much damage as they want to until they get bored. Beyond the dangers of anonymous trolling comes the problem of online harassment through intentionally anonymous targeted attacks. These can be done through fake account names (such as the earlier case of the fake Joshua Evans on Myspace), or through intentionally anonymous social media or messaging sites such as Reddit or Yik Yak.

Yik Yak was a social media platform where all users were anonymous. There were no links from the user's profile to their real name or face. When a person posted on Yik Yak, their post did not go to a group of friends or connections. It was posted to a location. Anybody with Yik Yak who was inside the radius of the creator of the post could see it and respond. But nothing could ever be traced back to the real person who posted it unless it merited a search warrant, executed by tracing the IP address. This became a major issue on college campuses since people could post gossip using the real name of the person with no fear that they would get caught for saying it. Donna Freitas, in her investigation of this app says "Yik Yak can also be terrifying. Anonymity is liberating, but sometimes it unleashes impulses that might better be kept in check." (Frietas, 2017, p. 136). The issue with this is that it helped people to be able to say things that they never could in person. These rude quips or indecent comments could now be expressed without fear of repercussion, and also without fear of seeing the damage done to other people. The emotional toll that this takes on the human psyche is astounding. Never before has cruelty been so easy to get away with, making people more vulnerable to it, but also more comfortable being cruel themselves.

This is not something that only happens on Yik Yak. The platform shut down in 2017, but the core concept of online anonymity remains more realized than ever. Fake accounts allow people to say whatever they want about whoever they want, wherever and whenever they want. Sherry Turkle examines the online world of confession boards in her book "*Alone Together.*" She found that people would go online to message boards (these are places where anybody can create a post, but all posts must be related to the topic of the board) and confess their darkest secrets. By totally removing the victim from the equation, it eases the personal guilt felt for committing the sin without offering any closure to the person offended. Since these people are going online and looking to find a place to confess anonymously, they are ending up in the same places, allowing them to find other people whoare as vile as they are. It creates an anonymous echo chamber of people who will be sympathetic to your cause and help you deal with the guilt, since they want to be free of it themselves. But this is, to quote Turkle "to confess, not apologize" (Turkle, 2011). There is no consequence to the offending person. In fact, they will likely find support.

The guilt that causes that pain can be beneficial to personal growth if handled correctly. By dealing with the awkwardness and pain that comes with apologizing to a person or confessing to a person who probably hasn't done the same thing will help you right the wrong, nurturing personal growth. It causes change. It makes a person not want to do it again. Online confessions stimulate none of that and allow the offending person to relieve their guilt because they at least told somebody and then they can begin to cope in their own way. This leaves the victim in a state that is much more likely to cause bitterness and revenge, lowering the probability that this issue will ever be resolved or put in the past. The Bible commands to "Confess your faults one to another, and pray one for another, that ye may be healed..." (James 5:16). Online confessions circumvent the very necessary pain that comes with admitting your failures to other people and confronting the issue directly. II Corinthians 7:10 says that "godly sorrow worketh repentance to salvation not to be repented of: but the sorrow of the world worketh death." Failing to address the situation biblically makes people more likely to remain in the same position that they were in prior to committing the sin, making them more likely to do it again. The internet essentially feeds emotional immaturity by giving every situation a back door.

BE YE ANGRY AND SIN AS MUCH AS YOU WANT

Message boards and anonymity do their share to defend the user from personal growth. The blame cannot be placed solely on the ability to be anonymous online: the nature of modern communication technology helps shield the user from discomfort of any kind. The internet allows people to communicate more than they ever have before. Dialogue about anything never has to stop, and conflict is no longer escaped by physically leaving the presence of another person. The general argument against this is that people can simply turn off their cell phones or not log in to social media so that they don't have to deal with the issue. After all, it is impossible to cyberbully a person who is not in cyberspace. To some people, this is a cut and dry issue that is simple to solve, and quite frankly, it is easy to say once you are on the outside looking in. To those who live online and have their entire personal life entwined with their social media presence, leaving is not an option. It is the dominant form of socialization for many people and leaving it would be social suicide. Since so many other people use it, you immediately become an outcast by not. This is commonly referred to as Fear of Missing Out, or FOMO for short, and it drives people to extreme measures. By staying active, you can maintain your presence in the mind of others and continuously build your popularity. If you go inactive, you risk missing something happening online, and those who are willing to use it more will outpace you in the race for social prominence.

Anger does not just drive the virality of news articles. Person-to-person conflict is what drives the virality, especially since nobody wants to admit that they lost an argument or walked away from something they think they could have won. News articles may prompt debate within their own comments sections, but they also make it simple to share the article on whatever social media site suits the sharer's fancy. To the media corporations, a share means traffic, so they will do whatever they can to make it easy to do. Once a user shares the article to their own profile, it opens up a whole new comments section that is specific to that person's page. Once a person makes their opinion known to their social circle, there is bound to be conflict. Now, rather than the conflict happening between two people who have never met each other, it now happens within the social influence of the person who shared it, meaning that it is very likely that it causes an argument between two people who already know each other.

This is where the subtle progression of anger is able to blossom into great personal conflict. Anonymous message boards and sites that use usernames rather than real names feed the part of the brain that produces anger. Ecclesiastes 7:9 states "Be not hasty in thy spirit to be angry: for anger resteth in the bosom of fools." Impulses that never would be said in person can be said without consequence to strangers online, and the tendency to become angry is fed. As the ability to get away with cruelty and vitriol become realized to a greater extent, it begins to seep into online interactions with people that the users do know. The worst impulses are fed by providing a "safe space" for them to exercise themselves. Once the worst parts of human nature are fed, they begin to be comfortable being used on people that they do know.

The screen has always enabled this kind of behavior since it allows the user to react however they want without seeing the consequences. This goes for anger, guilt, shame, or any other emotion that may cause the speaker humiliation in some form or another if done in person. Sherry Turkle interviewed many people on how they felt that communication technology had impacted their lives and provides quotations from many of them in her book *"Alone Together."* One such interview was with a subject regarding conflict resolution online. She described it by saying, "An online apology. It's cheap. It's easy. All you have to do is type 'I'm sorry.' You don't have to have any emotion, any believability in your voice, or anything. It takes a lot for someone to go up to a person and say, 'I'm sorry,' and that's when you can really take it heart. If someone's going to take the easy way out and rely on text to portray all these forgiving emotions, it's not going to work" (Turkle, 2011, p. 198). The lack of sincerity enabled by the use of a screen cripples the intended honesty of the user. Catherine-Steiner Adair says, "Texting is the worst possible training ground for anyone aspiring to have a mature, loving, sensitive relationship" (Steiner-Adair, 2013, p. 204). As was quoted earlier, the Bible clearly states in Romans 5:3-5 "...knowing that tribulation worketh patience; and patience, experience; and experience, hope: and hope maketh not ashamed..."

Screens help to mute the emotional turmoil that comes with acting immature. Since humility is never exercised, humility and empathy remain underdeveloped, while emotional extremes are worked excessively, creating an emotional imbalance in how people treat each other. Nobody enjoys pain in their life, but pain is essential, and screens help to mute that pain as much as possible. By being rude through a phone, people do not have to see the hurt on the face of another person. They do not need to witness them falling apart or having a breakdown. They can simply say whatever they want without having to experience any guilt. Since there is no fear of physical reciprocity, anybody can say anything they want, to anybody. Breakups are easier, fights are safer, and ultimately a culture of childlike immaturity is developed because the depth of humanity is removed from the equation.

Steiner-Adair, in discussing the impact of texting on developing teens says, "Psychologically, texting often promotes a pseudo-intimacy that easily becomes the stand-in for the real thing. Teenagers are so afraid of intimacy, the vulnerability of someone knowing and seeing you and the risk of rejection...The more they text, the less opportunity they have to develop basic relationship skills in face time conversation and hanging out. The less practice they get at face-to-face interaction over everyday things, communicating ideas and feelings in person, the less ready they are for relationships of greater emotional complexity" (Steiner-Adair, 2013, p. 201). Earlier, she quotes a middle school principal who believes that children are empowered by technology to act in this way, and they are fully aware of what they are doing. He says, "I really think that kids know what the impact is, and they're doing it specifically to generate that impact...I think it just makes it easier to be worse and to be more powerful the more removed you are" (Steiner-Adair, 2013, p. 190). In short, the internet does not make people into monsters. It just lets them be the monster that they already are.

CHILD CONSUMPTION OF ADULT CONTENT

The internet allows people to fully realize their toxic potential without fear of reciprocity or judgement. This goes beyond people fostering immature manners and into them using the internet to live out their worst sins. After all, the internet is simply a tool that smartphones make available everywhere and at all times. The problem with this is that it presents humanity with perpetual access to all of its vices simultaneously and without interruption. Online gambling and pornography are two of the most frequently brought into the limelight, as they should be. They have ruined countless lives of people who were only able to become subject to these sinful addictions due to their ease of access (Keen, 2008, pp. 146-150) (Steiner-Adair, 2013, p. 138). But the most disturbing issue here is not that this ruins the lives of adults. The two examples cited above by Keen and Steiner-Adair are examples of pornography and online gambling ruining the lives of *children*. Casinos, bars, and strip clubs are required by law to card people at the front door to keep children from getting access to things that can hurt them. These sins are more harmful to children because they lack the knowledge, self-control, and social awareness to understand what they are getting into. Adults are allowed to make those decisions for themselves. Despite a flawed nature, humanity is still born with innocence. The younger that this is stripped from them, the more trouble they have in their psychological development. So, while bouncers and bartenders may keep them from accessing these sins physically, the internet makes it all available freely. Age restrictions, content filters, and firewalls that block accessing online content reserved for "adults" provide little more than a speed bump in the way of determined and intrigued children. The content is out there and there will never be a firewall, content filter, or age restriction that children cannot circumvent to appease their curiosity. Technology belongs to the young, and they are better with it than they will ever be given credit for.

The availability of this content is amplified by the trend of modern culture to overemphasize sexuality. As America chases Europe in the death of social morality, sexuality has begun to force itself into the lives of children at a younger and younger age. What was once considered taboo for a woman to wear to the beach can now be seen on billboards on major highways, and there is no "content filter" on the back window of a minivan. Football games have cheerleaders, convenience stores sell softcore pornographic magazines at eye level, and social media lets people post anything that isn't technically nudity under the guise of free speech. Nancy Jo Sales, in her book *"American Girls,"* writes about how American Teenage girls interact on social media and disseminates her chapters based on the ages of the girls that she interviewed. Chapter one is about girls she interviewed who were thirteen. In it, she quotes from a Woman's Media Center Speech Project, who says, "…no one is talking about and of it [pornography] in terms of how it affects their behavior. Whether or not they're looking at it, our culture is permeated by a porn aesthetic" (Sales, 2016, p. 39). The fact that children are able to access information now that was only be sold in "adult" stores in times gone by means that children inevitably are accessing it. Although the law requires that users "verify" their age, there is no way to determine the age of a person using a computer. They can simply input whatever they want with no verification. A study conducted in 2007 found that roughly 42% of children between the ages of 10 and 17 had seen pornography online, and that two thirds of those children had viewed it without intending to (Keen, 2008, p. 156).

The damage done by pornography is far too extensive to cover in this book. It has burrowed into our culture and done irreparable damage to the moral fabric of the world. This was prophesied in Luke 17:28, as the second coming of the Son of Man is marked by the days of Lot returning. The most notable aspect of the days in which Lot lived was an unanimously hypersexual culture rooted in sexual deviancy. The Bible makes it abundantly clear that pornography is undoubtedly sinful and forbids the practice of viewing it. For the biblical support, read II Samuel 11-20, Psalms 101:3, Matthew 5:27-28, Proverbs 6, I Thessalonians 4:5, and James 1:15. There are numerous other examples throughout the Bible and the sinful nature of pornography can be indisputably proven using many more doctrinally accurate pathways than what have been provided here. Drawing back to Deuteronomy 6:24 where God promised the Israelites that he has made all of these commandments "for our good always," it is a foregone conclusion that pornography is bad for mankind. All of this is said to show that as this essay will take a slightly different approach to the detriments of pornography in culture, but the overall lack of content discussing it is by no means intended to minimize the wickedness brought about by it. The "rabbit hole" that would need to be explored on this subject is too deep to adequately expound upon without completely derailing the entire focus of this thesis.

The one key aspect of pornography that is to be examined here is the age at which children are becoming exposed to "adult" material. The issue lies not solely in pornographic images and videos, but in the "adult" world into which children are plunged at much younger ages. The average age at which a child sees porn for the first time is eleven (Steiner-Adair, 2013, p. 184). Developmentally, children that are exposed to sexual content at a young age tend to be traumatized by it. Katherine Steiner-Adair works as a child psychologist and speaks extensively on cases she has dealt with regarding children exposed to pornographic material. This can be anything from videos to language that they do not fully understand. In each case she discusses in her book, the child in her care is unable to cope with the adult knowledge that their brain is not yet equipped to handle. Her discussion on the harmful effects of pornography on children begins in her chapter on children in the age range of 6-10 years old. In some cases, it causes depression, anger, and anxiety (Steiner-Adair, 2013, p. 130). Furthermore, Steiner-Adair discusses at length that online pornography tends to be unrealistic, exaggerated, violent, demeaning, and played out by actors who are professionals, not people in love. Children in the modern era are tending to learn about sexuality through the worst possible source: people who make money on it. The full effects of this are unknown since it is impossible to conduct empirical sociological experiments, but based on all accounts given by a licensed child psychologist, it is entirely abominable. To quote directly from her book:

> "Boys and girls alike are easily traumatized by premature exposure to the media-based adult culture that cultivates cynicism and cynical values, treats sex and violence as entertainment, routinely sexualizes perceptions of girls and women, and encourages aggression in boys.

> Today's kids are growing up in this culture that normalizes lying, cheating, crass sexuality, and violence. These things are nothing new, of course, but prior to the Internet and personal tech that put it within reach, children generally did not have access to that world without parental permission. We have lost a protective barrier, individually as parents and collectively as a culture. When you go into a drugstore and see the Playboy magazine discreetly displayed under a partial cover behind the counter, it harks back to a sweeter, more innocent time when grown-ups at home and in the community together would protect children from premature exposure to unhealthy values and behaviors" (Steiner-Adair, 2013, pp. 41-42).

Ultimately, this exposure is causing extensive trauma in

the children of the Internet Culture that is difficult to accurately identify and treat. This is unprecedented in human history and the depths of its impact can only be speculated at. Biblically speaking, the world is rapidly approaching a culture similar to that of Sodom. It would be foolish not to assume some causation in the correlation of developmental damage caused by internet porn and rampant growth of sexual deviancy in youth.

EVERYTHING ALL AT ONCE

The internet allows children to access a lot more than just pornography. Social media allows people to post literally whatever they feel like, so long as it does not violate copyright laws, promote illegal activity, or violate the terms of use by the site. This means that a social media "feed" will host whatever the rest of the world felt like talking about that day. The nature of the feed is therefore chaotic and inconsistent by nature. All of this information, once posted, is framed in a standard format and then presented as the user's "feed." This feed then relays a near infinite supply of equally framed moments to the user. These moments can include heartfelt declarations of love, beautiful photographs of nature, vitriolic tirades against political figures, birthday photos, discussions about what was eaten for breakfast, emotional pleas for social change, aggressive assertions as to a person's personal rights, pictures of oppressed children in third-world countries, and discussions about what movies are coming to Netflix. The key here is not that there is emotional material present, or that some of it may be unpleasant to see. The key is in the variety of information presented in a similar light. Malaria-afflicted children in Africa are given the same amount of space as pictures of a family gathering at Denny's, and they are all listed in a procession that stimulates an emotional game of Twister. The heartstrings are pulled in every direction by news feeds because it is a representation of what the user's personal connections just happen to be thinking about or find interesting on that particular day (although it is rearranged by the platform to ensure maximum user engagement).

This is basically the equivalent of going on a never-ending emotional roller coaster while blindfolded. Sadness, happiness, anger, guilt, and every other emotion are pushed onto the user in order to gain their support via a like, comment, or repost. Combined with the fact that all of this information is displayed through a screen that further frames it in its own way, all of this information ends up being experienced in an entirely unintentional light: the cold, grey light of apathy.

This is a form of emotional whiplash that began its rise to prominence through the television, although it can likely further be traced back to the radio. Neil Postman describes the negative consequences of this in great detail, and his criticisms only amplify when proactively translated into the language of Internet Culture. When speaking of the television news media, he says "...we see the 'Now...this' mode of discourse in its boldest and most embarrassing form. For there, we are presented not only with fragmented news but news without context, without consequences, without value, and therefore without essential seriousness: that is to say, news as pure entertainment" (Postman, 1986, p. 100). Further on, he describes how the local news will describe world events of great importance, such as the inevitability of nuclear war (for context, his book was written during the Cold War,) with intermittent interruptions to promote eating at Burger King. Certainly, when considering the potential ramifications of a global thermonuclear war between the two most powerful nations in the world, interruptions for greasy fast food trivialize an event that had the potential (from a non-biblical humanistic standpoint) to eliminate the existence of mankind.

His conclusion of this matter ends with a lamentation for children who inevitably learn about life from television. He says, "The damage is especially massive to youthful viewers who depend so much on television for their clues as to how to respond to the world. In watching television news, they, more than any other segment of the audience, are drawn into than epistemology based on the assumption that all reports of cruelty and death are greatly exaggerated and, in any case, not to be taken seriously or responded to sanely. I should go so far as to say that embedded in the surrealistic frame of a television news show is a theory of anticommunication, featuring a type of discourse that abandons logic, reason, sequence, and rules of contradiction....in the parlance of the theater, it is known as vaudeville" (Postman, 1986, p. 105). He then justifies his assertion with a quote from television news co-anchor and executive editor Robert MacNeil, whom he quotes saying, "bite-sized is best, that complexity is to be avoided, that nuances are dispensable, that qualifications impede the simple message, that visual simulation is a substitute for thought, and that verbal precision is anachronism" (Postman, 1986, p. 105).

Consider now how much more fast-forward a Facebook news feed is than a television news broadcast. A broadcast is at least bound by how fast words can be audibly spoken to the viewers, they do tend to only mention one to two subjects in between commercial breaks, and there is no way to skip to different segments if one is uninteresting. Facebook and Instagram posts can be sped through nearly at the rate of thought. Siva Vaidhyanathan describes his experience of scrolling his Facebook feed by saying, "Nothing prompted me to think deeply. Everything made me feel something...But if you were to scroll through my News Feed the way I do most of the time...you would experience Facebook as an endless strand of disconnected and decontextualized images" (Vaidhyanathan, 2018, p. 43). Users are bombarded with every emotional stimuli that will provoke an interaction, since interaction is the currency by which all online content is judged (Lazarus, 2017, p. 183). This could be obtained through a guilt trip to raise support for a nonprofit, anger at an opposing political cause, jealousy towards a person with a seemingly more fulfilling life, sadness over the death of an irrelevant celebrity, or literally any other emotional reaction. An emotional reaction causes immediate action, and all posts require immediate interaction because everything posted to the internet has an entropic decay of attention after it is posted. The only way to lock down an interaction is to provoke an immediate emotional response because it is unlikely that a person will return once they have moved on. Since everybody is competing for the same thing using the same tactics, everybody continually has to "up the ante" in order to stay in the game.

This overabundance of emotional stimulation forces the brain to cope in the only way that it can: by desensitizing itself. The process of desensitizing is fairly simple. The first stimulus always generates the greatest reaction since the brain is unaccustomed to processing the provoking action. After a while, the brain comes to understand the action and commits less attention to dealing with it because it no longer perceives that action as a threat to its well-being. A new interaction requires attention, and a repeated one requires less each time. This is how the brain handles emotional stimulation on social media. Posts must outdo each other in terms of shock value, and eventually the part of the brain that handles that shock becomes fatigued, and things that should be shocking no longer are. When added in conjunction with the sharing of visuals for emphasized emotional shock value, emotional responses have to be reduced even further to prevent the brain from staying in a continual state of overload. Since pictures also require only a moment to experience, they can present all of their shock value immediately without the consent of the viewer. A disturbing story must be read and the reader, once sufficiently unsettled, can cease reading it at any time. An image can sear itself into the mind of the viewer in a moment. To put it in modern lingo, what has been seen cannot be unseen. It only takes a moment for an image to burn itself into your mind, and it can stay in there for the rest of your life. The pen may be mightier than the sword, but the picture is much faster on the draw. The intensified emotional stimulus combined with the rapid-fire nature of social media forces the brain to minimalize the seriousness of every situation in order to prevent the user from living in a perpetual mode of panic. The issue is that panic, whether stoked by anger or fear, is very profitable. Innocence drives curiosity, making it one of the most lucrative non-renewable resources that a person can give. Steiner-Adair, when speaking of the loss of childhood innocence says, "all those messages that used to come from family and friends are now being challenged by outside sources – programs, people, and profiteers with their own agendas. Protecting your child's innocence is not one of them" (Steiner-Adair, 2013, p. 44).

The end result of this is that apathy becomes the only way to cope with the complicated, scary issues of the day. The alternative is a perpetual state of anxiety, which is just as common. The world constantly trumpets out the dangers of climate change, global pandemics, international war, drought, disease, and famine. All of these threats have little to no impact on the average internet user since it is largely controlled by the developed world. People who do not have to worry about food can spend a lot more time sharing cat videos. The developed world perpetually lives on the brink of multiple life-altering catastrophes. This provokes the attitudes of apathy and anxiety. There is always a reason to panic or be worried, but there is little to nothing that you can do about it. All you can do is know and worry. Postman describes this state of mind as "In aesthetics, I believe the name given to this theory is Dadaism; in philosophy, nihilism; in psychiatry, schizophrenia" (Postman, 1986, p. 105). The brain is consciously deadened to the world around it, but subconsciously perpetually on edge. This is why the cell phone has become so addicting. It relieves the tensions of not knowing what is going on in the world around you at every point in time, while also feeding the addiction of perpetually knowing "some new thing" as per Acts 17:21 (Alter, 2017, p. 79). While many people know that their constant connectivity is unhealthy and controlling, they are unable to quit. After all, in his analysis on addiction, Adam Alter concludes that "addicts crave a hit without liking the experience...all addicts want the object of their addiction, but many of them don't like it at all…addiction persists even after appeal wanes, leaving intact the desire" (Alter, 2017, pp. 88-89).

CONCLUSION) BUILD-A-BASKET-CASE WORKSHOP

Emotionally speaking, the internet is a version of reality that the human brain is not equipped to handle. In some ways, it is like a gigantic sandbox. It is a safe place for people to go to say, do, or experience with no fear of anything that may hurt them. It encourages play without helping them to grow up. Emotions can be expressed without fear of repercussion, and unpleasant scenarios can be mitigated through the cold electronic light of a computer screen, rather than the visceral emotional risks that accompany in-person interaction. On the other hand, it is nothing like a sandbox. While sheltering the user from experiencing emotional discomfort, it reprograms them to live in perpetual emotional trauma. Children are preyed upon for their curiosity, drawing them into an emotional development cycle that forces them into an emotionally-charged world that they are utterly unequipped to handle. Donna Freitas finishes her book by making the following two conclusions: "I have come to recognize two things clearly. First, smartphones and social media have essentially taken over young people's lives. Second, young people don't feel they are well-equipped to handle this sea of change" (Frietas, 2017, p. 269). Although she speaks mostly in the context of social media interactions between young adults online, her statement also applies to how the rest of the internet functions as a whole, as this helps to contribute to the emotional online experience.

Adults have largely been grafted into the online world, as people over the age of 40 generally did not grow up with the internet and have adopted it into their lives after going through the majority of their personal growth without it. The greatest concern is that now there are children who are growing up that do not know life *without* the internet or social media. Screens have been babysitting children since they were brought into the home, and the children of today are a product of this culture. It shapes their brains emotionally during the critical years of cognitive development and rewires them into something that parents are struggling to handle. Even though connectivity does change adults too, it has had a greater impact on the children it has raised than the parents that it has adopted. The Law of Neuroplasticity dictates that the surrounding world continuously changes how the brain functions, but the law has diminishing returns over time as the brain ages. Internet Culture and Facebook *can* turn your grandmother into a basket case, but it *will* turn your child into one.

The reality of the situation is that this culture attacks the emotional centers of the brain in two ways that build off each other. The emotional immaturity of the brain is maintained, while simultaneously flooding it with problems that require a great deal of emotional maturity to handle. By protecting the users from the potential discomfort of human interaction, users are able to maintain their own personal flaws without realizing how important it is for them to change. This produces a generation of emotional babies that never learn how to communicate with those around them with the depth that previous generations have been able to. They are then perpetually bombarded by the news media and social media with problems that must be hyped up to the point of crisis in order to outsell all of the other sites and people posting about their own crises. All of this is entirely overwhelming and places the latest generation in a position where they see more problems in a worse light and are less capable of handling. A better analogy would be that using the internet is like trying to grow up in a sandbox. While it may have some benefits to a small child, an adult has no place there, and living in it will eventually cause death due to exposure to the elements.

The result is emotional apathy as a defense mechanism. The nihilistic world view is growing amongst children in this day and age. Dr. Jean Twenge gathered the data from a standardized test that has been administered to schoolchildren for more than 50 years. The questions on it remain unaltered as to ensure that the data is collected as empirically as possible. Some questions have been added over time to address rising social issues. The data collected shows that the number of high schoolers who reported feeling "very happy" is higher than it was in the 90's, but is beginning to decrease, with the inflection occurring around 2012. The number of high schoolers who feel dissatisfied with themselves and with life as a whole is at its lowest point since the data began to be collected in 1976, with this feeling skyrocketing around the year 2012. The number of high schoolers who feel left out or lonely is increasing dramatically, with this trend beginning around 2011. The number of high school males who experience depressive symptoms has been relatively stable with a slight overall decline since 1991. However, depressive symptoms in females followed the same trend until 2012, where it began a rapid ascension from 22% in 2012 to 33% in 2015. The number of undergraduate college students who feel overwhelming anxiety or became too depressed to function has been gradually trending upward since 2011. The number of girls experiencing major depressive episodes declined generally from 2005-2012 from about 13% to 11%. From 2012 to 2015, it increased from 12% to over 19% (Twenge, 2017, pp. 95, 96 97, 103, 104, 109). These numbers all experience general trends that seem to begin to alter significantly for the worse around the year 2012, which is the time that smartphone use became mainstream in modern culture. Again, correlation cannot be imposed over causation, but the relationship between these two factors is uncanny. To assert that smartphone usage is beneficial to the emotional development of children and teens is utterly unfounded, and to assume that it does not impact the mind of an adult in a negative manner is unscientific.

Internet Culture has created an indelible mark on the emotional capacity of those ingrained in it. Social data, testimonials from psychologists, and experts on communication media all agree that the manner in which the internet is used to communicate is having many negative impacts on the minds of those who use it. The ending result of this usage is apathy and anxiety, which plague the generations that are being raised in it. Analyzing social trends scientifically has always been difficult since it is impossible to empirically establish a social control group, nor is it humane to conduct lifelong experiments on human beings. Fortunately for science, what conclusions it is able to draw do align with the biblical view of the continuous decay of human nature (II Timothy 3:13), and the Bible not only prophesies that this will happen, but it is also the greatest commentary on human nature ever written. In the following section of this thesis, the emotional changes in society due to Internet Culture will be analyzed in terms of their spiritual ramifications, as well as where the Bible says that these trends are headed.

The impeding alterations to the natural mindset that are being imposed on developing generations are largely unknown by the scientific world. This is to be expected since it is not ethical to formulate social experiments on children, and simulating realistic circumstances is not feasible. Children today will live their lives knowing that the internet, which is the world in which they live, holds a great deal of content that looms over their heads like the blade of a guillotine. Their every action online will be recorded and judged by the will of the mob. This could be compared in some way to children raised hundreds of years ago under the knowledge that their every action would be judged by an almighty and omniscient God. The key differences lie in the standard by which they will be judged and the punishment for their trespasses. The fear of wrath from God based on biblical principles is foundational to the conversion of every Christian. The fear of wrath from the internet, which is the unfettered collective of human consciousness, is based on an everchanging, progressive standard and is a catalyst to an entirely different kingdom. What is clear is that the internet is here to stay, and it is changing the world in a negative manner faster than anybody can understand or adapt to.

A small glimmer of light is that America as a nation does remain a bastion of free speech and religion in the world. It was founded on the principals of free speech and that concept still remains at the core of American society. As long as this remains a tenet of American culture, the ability to preach the gospel unimpeded will help to stem the overwhelming flood of Internet Culture. But the world wide web surpasses all borders. Unlimited connectivity impedes upon the American way of life and allows the one-world system to freely impose itself on all who are touched by it. It is the first truly global system. Siva Vaidhyanathan states that Facebook has "universalizing tendencies and embodies a globalist ambition" (Vaidhyanathan, 2018, p. 27). Franklin Foer blames the internet as a whole, stating, "If the planet was gliding toward the End of History, a globalized, liberal order, then the Internet was going to carry it all the way toward that glorious resting point" (Foer, 2017, p. 184). Social media, and by proxy the internet are not contained by governments or walls or cultures (with the notable exceptions of China, North Korea and Iran), which facilitates the global homogenization of culture.

If human nature were innately good and there were no unholy spiritual forces at work to bring in the kingdom of the antichrist, global hegemony could, theoretically, be good. The reality of the situations is that human nature is sinful and brings forth fruits that are against the will of God (Galatians 5:19-21). The spiritual darkness brought about by this sin enables Satan to work at bringing the whole world to him (Ephesians 2:2). This means that the unification of humanity will be for the direct purpose of accepting the Devil and rejecting Jesus Christ. This concept is key to understanding the Second Advent and the wrath of God on the nations of this world. The Bible speaks of how, at the end of the Tribulation during the reign of the Antichrist, the nations will assemble as a unified whole. This will be in rebellion to God and in service to Satan. The unification of the world against God is prophesied directly in Zephaniah 3:8, Revelation 19:17-21, Zechariah 12:3, 14:1-3 and Isaiah 8:9, 34:2, 66:18. This unification, though against God, is ultimately directed by God in order to purge the world of those who would reject Him and His Son. This is stated overtly in II Thessalonians 2:11, and the theme is repeated too numerously throughout the Bible to provide a complete list. It is made highly evident by Jeremiah 13:16, Isaiah 66:4, Ezekiel 14:9, and Psalms 125:5. The internet is simply the key to bring about the establishment of this global order.

The Old and New Testament both make it abundantly clear that the general progression of the world is towards a globalized, unified kingdom under the Man of Sin. This premillennial point of view redefines the meaning of the word "progressive". The word "progress" comes from pro, meaning forward, and gradus, which indicates movement. Every biblical age of mankind has ended with the failure of those living under it to live in accordance with that which has been dispensed to them by God. The Church Age is no different and is prophesied in Revelation 3:14-22 to end with the church of Laodicea, which is rebuked more staunchly than all of the other churches. This end is marked by the rapture and the beginning of the ministry of the Man of Sin. Therefore, any *progress* taken by the world is movement in the direction of the establishment of the rule of the antichrist.

Ironically, mankind, even without God, is becoming moderately aware of the impending doom brought about by the internet. The overall detrimental impact that Internet Culture has had on the development of our society as a whole is a conclusion unanimously and independently drawn in *every source* gathered and cited in this thesis except for one. The only source claiming that the internet as a whole is beneficial to mankind acknowledges that it actively contradicts scientific data because science does not account for "sociocultural context", which is progressive doublespeak for denying all evidence that contradicts progressive ideology (boyd, 2014, p. 93). The information presented flies in the face of hundreds of years of academia and years of clinical practice provided by all other sources. During the research process, no attempt was made to obtain sources biased towards the viewpoint that the internet does more evil than good. The research presented stems from books written across the last 100 years by authors whose expertise ranges from child psychology to marketing to history. All of the books that make a judgement on the direction of society indicate that the general trend is negative, and a massive overhaul is needed in order to prevent humanity from an oncoming collapse. And, unfortunately, all of them, being humanists at heart, come to the conclusion that we will save ourselves in time with education or social reform. All of them bring about a light of hope for the future of man with his newfound tool, and believe that once we adapt correctly to it, we will be a better world for it. Every cited work provides some hope that the end is not inevitable, humanity is inherently good, and we can all get through this together. All of them, that is, except for the King James Bible.

As the infallible word of God, it can be taken as a standard by which all other information must be judged. It sits in judgement of books on history, scientific research, the philosophies of man, and any other study that claims to provide a definitive truth. Any literature that contradicts it can be dismissed as corrupted, and in any situation where the world aligns with it indicates that somebody with a sincere desire for truth has accurately written about the creation of God Almighty. For years, preachers have railed on the negative effects of the internet and social media use, based solely on the fact that it enables the sinful nature of mankind. These men were largely ignored and some of them have fallen prey to what they once condemned, just as the previous generation fell to the television. In recent years, most notably since the 2016 American presidential election, authors have begun to realize that the internet might bring with it unintentional negative side effects. While their motives were largely impure (to attack a president whom they disagreed with politically), the facts unearthed are true, in spite of the attitude of the speakers. Sherry Turkle (in 2011) made a comment which has already been presented but bears unparalleled significance on this issue. She says, "We cannot blame technology for this state of affairs. It is people who are disappointing each other. Technology merely enables us to create a mythology in which this does not matter" (Turkle, 2011, p. 237). And so, science finally began to catch up with a book that was finished 1,900 years ago and translated into English 400 years ago. The great minds of this world began to catch up with the preachers who don't have high school diplomas, much less doctoral degrees in psychology or years of higher education and research. They did not need peer reviewed studies, periodicals in science journals, or literally hundreds of thousands of sociological test results spanning more than 40 years. They had an old book and a walk with God and that helped them warn people decades ahead of the scientific community. I Corinthians 1 rings ever true.

The reason that they were able to do this stems from Revelation 19:10 which says, "…I am thy fellowservant, and of thy brethren that have the testimony of Jesus: worship God: for the testimony of Jesus is the spirit of prophecy." The speaker talks of his walk with God, and that the testimony of a follower of God is that they are able to tell the future through prophecy. The ability to accurately describe the future in great detail and without error is an ability reserved to God alone. This means that anybody who is able to accurately describe the future must have been provided with their premonitions by God and only God. It is the litmus test by which all predictive information can be judged.

God has provided His children with all that is needed to maintain a healthy walk with Him. This book may provide new information on the granular aspects of Internet Culture on the lost world and Christianity alike, but up to this point presents nothing new in terms of the overall message: the internet influences both the lost world and Christians to be more sinful. This thesis only reinforces this concept that has been preached by men of God for as long as the internet has been ruining the lives of those who fall prey to both its subtle and not-so-subtle pitfalls.

Continuing on, this thesis will directly address the spiritual implications that the emotional and cognitive changes have caused. This will evaluate the conditions of both the Christian, as the church fully embraces the Laodicean Church Age, and the lost world, as it prepares to embrace the kingdom of the antichrist. While the end of this age has always been clearly stated in the Scriptures, the means by which we will arrive there have always been generally speculative. As the day approaches nearer, the exact workings of Satan become clearer, and it is the intention of this labor of love to shine the spotlight on the role that the internet will play in achieving his purposes.

God help us.

Section 3) Why

CHAPTER 6) SPIRITUALLY SPEAKING

Technology is basically defined as anything that is developed into a more complicated form for the purpose of completing a specific task. While it is generally used throughout this book as a blanket statement, technology is simply anything that man has created to do something easier. Since technology is a concept that describes physical objects, all technology is therefore hermeneutically neutral. In Romans 14:14, Paul says, "I know, and am persuaded by the Lord Jesus, that there is nothing unclean of itself..." Technology is not an evil thing that should be shunned and totally abandoned. Humanity is able to live with it without fully corrupting itself into a sinful abyss. What technology does is make sin easier to commit, more accessible at all times, and addictive, all while delaying the harvest that is reaped from these sins.

These sins, which are enabled by modern communication technology and promoted by Internet Culture, are detrimental to the spiritual climate of society. As sin takes a more prevalent position in everyday life, it becomes normalized, sanitized, and accepted. The shroud that this casts over the developed world results in a decay of the efficacy of the working of the Holy Spirit. Proverbs 14:34 says, "Righteousness exalteth a nation: but sin is a reproach to any people." As the sin moves in, God moves out. Sinners build their immunity to the gospel call and Christians lose their fire for serving the Lord. This has been the case ever since sin drove man from the presence of God in the Garden of Eden in Genesis 3. For the Christian of the Church age, the continual battle of sin is detailed by Paul in Romans 6, where he describes the war between his flesh and the Holy Spirit as he tries to fulfill the perfect will of God.

This chapter will dive into how these sins harm a Christian's walk with God, followed by how these sins prevent the lost world from coming to Him, and will conclude with the trends that the world is following as it begins to embrace the doctrines of Satan as a world system. This also begins the "Why" portion. Until now, the emotional and cognitive effects have been analyzed in terms of what their impact is on human psychology. Considering the bigger picture, which is the spiritual world, this only matters in terms of how it impacts the spiritual state of individuals. Satan is only concerned with warping the collective human will to accommodate his will. This section will examine how the internet enables him to fulfill his purposes.

CHRISTIANITY) ALONE IN THE GARDEN

Exodus 24:2 – And Moses alone shall come near the LORD:

There is a common denominator that runs through the relationships that all great men in the Bible have with God, regardless of the dispensation or their calling. That singular feature is that in order to communicate extensively with God, each man individually had to spend time alone with Him. Adam walked with God, alone, in the cool of the day. Enoch walked with God in a wicked world and God was so pleased that He took him and him alone. Abraham was told to get away from his kindred in order to follow God. Jacob reconciles with God when he wrestles with the angel, alone, after sending all of his family and possessions ahead of him to meet Esau. Moses gets the Law and all of the commandments from God when he goes up into the mountains alone. Gideon is called by God to defeat the Midianites when he is working alone. Samuel gets called by God when he is sleeping by himself. David begins to write the Psalms when he is alone as a shepherd. Solomon receives two messages from God when he is asleep. God answers Hezekiah's prayer for a longer life when he prays alone in his room. Daniel prays alone and is given revelations about the end of the world and the end of the Jewish captivity. Paul receives the doctrines of the Church Age, alone, in the desert in Galatians 1:17. And most importantly of all, Jesus Christ leaves the disciples to pray alone in the Garden of Gethsemane, just before He is arrested and crucified. Throughout the Bible, God's men grow their relationships with Him by getting alone and learning the heart of God.

This concept runs across all major Bible characters. It is also a concept that runs true in the personal lives of individuals who want to grow relationships to a deeper level. Men and women determine if their relationship is suitable for marriage by spending time alone with that person. This enables them to decide if they feel they are compatible. This is because in order to get to know a person better, you have to become vulnerable around them and allow them to understand who you are as a person. This is much easier to do when there is only one person that you do trust, as opposed to a group of people who you may trust. The relationship becomes personal when all other people are removed. This works romantically and in terms of friendships. The fewer people there are, the easier it is to establish unity of thought, and the will of the crowd is easier to ignore.

One of the great detriments, therefore, of the internet is the mindset of perpetual connectivity. This plays off of the tendency to connect perpetually due to smartphones, and the subconscious attenuation to the world system. Smartphones allow us to connect with anybody else in the world who has access to a phone or the internet, which is a number that is continuously increasing proportionally to the population of the earth. Since humans are inherently social creatures (Genesis 2:18) this is a desire that runs in our nature and is not something that is sinful by itself. After all, God did provide Adam with Eve to alleviate the loneliness. The issue is that perpetual connectivity eliminates solitude. The only way to grow a relationship with God is to pray and read the Bible. All other aspects of the Christian walk stem from these two activities, which represent a conversation between God and man. Reading the Bible is how God speaks to man, and prayer is how man speaks to God. This conversation grows the relationship but requires solitude and concentration, neither of which can be achieved when in the presence of other people, be it physically or virtually.

This plays into the second aspect which is that the ability to connect perpetually brings with it a subconscious awareness of the social opinions of the world. While the world as a whole has never acted in accordance with the will of God, it is continuing to "wax worse and worse," as per II Timothy 3:13. Combined with the policing effects of "two billion little brothers" and the cancel culture that permeates the internet, there is now a greater fear than ever of a failure to comply with the world system. The world is able to follow us into our homes, our bedrooms, our churches, and anywhere else we choose to bring a smartphone or computer. Smartphones and computers exist primarily as a tool of connectivity, and the connection provided is purely between mankind and itself. Communication from man to man has never been faster, easier, or more available. Because technology makes this possible, human nature pushes us to communicate with each other more than ever and with God less than ever.

The most important thing that a Christian can do in their life is to walk with God. This is what Enoch did, and God loved that he walked with Him so much that God chose to create an exception to His own rules and take Enoch, preventing him from ever dying. A Christian who walks with God on a moment-by-moment basis and allows the Lord to direct his every step will do everything else that a Christian should do because he is constantly in tune with the will of God. What cell phones do is eliminate the breaks in everyday moments with a petty form of amusement, whether from texting, mobile games, or social media. Any moment that people experience boredom, a wait, awkward conversation, or anything else causing even the slightest amount of emotional disinterest, results in them generally pulling out their smartphones for some amusement until the moment passes. What would have once been a prime moment for prayer is now filled with pointless communication with other people.

Furthermore, a perpetual awareness of the world system subconsciously wears against a Christian's command to not conform to the world (Romans 12:2). The more aware of the world, its opinions, and the punishments that exist for contradicting those opinions (shown through the news media and social media), the more difficult they are to reject. The more a person connects with the world as a whole (aka, social media), the more that they will tend to be like the world. There has always been a battle between the Christian and the world, but as people communicate with each other more and communicate with God less, the outcome of Christianity conforming to the world system is inevitable. Even association with other Christians becomes difficult as Christianity continues its decay into Laodicean tendencies. A Christian must maintain their walk with God by simply walking with God and God alone. Each and every Christian must isolate themselves in order to draw nearer to God. Social media and communication technology are subconscious weapons that draw the attention of the user away from God and push them towards a more social, and less spiritual mindset.

DELAYED GRATIFICATION

Ephesians 4:15 – But speaking the truth in love, may grow up into him in all things, which is the head, even Christ:

Whan a Christian is born again, they are described as being a baby in terms of spirituality (I Corinthians 3:1). If fed, nurtured, and protected appropriately, that baby will eventually grow into a fully function adult capable of reproducing Christians and nurturing them (I Peter 2:2). What is universally true of the human development cycle is that this process simply takes time and effort. The correct conditions must be applied for growth, and then that growth must be allowed to run at the pace of the believer. While this may be faster for some than others, fully developing as a Christian takes time. Some new Christians will immediately begin to win others to Christ and may read the Bible as much as they are able to, but it is impossible to read through the Bible in a day. Based on the size of the print, most Bibles tend to run around 1500 pages. Nobody is able to read, retain, and understand the word of God in a lifetime, much less in a few years of fervent reading.

The church is described in Ephesians 5 as the Bride of Christ. Since the church has a similar relationship with God as a wife does with her husband, there are parallels that can be drawn from it. The most notable aspect, for the purpose of this section, is the tendency of love in a successful marriage to grow with time. After years of marriage, men who are still happy with their relationship will say that they are more in love with their wife than they were on the day that they married her. The same goes for the opinion of the wife. This comes through years of trials, hardships, and a consistent effort to make the relationship work in accordance with the biblical standard. They may have loved each other as much as they could on the day that they got married, but their capacity to love each other grew through time in a way that only time can grow it. The same is the case with a believer and their walk with God. The love that a Christian has when they get saved may be as much as they are capable of loving. However, the only way to fully appreciate the blessed hope is to experience tribulation (Romans 5:3-5, Titus 2:13) and determine to grow spiritually though it. The full understanding of the Christian life comes not through a factual understanding of the contents of the Scriptures, but through living life according to the precepts described therein.

It is critical to understand that the growth of a Christian simply takes a long time. This is key because modern communication technology and Internet Culture all promote a common theme: instant gratification. The speed at which the internet can be streamed to a phone or through wi-fi is a continual selling point in advertisements for smartphones, computers, Internet Service Providers, and software. This speed enables seamless access to everything provided on the internet, thus preventing any delay in the flow of information. This plays into the previous section on eliminating pauses in life for prayer or reflection. The Devil is intent on driving the world into Hell as fast as possible, and the best way to ensure this is to make sure that there is a constant availability of distractions available to prevent people from stopping to think if there is something wrong.

A greater detriment is caused by the reduced investment required for an immediate return. On the internet, information can be researched through a search engine that provides answers to nearly any question that can be asked (Google, Yahoo or Bing can almost always provide an answer, though not necessarily the correct answer). The goal of each of these sites is to make sure that the person gets the information that they need as easily as possible so that their service will be used in the future. This ensures profitability through advertising and harvesting metadata. Google will often provide a statistic in the top corner indicating the number of discovered responses in relation to the amount of time it took to gather those responses. The answer is often that it is able to retrieve millions of responses in less than a second. This makes more information available to an internet user in the time it takes to blink an eye than a person in the enlightenment would be able to gather in a lifetime. These engines take great care to provide the link most pertinent to the query on the first page, meaning that there is often little to no investment in the acquisition of information.

Building on that concept, the online news media must provide the most up to date information as quickly as possible. They must also ensure that many related articles are available, rather than a single, cohesive analysis, since quantity trumps quality in terms of profitability on the internet. Information must be quick, shallow, and emotional in order to drive the most traffic. One of the major impacts of this is that it passively teaches the readers that complicated issues can be explained using simple, short descriptions. Complicated issues are stripped of all nuance or complication because complication slows the reader and causes them to think, which means that they aren't clicking on more articles and making the news media more money. Rather than reading books, which are cohesive logical arguments that address the complexity of issues, people have degraded to newspapers, to radio, to television, and now to the internet. As the complexity of the analysis has decreased, so has the appetite for any amount of deep understanding.

Tying the concepts listed in the previous paragraphs together is the concept that the internet promotes immediate gratification in terms of understanding complex issues, while the Bible teaches that the complexities of the Scripture, when lived out across a long period of time, end up producing a Christian that fulfills the perfect will of God. The nature of the internet is contrary to the nature of the Christian walk. One promotes instant gratification while the other promotes delayed gratification. Since the human mind adapts to what it is exposed to the most, a Christian will have an easier time experiencing whichever world they choose to immerse themselves in the most. The internet does not promote the development of patience, and without patience a Christian will never complete the race that is set before them (Hebrews 12:1). Using the internet does not make this impossible, but the more that a person uses the internet, the more weight they will carry in their efforts to run for Christ.

SIN AND SIMPLICITY

Matthew 6:13 – And lead us not into temptation, but deliver us from evil:

A concept that was explored earlier on when discussing addiction was the concept that a person's proximity to their vice directly correlated with their tendency to fall to it (Alter, 2017, p. 275). This is why God offers the victory over temptation primarily to the Christian by avoiding it. In I Corinthians 10:13, God promises that He will always "...make a way to escape, that ye may be able to bear it." The solution to fighting some temptation in life is to distance yourself physically from them as much as possible. This may include finding new friends, changing occupations, or stopping some activities that are associated with sin (such as adult softball due to its correlation with alcohol or playing cards due to the affiliation with gambling). In each case, physical distance is created between the person and the temptation, making it more manageable.

The problem with the internet is that it makes all sin more accessible to the users. Gossip is easier through social media. Lust is easier through pornography. Covetousness is easier through online shopping. The internet allows people access to whatever they want. Human nature is sinful, and the internet is driven by whatever makes the most money. Combining these two factors makes it easier than ever to access whatever the besetting sin of a Christian may be. As the internet has invaded all aspects of our lives (doctor appointments, paying rent, buying clothes, banking, etc.) and has been placed on steroids since the rise of COVID-19, living life without an internet connection is becoming continuously more difficult. Access to the internet cannot be compartmentalized meaning that it is impossible to restrict access to only the parts that are necessary for everyday life. If an Internet Service Provider gives you access, it gives you access to everything on it. While the intent may be to only use it as needed, having an internet connection brings with it the siren call of the knowledge that every sinful practice is out there as well, waiting to be toyed with.

The internet also serves to virtualize the temptations. Sins that once required physical action, purchases, or movement now require only a few moments with a screen. Lust used to be pushed through dirty magazines and movies, which could only be bought at adult stores or sleazy gas stations. You had to go to the place, pick something out, interact with the cashier, take it home, and then keep it hidden. There are risks and drawbacks associated with all of these actions that helped to keep it in check for years. Now porn, which is more damaging than the static images on a magazine, is available in greater quantities and variety than what can be put on a VHS tape. There is no shame of having to talk to a cashier, and no risk of having to hide a physical book or tape, since it is all purchased by watching ads and streamed through the screen. Since it is available on smartphones, which can be used anywhere. Since all devices are protected by passcodes, you (and your kids) are much less likely to get caught than if it had to be played on the television screen in the living room at 3 AM. Smartphones and the internet remove all of the barriers to commercialized lust and mental adultery. Unsurprisingly, this correlates directly with the rise in the number of people that view pornography, its cultural acceptance, and a decrease in the age at which children are exposed to it.

The internet removes obstacles to all sins. Gambling no longer required going to a casino. Finding people to "hook up with" no longer requires going to a bar. Gossip no longer requires looking a person in the eye or experiencing any in-person reciprocation. Even activities that are not sinful, such as making crafts at home on Pinterest, can become sin through excessively exploring the nearly unlimited amount of content available online. It is easy to pinpoint the visible sins such as lust, swearing, or gambling online because they are so easily identifiable and have been preached against for years. It is not so easy to identify when the internet turns a hobby into an obsession and begins to eat away at more important things in life. These passive sins are enabled just as much as the active ones and can do a substantial amount of damage on their own.

All these sinful practices inhibit a Christian's walk with God and are now easier than ever to indulge in and conceal. This is simply due to the fact that the internet exists with all of this content on it. Human nature drives us to sin based on how easy it is to do (and also how likely we are to get away with it). While no sin is ever truly gotten away with (Proverbs 15:3), sometimes the social consequences of it, when it is done in person, are enough to keep people pure until the Holy Spirit can convict the heart.

SEEING SHOULD NOT BE BELIEVING

Hebrews 11:1, 6 – Now faith is the substance of things hoped for, the evidence of things not seen...But without faith, it is impossible to please him:

The internet is rife with visually based messages. The introduction of the television into the home began to reprogram the human mind in a way that processed visuals, quite literally in a different light. Now with the addition of pictures, the only words that a person watching television will read are the headings at the bottom of the screen during the news. Any other visual presentation of words is purely incidental, and their use is minimized to the greatest extent possible. After television rooted itself in the center of the world's culture, the internet craze swept across the hearts of men with ease since, in part, because of how easy it was to send and access the visuals that it has become accustomed to. Since the human mind will always tend towards the easier of the two pathways, visuals continued their rise in the human heart as a means of communication.

The internet is an emotional place to be. This has already been established and the evidence points towards the fact that people are now more emotionally driven than they ever have been before. Pictures can instantly set the desired emotional context to frame any information, promoting the ability to sway the heart without thinking. Since the internet is run by the love of money, corporations will always use the most effective methods to win over audiences, which has caused the advertising industry to balloon into the monstrosity that it is today. Pictures make us feel, not think, and feelings drive traffic and sales.

The rise in visual communication also correlates with the decline in the usage of print media, as well as the linguistic skills of the general public. The more that people use the emotional parts of their brain, the more exercised these portions become. As people use their intellectual thinking capabilities less, those parts of the brain become weaker. The internet cannot be proven to cause this to happen, but it does correlate exactly with the primary communication methods of the day. Twitter, one of the dominant social media platforms of the day limits each tweet to a maximum of 280 characters. It effectively eliminates the ability to pose an intellectual point of view unless an author posts a string of posts, circumventing the platform's intended use. Instagram and Snapchat both are based mostly on pictures or short videos, with only comments sections to engage literacy. YouTube follows the same formula but is for only videos and again, allows for literary correspondence in the comments sections. Social media platforms as a whole are designed to promote short feedback in terms of likes, shares, and comments, while promoting visuals over words, since pictures have been proven to draw more attention.

The emotional overload that these platforms provide causes people to communicate at a much shallower level. When a Christian spends much of their time in the digital world, it severely cripples their ability to understand a God that expresses himself to the world primarily through an extensive written work. God expects His people to read, study, memorize, and meditate of what He has given them (Isaiah 34:16, Psalms 1:2, 119:11, II Timothy 2:15). These actions are based on committing attention to the literary aspects of the Bible. All of this is made more difficult when the mind is constantly flooded with a world of visual content that promotes feeling rather than thinking.

This is not to say that a Christian should be an emotionless robot that coldly applies Scripture without feeling to every situation. Jesus demonstrated a wide spectrum of emotions from joy (Luke 10:21), sorrow (John 11:35), compassion (Mark 8:2), and anger (Mark 3:5). The focus here is that the internet feeds the emotional core of the brain while starving it intellectually. The problem is not experiencing emotion but becoming emotionally imbalanced. God provides a stern warning against this state of being in Proverbs 25:28 where he says, "He that hath no rule over his own spirit is like a city that is broken down, and without walls." The internet immerses the believer in this culture, making it difficult for the correct balance to be maintained. In some cases, people become overly emotional and unstable, while others become desensitized, cold, and emotionless. This leaves them open and vulnerable to the attacks of the Devil. Since online interactions are public by nature, it allows the Devil to publicly declare and archive the weakness of modern Christianity for all the world to see.

SELFIES AND SELFLESSNESS

Matthew 16:24 – Then said Jesus unto his disciples, If a man will come after me, let him deny himself, and take up his cross, and follow me.

There is no denying the purpose of social media, which is self-promotion. All social media platforms take great care to numerically quantify the popularity of every single user. This is why the number of followers and friends is visible on every profile page, and statistics such as the likes and favorites are the first metrics shown on each post. Whatever the initial goal of any user may be, their quantifiable popularity will indisputably come into play throughout their continued use. Some people may begin using social media to stay in touch with distant family, to engage in a community of their interest, or just to fit in, but the temptation of popularity corrupts every user that enters their realm. The primary goal may never become the never-ending rise to limitless popularity, but the draw is undeniable and will impact the quality and quantity of content created.

All posts on social media are judged. This happens regardless of the number of friends or followers that a person has. When something is posted, the judgement comes in the form of how much interaction it does or does not generate. If a post receives little interaction relative to the total number of followers or past postings, then it is considered unpopular. If it receives a lot, then it is popular. This popularity may be achieved through love or rage, but popularity is popularity, and there is no bad publicity when it comes to marketing. This is true even if you are simply marketing yourself. The perpetual threat of negative judgement by the people that a user has chosen to associate with provides a persistent passive influence over the content that is created, how it is framed, and how much of it is created.

The mindset of acting in a way that is pleasing to the crowd, especially if the crowd consists of a large number of unsaved or progressively minded individuals, is contradictory to the teachings of the Bible. This is true for many reasons. Primarily though (and most obviously) is that if a Christian is connected to the lost world through social media, anything they post will be viewed by the crowd. As the Overton Window has shifted more towards the progressive ideologies of the political left, even among modern Christianity, biblically true statements have become more and more outrageous. The rise of the internet rage mob and cancel culture has created an entirely new threat against Christian beliefs. Christianity has long been part of the core of American culture but voicing these beliefs on the internet subjects the user to the potential that their online presence will be silenced. It also brings with it the threat that online activists will mobilize and attack their personal accounts. The looming threats that hang over the avid users of social media will eventually begin to take their toll on the content that they post. This may manifest itself through a conscious decision to compromise or a subconscious reduction in the poignancy of what is posted. The costs of being cancelled online are bleeding more and more into the real world, and this threat is more than enough to quell the more unpopular doctrines of New Testament biblical Christianity.

Beyond the threat of posting spiritually controversial content comes the fact that when a post is judged favorably by the online community, it bears with it the potential for nurturing the pride of the user. In evaluating what is posted, the reason for why a person is posting something should be called into question. In what way will this provide a positive impact on the overall spiritual condition of the person posting it, or anyone that they are connected to? Any purpose not rooted in conveying spiritual or functional information to others is effectually meaningless in the scope of eternity. Since the posts will be judged by the community, it is likely that the post in some capacity serves to inflate the ego of the user. The success of the post is judged by the reaction of the crowd, so the user must create posts that will be approved of by others. This act of self-promotion flies directly in the face of II Corinthians 10:12 which says, "For we dare not make ourselves of the number, or compare ourselves with some that commend themselves but they measuring themselves by themselves: and comparing themselves among themselves, are not wise." Social media, as was discussed earlier, forces the comparing of the user with other users.

Understandably, this has always occurred in social circles among Christians. Paul wrote II Corinthians before social media existed, which means that this tendency is not unique to the online world. What should be understood through this is that social media, because of the nature of how it is programmed, makes it much more difficult not to compare yourself to others. There is a strong conscious and subconscious influence placed on the user to conform to the sinful practices that social media facilitates. Social media enables human nature to exercise itself, and the sinful Adamic nature must be suppressed in order to lead a life that is pleasing to God.

EVERYTHING WANTS TO BE WANTED

I Kings 21:6 – And he said unto her, Because I spake unto Naboth the Jezreelite, and said unto him, Give me thy vineyard for money; or else, if it please thee, I will give thee another vineyard for it: and he answered, I will not give thee my vineyard.

There is no free lunch. On the internet there is a phrase that is often uttered when discussing the issues of online piracy or copyright law, and that phrase is "Data wants to be free." The internet does what no other invention has ever done before. It can take any creative work, be it a painting, movie, or novel, reduce it to computer code, and transmit it to anybody in the world on demand. As the speed at which data can be transmitted in bulk increases, the cost of doing so decreases. The internet has quickly become the greatest threat to intellectual property that the world has ever known. Because information is so easy to share freely, it has become exponentially more difficult to keep it guarded. After all, it only takes one person to get their hands on the data for it to be copied and distributed practically an infinite number of times. To combat this, websites decided to take a different approach to monetizing their content: advertisement.

Advertisement is the only way that any online company that does not actively sell a product or service can make money (apart from stealing or monitoring your personal data, which they then sell to advertisers, so the effects are basically the same). Rather than charging the user to view something that they want, they simply allow other companies to advertise their content next to, before, or in the middle of the content being viewed. This has all been discussed earlier, but it is essential to understand that most of the money that circulates through the world of the internet circulates based on advertising. This business model has flourished because it has the highest return on investment. Unfortunately, this business model is rooted in the sinful act of covetousness.

Covetousness is the engine upon which the entire internet runs. Any internet service or information that is made available freely must generate a profit for the laborers who created it. Advertisers would not have fully embraced this business model if it did not work. Advertising drives consumption and consumption funds the free portions of the internet. Thanks to the value contained within the seedy market of metadata harvested from users, advertisements can be targeted directly to individuals for increased effectiveness. Since the only desire of these companies is to drive their own profit margins and not to protect the spiritual condition of the denizens of the internet, covetousness is now being exploited at levels never possible before.

The Bible makes it an adamant point that covetousness is sinful. "Thou shalt not covet" is the tenth commandment given in Exodus 20, and it is continuously preached against across the remainder of the Scriptures. Paul takes time to condemn this sin in Romans 1:29, II Corinthians 9:5, and Ephesians 5:3. It is condemned in Hebrews 13:5 as an opposition to the contentment that should be present in the heart of one who trusts God. Colossians 3:5 identifies covetousness directly as idolatry, which in the Old Testament context was punishable by death. What covetousness is, essentially, is a desire to have something that eventually coerces a person to sin in order to obtain it. This may be as obvious a sin as stealing it, or as seemingly minor a sin as misusing the money that God has provided to obtain something He did not intend for that person to spend it on. The point is that covetousness is equated with idolatry because the item that is coveted eventually takes the place of the will of God and the desire to obtain it surpasses the desire to follow the will of God.

The internet, once again, does not *force* a user to become guilty of covetousness, and a user does not become guilty by proxy through using it. It is entirely possible to use the internet without coveting anything advertised. The point is that this is, quite frankly, nearly impossible to do on a daily basis. Internet ads are present on nearly every site and are used so much because they work so well. Since companies can now tailor advertisements to the user, their location, the time of day, and any other factor that may persuade them to purchase something, covetousness is now harder than ever to avoid. The more time that a user spends immersed in this environment, the more likely they will be to fall to it.

CONCLUSION) THE MENTAL MINEFIELD

The internet is, ultimately, a tool. It is a creation of man that is designed to allow humanity to communicate information instantly across large distances. It is not like cigarettes or alcohol which are expressly forbidden because the use of them is undeniably sinful. The internet is a simple tool, and how it is used is determined entirely by how the user chooses to engage with it. The issue lies in that it this tool is a reflection of the heart of the natural, fallen man. The pale blue light that a screen gives off is in no way natural and everything that exists on the internet exists on there because some human decided to create something *in their own image.* There is no such thing as the natural internet. God did not create the world of the internet and as such, it does not reflect His character or His message to mankind. This is the world that humanity created for itself.

Since the internet is developed purely by man, it is a reflection of the ambitions, introspections and creations that humanity has derived from the desires of its own heart. As human nature is irrevocably broken outside of submission to God and the majority of humanity has always rejected God, the internet reflects the sum of its parts: a total rejection of God. The result is that the internet passively promotes lifestyles and personality traits that Christianity is commanded to reject. The sins of covetousness, emotional instability, impatience, and pride are all traits that are rewarded by avid internet use, especially those who spend a great deal of time on social media. There is a continual, subconscious awareness of the spirit of the lost world that permeates the internet, making combat against it much more intimidating than combating the influences of the world within where they can physical be. Christians have always known that the entire world is against them, but now the rest of the world makes that knowledge much clearer. Furthermore, the internet makes it much easier to dabble in, obsess over, and conceal the committing of any besetting sin that hounds the path of the believer. All of these threats to the spiritual walk of a Christian hang over their head, and the more time that a Christian spends in this environment, the more they will be tempted by it and the more likely they are to conform to the world around them. The internet is only a tool, but it is a tool that wants to be misused. It is a minefield of sin, and even though not everybody who walks through the field steps on a mine, everybody in it tends to walk a little differently.

THE UNSAVED INDIVIDUAL)

WHAT DOES EVERYBODY ELSE THINK?

The ability to transmit a near infinite amount of information at the speed of light has changed how people choose to communicate with each other, and what they choose to communicate. The intent behind this was to connect people with other people and to draw the whole world together into a cohesive whole. Silicon Valley is actively run by members of the hippie generation who stimulated the tech explosions and brought with it their socialistic and communal philosophies. This is historically documented by Franklin Foer in his book, *"World Without Mind,"* in which he highlights the involvement of modern technology's fathers in the "peace and love movement". He then draws parallels from how the ideals of those movements are preserved in the technology that these men developed. The ultimate goal is a humanistic harmony that is enabled through the brotherhood of man and uses communication to help everybody get along. As was stated before, if human nature were innately good and there were no supernatural forces drawing this world to a universally sinful one-world government, this would probably be a good thing. Unfortunately, they are incorrect, as human nature is in a fallen state due to the sin of Adam and Eve, and the future of this world is revealed through the prophesies given in the Bible.

When connecting everybody together and allowing them to communicate without bounds, many unfortunate consequences arise. One such issue is that now, all information and opinions are available at all times. The normal reactionary response is that this should be a good thing. After all, people now have access to the truth. But they also have access to all of the lies in the world, as well as the opinions of the rest of humanity. Those opinions may be passionately presented but ultimately unsupported, illogical, or based in falsehood. There is such an abundance of information in the world that truly knowing anything certain now feels like an impossible task. Not only is the truth out there, but so is every lie, exaggeration, caricature, and intentional omission that people can come up with. Truths, half-truths, creative interpretations, and passionate opinion pieces litter the internet and create such a hodgepodge of differing viewpoints that actually identifying the truth is not only impossible but also apparently pointless. Having a perfect knowledge of any single subject and expressing it would only be met with criticism from those who disagree and the presentation of disinformation to support it. The internet allows the spread of information but also encourages people to interpret it in any way that they choose and then to add in their own position. The comments sections on websites encourage people to say what they feel, which may make them money, but also means that their articles do not present the absolute truth because people are encouraged to disagree with what is presented. This is why the Bible does not have a comments section; it is true, regardless of what anybody says, and God did not ask for any opinions when writing it.

The internet also feeds the emotional side of the brain while starving the intellectual. The internet subtly influences people to be more emotionally reactive and less logically empirical. To summarize previous sections, the content posted on the internet must be emotional and short to make money. The same rule applies for gaining popularity on social media. Search engines make it their goal to answer each query in as simple a manner as possible in order to ensure they retain the most traffic and therefore can charge the most for their premium advertising space. As people continue to spend more time on this media and less on intellectually-based medias (aka books), the brain adapts to what it is subjected to the most. This makes reading books less appealing, because the fewer of them a person reads, the more difficult that it becomes to read them critically. The problem is self-defeating. The internet hinders critical thinking skills, which is a problem that can only be countered by exercising critical thinking skills. Thus, the task of dissecting all of the conflicting points of view, facts, alternative facts, outright lies, and slants becomes a much more difficult task than it would for a highly literate public.

Since there is already so much "fake news" out there, finding the truth is inadvertently discouraged since there is no reward for doing so. As such, "truth is fallen in the street" (Isaiah 59:14). The truths that people arrive at therefore tend to be in alignment with whatever social circle they align with. Any information that contradicts their world view is easily dismissed as "fake news" or disinformation. Truth becomes relegated to the preconceived notions of the user and their personal fear of being rejected by the mob. Although the conservative and progressive political parties are both active on the internet and social media, the internet belongs to the young, who tend to lean more towards the progressive mindset. Ultimately, the internet drives the world towards "progress," and any story, article, or fact that is contradictory to this mindset is pushed off of the internet.

Ultimately, the internet makes the truth nearly impossible to find. There is entirely too much information out there from too many sources of varying reliability. Actually locating the truth of the matter is complicated, which is a reality that few people want to face, as it often results in conceding that the opinions of people that users choose to associate with are incorrect. There is no victory in finding the truth because for every person who is willing to put in the effort to determine what it is, there are many more who do not have the time, patience, determination, or humility to look for it honestly. This mindset seeps beyond the internet that propagates it and into the hearts of the users who obsess on its use, resulting in what is not only a lack of the truth, but an apathy in trying to determine what it is.

SAYS WHO?

The internet as a medium for communication enables and encourages people to say anything that they wish at any time. This, again, at surface level, seems like it would be a good thing. The issue lies in how this changes the perception of authority structures that are in place in our culture. Internet Culture promotes information communication through short messages delivered instantaneously. There is no need for formality or for writing content of any length, as follow-up messages can be sent immediately for clarification, or simply to maintain the cadence of the conversation.

While social media accounts generally are associated with the real name of the user, most accounts on other sites are not. The website Reddit creates discussion threads for every topic that its users want to create and is one of the most heavily trafficked websites on the internet. In creating a profile for this website, there is no link between the actual name of the user and the username that they choose for themselves. Their personal profile page only has the contact information on it that they choose to display. This means that an account can be created that will have no impact on the rest of the life of the user. Misbehaving on reddit comes with a free pass. So does trolling. This is why some accounts have names like "burneraccount01" or "fakeprofile" or "insertusernamehere". The people who have them do not want the rest of their life associated with what they do on Reddit. This can be true for other popular social media sites like Twitter or Instagram. It effectively makes these places "safe spaces" for people to act however they want to whoever they want, so long as their actions do not merit a government-backed investigation. This gives all of its users a free pass to say whatever they want to whoever they want, whenever they want, as much as they want.

In the past, people could send anonymous letters, but that required both work and money to mail it to somebody else. These websites exist on the internet where the physical and temporal limitations of reality do not exist, meaning that harassment, abuse, and disrespect can be exercised until they are strong enough to invade the lives of the users. As a person becomes more accustomed to disrespecting authority, or anybody for that matter, on the internet, this action becomes a well-exercised aspect of their personality. It has now become common to hear a person saying anything that comes to mind about people who, according to the Bible, should be reverenced. This is described clearly in Jude 1:8, where it says, "Likewise also these filthy dreamers defile the flesh, despise dominion, and speak evil of dignities," which seems to be an incredibly accurate description of America after the 2016 presidential election. Disrespect for those in authority has always been a facet of American culture, but since the election of Donald Trump there seems to be no limit on what cannot or should not be said about a sitting authority.

This is made easier by the fact that the internet and cell phones do not require in-person interaction to ensure communication. Screens not only hide identity but also shield the users from the guilt or fear that they may have when getting into an argument with another person, they also remove all body language from the equation and protect the speaker from experiencing any negative feedback that their words may elicit. This hinders empathy, which is a key element of conversation, especially when differing viewpoints are held. Social interactions are moving heavily towards the online world rather than in person, meaning that the skills associated with in person communications are declining. This makes it much more difficult for people to develop functional, in-person communication skills. It also further enforces the development of negative behaviors because rude and spiteful messages can be relayed without the sender having to see the negative impact of their words. This helps to eliminate the natural guilt that is felt when sinfully offending another person. Be it intentional or not, the lack of negative reinforcement allows brash, insensitive and irreverent tendencies to develop.

All of this boils down to the fact that the nature of the

internet supplements a user's ability to disrespect authoritarian figures. Any person in power can be attacked, undermined, or disrespected with no consequence. Outrightly attacking the personal characteristics of the sitting president to loyal supporters can get you a bloody nose, if it's done in person. If it's done online, your body is physically safe. Seeing people of opposing viewpoints become enraged also helps to fuel personal pride, meaning that dong it online doesn't just remove the risk, it also *feels* better because you can push people further than you ever would in person. Doing this safely through online message boards and usernames that do not link back to the user's real life protect from any form of damage to their person, as well as their career, friends, or family. The internet gives humanity the ability to write freely about anyone with no fear of repercussions. If human nature were good, this would be used solely to topple dictatorships, oust corrupt officials, and promote humanitarian forms of government. In some cases, and in some countries, this is exactly what has happened. But since human nature is fundamentally flawed, the tendency is for this not to happen. While evil men and women in power can be denounced and harassed, so can good people. Since society perceives concepts such as "good" and "evil" in the light of the prevailing public opinion, the people who are attacked online the most are those who are seen as "evil." The people on the internet that are seen as the most "evil" are those who disagree with the majority of the most influential social media users. This just happens to be anybody who is in the way of the progressive social agenda. Thus, anybody who stands against this movement is literarily crucified without any respect for their person, authority, or achievement.

This feeds a sentiment that is key to driving humanity away from God. Since the authority of individuals can be assaulted by anybody at any time, authority becomes resented. Since it is impossible to defend a reputation on the internet, gossip abounds. The internet facilitates the spread of lies about their person, past sins, or personality flaws, and with enough time it can make any person appear to be unfit to hold authority. Since every reputation can be dismantled one way or another through the internet, it appears that no person is fit to hold authority. While all people are flawed, God does see fit to set people in authority over others. He establishes the role of pastors in I Timothy 3, parents in Ephesians 5-6, and kings in Daniel 2. According to John 19:11, all authority comes directly from God himself. By attacking authority that is inherent to social, political, and religious structures, society diminishes its perception of a God who holds total authority over all things. Nothing is sacred, so God, if He is real, must not be either. Once the perception of authority becomes flawed in society, it no longer looks to God for guidance on morality, politics, or daily conduct. This results in a society similar to that of Judges 21:25, which states: "In those days there was no king in Israel: every man did that which was right in his own eyes." With no king, every man is king of himself. The internet is actively removing every "king" of anything by permitting open disregard towards authority. Interestingly enough, immediately after this statement is made, the Jews begin to demand a king. And king that is a man that is appealing to all of Israel. And that king is one of the greatest types of the antichrist is the Old Testament.

MY WORLD, MY RULES

The combination of an inability to determine any form of truth and the total disregard for all personally disagreeable authorities to be fit for leadership creates a rather unpleasant societal cocktail. Since truth is unattainable and nobody has the authority to establish it, nothing can be established as truth. All facts are presented with contradictory facts. Studies are counteracted with other studies. Truths are met with lies, and neither can be proven. Since nothing can be said for certain anymore without *somebody* contradicting it with their own understanding of reality, society has begun to doubt that anything can ever be said to be true.

This is further emphasized through the death of the intellectualism that was brought about during the Enlightenment.

The internet helps to short-circuit the brain by feeding it a continuous diet of emotionally saturated content devoid of any critical thinking. This makes it harder for society as a whole to agree on anything since emotional manipulators are continuously trying to vie for the attention of others to drive up their advertising revenue. Being controversial is lucrative, and there is no better way to do this than to attack established truths. These diatribes against reality appeal to the emotional centers of the brain to drive internet traffic, tearing apart any and every concept held dear enough to the general public to garner a reaction. This tears apart social fabric, unity, and morality, leaving each individual with personally held truths that are unique solely to themselves.

This reveals a rather insidious truth of its own. The Devil has created a rather fascinating lie with which to ensnare the world that is unlike anything known to humanity up to this point. Throughout the Dark Ages, Satan attempted to violently suppress the truth with fire and sword which, did not succeed. In some ways, it actually accelerated the growth of the Church. When the age of enlightenment arrived, the Devil pivoted to a new form of global deception. He decided that instead of trying to eat the seeds (Matthew 13) he would simply poison the ground. Instead of destroying the truth, which is scripturally impossible as per Psalms 12:6-7, Matthew 24:25, Isaiah 30:8 and a host of other verses, he has chosen rather to destroy the concept of truth. He has made the only truth to be that all truth relative and left to the discretion of the individual. If no truths can be proven to be universally sound, then truth itself cannot exist beyond the personal views held by each unique soul.

There are a host of issues that arise from this, but the key is that if a person does not understand that truth exists, then it becomes much more difficult to convince them of the truths presented in the Bible. If a core belief of a lost man can be contradicted through the Scriptures, that man must choose between believing the Bible or believing what he already holds to. If he believes that the Bible is the word of God and therefore true (as many unsaved members of western society have until recent years,) and if he is an honest man, he will conform to the word of God and eventually ask the Lord to save him. If the there is no universally held truth, then there is no need for him to conform to anything that contradicts his personal opinion. The word of God may be true for a Christian, but that in no way makes it true to him if he chooses to not believe it. Truth becomes whatever a person chooses to believe since the human heart (again) is sinful. People will tend to believe whatever makes them feel the best. They will only change if they feel that another version of reality would be beneficial to them.

While this may seem to be a ludicrous argument (which it is), this is becoming a more societally accepted position to hold. This philosophy of personal absolutism is enabled simply because of the way that the internet works. It passively teaches the concepts necessary to convert society into this method of thinking by making it possible and nurturing the personal outcomes attained by ascribing to this train of thought. Simply by existing as a limitless tool of person-to-person communication, the nature of the human heart (and to an extent, the unseen hand of Satan himself) has guided the technologically developed world to this point.

CONCLUSION) ROCK THE CRADLE, RULE THE WORLD

The plan to eliminate the concept of absolute truth has been so flawlessly executed that the concept of personal, relative truth as the standard by which all things should be judged is taught and encouraged throughout the connected world. It is taught in universities across America. Hollywood and television propagate the message promoting the importance of the individual, the importance of autonomy, and the importance of developing "your own truth." Schools promote self-esteem and taking pride in your own work, even if it is incorrect. Children today are overloaded with messages dictating the importance of themselves and the failure of established systems to provide for them. They are told that those in power suppress all minorities and women, are destroying the planet, and are leaving them with unpayable debt while keeping all of the money for themselves. They are told that their lives have been ruined before they have been lived by people who will die before they have to meet the consequences of their actions. This would account for the decay in the attitudes of high school students towards how well institutions are living up to their purpose. There is a general decline from 1976-2016 in the overall opinion of how well high school students perceive the actions of public schools, universities, the news media, and the Federal US Government (Twenge, 2017, p. 279). This correlates with a general decline in the number of high school students that believe there is a God (86% in 1990 to 67% in 2016), ever pray (83% in 2006 to 74% in 2016), or believe that the Bible is the inspired word of God (83% in 1984 to 73% in 2016) (Twenge, 2017, p. 127). There has been a general increase in the number of students who believe in an afterlife, but this number has begun to decline in recent years, as all of these statistics tend to start a steep downward trend around 2005.

What is clear from all of this data is that children today are being stripped of any and all respect for authority. This correlates with a decline in the belief of absolute truth. With no absolute truth, a mindset rooted in the libertarian philosophy of "live and let die" is flourishing in the world today. This may seem to be beneficial, as a libertarian society would allow for religion to be practiced without fear of oppression. There is a singular caveat to this system, and that is that there is only one unpardonable sin in the setup that modern society seems to be trending towards: intolerance. Everybody must be allowed to live as they please as long as their truths do not infringe in any way into the lives of other people. Each person holds their own unique truths that they have concluded from within their own minds, and they must all be allowed to live as they please without fear of and form of infringement from others. Judgement of any kind infringes on the ability of the individual to develop as they see fit. Individuality is worshipped in modern society, to the point that each person must be allowed to develop their own personal truth in the manner that they see fit. They should never be exposed to world views that they do not wish to think about, and anything in disagreement with their opinions causes damage to their persona and sense of self-worth. They would have to admit that they were wrong. Anybody who tries to convince another person of their lack of personal importance (Job 35:6), their sinful nature (Romans 7:24) or their need to conform to a standard that they may not agree with (Romans 12:2), must be silenced because it violates the personal expression of the individual.

In short, the coming generation is its own god. This is not necessarily because they have chosen this view for themselves, but because it has been forced onto them by every established institution that hearkens to the progressive agenda. They are told to see reality as they choose to, and as such, they believe that they hold a power reserved for God alone: the ability to create truth. Jesus said in John 14:6, "I am the way, the truth, and the life." In this statement, Jesus claims that there was only one truth: Himself. Anything else therefore must be a lie, and Satan is the father of lies, according to John 8:44. The current generation believes that every person is their own god because they each have the ability to decide what is true for themselves. They believe that they are gods, not because of a divine heritage or spiritual attainment, but simply because they are ordinary people. The god of the new age is no idol or demon. It is a base human.

This mindset is blasphemous and utterly ridiculous. It is a mindset that is contradicted by biblical law, empirical science, thousands of years of true philosophy, and common sense. A human is in no way capable of manipulating reality simply because they choose to change how they feel about any given subject. This way of thinking does not have any greater impact on reality than the imagination of a child. It simply allows those who ascribe to it to assume that their opinions are facts that apply only to them. Opinions are a fine thing to have, but opinions are not facts.

Furthermore, even opinions that may become universally agreed upon by a globalized society do not in any way alter the truth of the word of God. The truths given by the Bible are absolute (Psalms 19:7), eternal (Psalms 119:89), and not open to human interpretation (II Peter 1:20). They are not subjected to the whims of the cultures or times into which they are applied. They are provided in the Bible and divinely understood through establishing a relationship with the Author on the terms that He gives (Isaiah 66:2). It is by the words that God has given man that God Himself will judge man. This makes the words of God, by His own admission, the highest authority in the universe (Psalms 138:2) and the standard to which each individual must conform themselves in order to please God. The opinions of individuals, in light of this judgement, are entirely irrelevant.

CHAPTER 7) **FURTHER ONWARD AND DOWNWARD**

Each author cited throughout this book addresses a balance of benefits and detriments that modern communication technology and Internet Culture have brought to humanity. Each considers the implications that they bear on society through a different lens. Some address it purely in light of the social changes brought upon children, college students, or teenage girls. Others address the direct impacts on the human mind using scientific studies to address topic such as addiction or cognitive development. Some simply present the facts as they stand in an attempt to let the stories speak for themselves. What all of these sources have in common is that they all end with the exact two same conclusions:

1. *Communication technology/Internet Culture is doing more harm than good to society.*

2. *If we work hard, come together, and learn, it will eventually do more good than harm.*

While some authors seem to show a great deal more concern than others, all of them agree that the damage that is being done can be undone. Once humanity bands together and figures out how to make this tool work to our benefit, the human race will enter a golden age of unfettered knowledge, tolerance, and technological development.

Of the two conclusions, only the first one is accurate. Technology is doing more harm than good to human society. This is proven through hard science, social studies, personal accounts, and a complete lack of evidence to the contrary. All of this data accurately reflects the biblical position of technology. Throughout this book, the Bible has been referenced repeatedly in order to show that the Bible does speak on the issues that are present in the 21st century. The Bible does speak of how the setup of the internet negatively impacts the human mind. This position has been echoed by preachers since before the scientific community began to wonder if it were possible that all of the scientific developments (and social developments enabled by them) might actually be bad for the whole world. Every statement regarding the impacts of Internet Culture on the human mind made in this thesis can be proven true with a Bible. The assertions made by the intelligent minds of the world today using data or stories gathered serve only to establish that the Bible is in fact accurate to the skeptic of old-fashioned preaching, and also to provide additional commentary on the current condition of the world.

The second conclusion is provided by each author as their own opinion. Since the sources used were written mostly by non-Christian individuals, it is understandable that they would arrive at this conclusion. The alternative is so horrible that they want to drive society to avoid it at all costs. To conclude that humanity is in decline and a collapse is inevitable would be blasphemy to the progressive world agenda, and contrary to the widely held human belief that human nature is innately good. The generally used analogy is that since the internet is new, human nature is basically childlike in its approach to appropriate use. In time, we will mature and begin to use it correctly for the greater good. In this assertion, each author demonstrates fear that we may not survive long enough to reach this point, and that we must persevere by a variety of social programs, legislation, sacrifice, and education.

These opinions are contradictory to the teachings of the word of God, and as such, they can be discarded as false hope. The Bible teaches that each age of man ends with the failure of mankind, and the church age does not provide any exception to that rule (II Thessalonians 2:1-3, Revelation 3:14-22). The global decline of morality and the rise of a kingdom governed by Satan himself is prophesied through the Old and New Testaments (Zechariah 14:1-3, Revelation 13:3-4). All of the kingdoms of this world will fall to the influence of the antichrist and at the end of the Tribulation, they will gather in the Valley of Megiddo to attack Jerusalem. Mankind will fulfill every prophecy in the Bible exactly as it is written. In doing this, God has not forced humanity to act in the manner against its own will. He has simply recorded what will happen in the future because He has a perfect understanding of human nature and the universe that He has created. The only way that a person can alter this in any way is to determine what side of history they personally want to be on. The prophesies made by God do not force any individual to conform to one set of beliefs or another. He simply shows the future of whatever decisions we choose to make and then lets us make them for ourselves. The world will fall to Satan's rule during the Tribulation and then be conquered by Jesus Christ, and no amount of education or social reform can keep humanity from that fate.

The condition of the world system is laid out very intricately in the Bible and the world must match this description before the Devil will be able to step in as the ruler of this world. He is using many schemes currently to alter the global society into what he wants it to be, so not all of the points made here are completely conditional upon the internet. Factors such as the world economic systems, communism, climate change, the United Nations, and Covid-19 all play into his plans. Consider that regardless of the views held by anybody on any of these subjects, such as their legitimacy or even existence, the impact that they have on the world as *concepts* is entirely real. When a large group of people believes that something exists and influences their lives, the influence does change their lives even if the thing does not exist, or is not actually as they understand it to be. The internet is only one of the pawns in play, but it does occupy a key position on the playing field. If organizations such as the Illuminati or Knights Templar are currently playing a role in the downfall of civilization as we know it, they are still only pawns used by the Devil to achieve his ends. Exposing, eliminating, or bankrupting any of these organizations would not change the fate of the world. Fighting against these concepts, organizations, governments, or anything else will not change the immutable fact that this world will eventually unite under the Antichrist. The only impact that a Christian can (and should) have is how many people end up in it. A Christian's only recourse is to win and disciple as many other people as they can. This will not alter the future course of human history, but it will alter the future of individuals who will be grateful to Jesus Christ and them for all eternity. The rest of the world will conform to the biblical prophesies that the Bible gives about the path of humanity.

There are many features of the upcoming world system that the internet enables. The internet and smartphones are simply tools in the hands of the ones that use them. But they are tools that help to amplify the corrupted human nature into a form that it has never taken before. The goal of this chapter is to establish the parallels between what the internet and communication technology enable and what the biblical prophesies for the condition of the heart of man during the Tribulation are. As mankind conforms to the conditions set forth in the Tribulation, the nearer the event of the rapture must be. No Christian wants to see the word decay into a sinful state of Hell on earth, but once this condition is reached, the Church gets to go home. This should be a warning to the unsaved, and in a roundabout way, a comfort to the Christian.

AN APPOINTED END

In her book *"iGen,"* Dr. Jean Twenge uses a very impressive amount of data gathered from social surveys to analyze trends in society using a consistent methodology. The tests are administered to high school students and have maintained the same format since many of them began in the 70s. Some questions have been modified to accommodate changes in how words are used in social contexts. Some questions have been removed since they have become outdated and sat at roughly 0% for years, while other questions had to be added in, such as questions about technology. Ultimately though, the format remains unchanged, and she is able to make many factual observations about the children of today in comparison to years gone by. Some of these observations are highly controversial. Some are counterintuitive. But ultimately, she allows the data gathered to direct her analysis and conclusions rather than preconceived bias. By using results from tests that do not change with time, she is able to determine how attitudes about issues change over time, without having to rely on the memories of older subjects. She can see how everybody answered the same questions when they were in high school.

What is remarkable about her data is that so many of the line graphs depicting varying opinions or general attitudes show the start of a sharp change between the years 2008 and 2012. These are not subtle changes, nor do they tend to align with previous trends. There is a notable decline in mental health that is consistent across most of her data that indicates that *something* began to take a serious mental toll on the youth of America roughly in this time period. During this time, America did not get a new president, but did come out of an economic recession. Other cultural events changed society, but no major wars were started or finished, and the second term of President Obama is considered to be largely uneventful. What changed around this time was that this is when smartphones began to become mainstream in American society. The number of 12th graders who spent 10 or more hours a week online increased from 23% in 2009 to 44% in 2015 at a generally consistent rate of increase (Twenge, 2017, p. 75). One graph shows that smartphone ownership rates and depressive symptoms increase at nearly parallel rates over the years since smartphone usage began to be polled in 2010. On the same chart, Dr. Twenge shows that these increases correlate with a decrease in unemployment, indicating that the depressive symptoms among young adults do not follow economic trends (Twenge, 2017, p. 106). As the number of people who could connect to the internet on-the-go increased, the general mental health of teenagers began to decrease. Since this is social data, causality cannot be inferred (as there is no control group in societal experiments) but given that there are so many other factors linking Internet Culture to mental health, the correlation would seem to go far beyond coincidence.

The purpose for noting this is to underline that the passive changes that continuous internet use seems to have on the mind. The scientific community can only speculate with a good amount of certainty that the correlation is a causation but cannot say for certain. In taking into consideration the authority of the Scriptures, it is evident that the negative, subtle, spiritual influences that originate from internet use directly cause harm to the mind and soul of any user who spends a significant amount of time on them. The spiritual hindrances take their toll on any person's desire to know God and better their relationship with Him. With this God-given desire subdued, ignored, and overridden, the benefits that biblical living have provided to society begin to decline rapidly. Biblical law was established by its Maker, "for our good, always" (Deuteronomy 6:24) according to Moses, and deviation from it separates humanity from the good made available to them by God.

Since this connection to God is being replaced with a connection to man, as these trends continue, they will eventually begin to change exponentially. The decrease in spirituality is replaced by carnality, thus allowing carnality to build on itself, resulting in massive changes to what people think about and thus, how they think. In considering this fact, it becomes evident that there may be a societal "tipping point," at which society would begin to dissolve into a disorganized conglomerate, unable to support itself. This may be a debatable question among the philosophers of our time, as to if the civilized world has reached this point yet, or if it is avoidable. To a Bible-believer, this is not a question of "if" humanity will reach this but "when." The Bible speaks heavily on the condition of man at the end of the church age, and the parallels between what is biblically prophesied and the current trends in society are highly evident.

Jude makes several remarks describing the condition of

man, stating, "[1:8] Likewise also these filthy dreamers defile the flesh, despise dominion, and speak evil of dignities... [1:12] These are spots in your feasts of charity, when they feast with you, feeding themselves without fear...[1:16-19] These are murmurers, complainers, walking after their own lusts; and their mouth speaketh great swelling words, having men's persons in admiration because of advantage. But, beloved, remember ye the words which were spoken before of the apostles of our Lord Jesus Christ; How that they told you there should be mockers in the last time, who should walk after their own ungodly lusts. These be they who separate themselves, sensual, having not the Spirit." In II Timothy 3:1-7, Paul states: "This know also, that in the last days perilous times shall come. For men shall be lovers of their own selves, covetous, boasters, proud, blasphemers, disobedient to parents, unthankful, unholy, Without natural affection, trucebreakers, false accusers, incontinent, fierce, despisers of those that are good, Traitors, heady, highminded, lovers of pleasures more than lovers of God; Having a form of godliness, but denying the power thereof: from such turn away. For of this sort are they which creep into houses, and lead captive sully women laden with sins, led away with divers lusts, Ever learning, and never able to come to the knowledge of the truth.[1]" Romans 1:20-25 states, "For the invisible things of him from the creation of the world are clearly seen, being understood by the things that are made, even his eternal power and Godhead; so that they are without excuse: Because that, when they knew God, they glorified him not as God, neither were thankful; but became vain in their imaginations, and their foolish heart was darkened. Professing themselves to be wise, they became fools, And changed the glory of the uncorruptible God into an image made like to corruptible man, and to birds, and fourfooted beasts, and creeping things. Wherefore God also gave them up to uncleanness through the lusts of their own hearts, to dishonour their own bodies between themselves: Who changed the truth of God into a lie, and

---

[1] The word "incontinent" is defined as having no self-control

worshipped and served the creature more than the Creator, who is blessed for ever. Amen."

These passages need no commentary. They show the true prophetic power of the Bible by perfectly describing the trends arising in the globalized society of the internet. These traits are all endemic to human nature, and thanks to the "magic of the internet," they are transformed from repressed traits to fully realized and exercised traits. The promotion of mankind as the epitome of evolution, the denial of the providence of God, the inability to come to the truth, the rampant sensuality, and the blatant disregard for authority all thrive because of the nature of how the internet functions. As the internet connects all of humanity together, it is only a matter of time before this condition exerts itself globally. This end is unavoidable, and humanity will reach the condition described above. Internet Culture is simply the vehicle by which the human race will arrive at this destination. It can only be described as the mercy of God that the spiritual decay of the human condition has been postponed until today.

God saw that this future would come, so he chose to prophesy of it in his word, both to warn us, and the prove his deity (Revelation 19:10). Any attempt to preserve humanity or prevent this condition from being reached, on the global stage, would be futile. The general state of humanity will decay, and the Bible is simply a reflection of the foreknowledge of God.

What is not set in stone is how many people will personally embody this condition. The world as a whole must conform to the disgusting state as described in the Bible, but in no way is the *individual* confined to this fate. God has, and always will, offer salvation to any individual who comes to God on the terms that God has provided them with. This is shown through Matthew 11:28-30, Romans 5:18, I Timothy 2:6, Revelation 22:17, and a host of other verses that span across all biblical dispensations. Salvation is an opportunity for each person that comes into the world. God provides a way to Heaven and it is His desire that each individual will take that route in their own life (II Peter 3:9). This is where it is crucial that God's foreknowledge is differentiated from God's for-ordination. God ordained that whoever comes to him, he will grant eternal life (John 1:9). However, in His omniscience, He knows that the majority of humanity will choose not to come to Him (Matthew 7:13-14). The human race will not fall to the ploys of Satan because God ordained it to be so. The world will fall to Satan because of the corrupt nature of man and the workings of Satan. God has simply made note of this because He knows that it is true. As the Creator of the human soul, He has a perfect understanding of the future humanity will create for itself, but He will never force it to comply with His own will.

This knowledge should arm the Christian with an intense desire to rescue as many individuals as possible from the fate of the rest of the world. It should also drive them to fulfill Romans 12:2, which states, "And be not conformed to this world: but be ye transformed by the renewing of your mind, that ye may prove what is that good, and acceptable, and perfect, will of God." The Christian should be concerned with not following the downward path that the world is taking as a whole. Their mind and heart should be fixed on pleasing God through the words that He has provided them and helping others to do the same. This means reaching the lost through evangelism and supporting the growth of other Christians. While the world may be in spiritual decline, there is no scriptural implication that the world must remain decayed for a great deal of time before the rapture occurs. The prayer that "your flight be not in the winter, neither on the sabbath day:" of Matthew 24:20 may indicate that while the rapture may be a set date in history, the date of the establishment of the kingdom of the Antichrist *may not be*. God tends to ordain key scriptural events to happen on mathematically established dates that are prophesied. So, while the rapture cannot occur until the requirements have been met, there is no scripturally-given link as to an exact amount of time that must transpire between these two events and the rapture. It is not inconceivable to think that the more that the church spiritually resists these influences, the longer this inevitable fate can be avoided. The more it is delayed, the less suppression the gospel will be subjected to before the rapture, hopefully resulting in the salvation of a greater number of souls. The acts of individuals can potentially delay the timing of this ungodly event. As it draws nearer, the influence that an individual can have will likely become more apparent. Christians at the end of the church age would do well to stay busy.

TERMS AND CONDITIONS

The digital revolution is rapidly imposing itself into every facet of the developed world. Socializing is now done more frequently online than in person. Covid-19 revealed the viability of teleworking on a broad scale, with all interaction taking place through video conference calls, phone calls, texts, and emails, rather than face-to-face conversation. The coronavirus also expedited the death of physical currency in lieu of credit and debit cards. Cryptocurrencies, which exist only in the digital world and have no backing of any kind, have caused a global shift in how people perceive and exchange money. Banking, communicating, purchasing, working, and a host of other activities have all become possible through the internet, and are growing in their influence across the world. This is unprecedented in human history, and to a world that does not seriously consider biblical prophecy as truth, the future of this is largely unpredictable beyond a conceptual level.

To a Bible-believer, the mass exodus of physical activities to the digital world helps to illuminate an interesting Bible truth. There is a prophesy that is plainly spoken but has not been able to be understood without analyzing the world as it exists today. This is a truth that could not be understood simply because it described a technological world that could not even be speculated at until recent years. In Revelation 13:16-17, John states: "And he causeth all, both small and great, rich and poor, free and bond, to receive a mark in their right hand, or in their foreheads: And that no man might buy or sell, save that had the mark, or the name of the beast, or the number of his name." This passage is simple and to the point. It makes direct statements that are not obscured in any way. What commentators have struggled to expound up until the mid-1900s is *how* can you force a society not to buy or sell without a mark? Each transaction would be left up to the discretion of both the seller and buyer. Violating this principal would be simple. This is because in a world without computers, the decision to enact the transaction is left up to the humans that wish to engage in it. They are able to make their own choice. However, when you insert a computer into the mix, things get a bit dicey.

Computers run on code. This code is written by a person who intends to make the computer complete a desired function. Once a computer has been given the authority over anything, it can only operate in the manner that it has been programmed to operate. If the computer is programmed to play chess, it can only play chess. If it is programmed to imitate conversation, it can only imitate conversation. And if it is programmed to manage money, it can only manage money in the way that the designer has programmed it to. This means that if all transactions were relegated to the digital world, then performing a transaction must be done in compliance with the manner in which the computer has been programmed. A dollar bill has no will of its own to refuse to be handed to another person. But a computer can establish prerequisites for performing a digital transaction.

Returning to the subject of buying and selling in the Tribulation, it becomes apparent that if the Antichrist is able to control the means by which money is transferred, he can control all of the money in the world. Money, after all, is completely valueless unless it can be traded for goods or services. In time, paper and coin money will be eliminated from society and all transfers of wealth will be electronic. The push to enter a world of purely digital transactions will come from a range of arguments. It will come in part through appeals to justice, since physical money cannot be traced and can therefore be used for criminal activities. It can also be argued using an appeal to personal health, since germs, viruses and bacteria can all spread through contaminated physical objects, and the whole point of physical money is to be handed to another person. The coronavirus scare has demonstrated that fear of death can bring the entire world to its knees (although this fact was already documented in Job 2:4 more than 3,500 years ago) so eliminating a known germ spreader is something that a lot of people can get behind now. Influence could come through the security offered by cryptocurrencies in conjunction with blockchain. This is also emphasized through the fact that cryptocurrencies, like the internet, are not bound to a singular county, and would be an ideal method for unifying a world economy. There may be other factors that will argue in favor of this outcome, but the key takeaway is that this outcome is inevitable, and it has been a long time coming. It is the perfect method to enact the prophecy of Revelation 13:16-17. By putting all of the transactions on computers that are connected to the internet, and removing paper money, he can control who can do literally anything by restricting access to the internet.

The overall process for controlling the world is actually quite simple. First, all key activities in human life must be relegated to a single platform, aka the internet. Second, activities that enable a fulfilling life outside of the outside world must be minimized. This can easily be done through enforcing the lockdown due to health crisis, political unrest, environmental dangers, or simply anything that can drive public fear through news media indoctrination. The news media has a continuous supply of things to make its viewers afraid of, so this is not an issue in the world of today. This will only get worse as the Tribulation will bring about many things that will actually merit fear. Once everything of significant importance is accessed through the internet, then the third step is quite obvious: limit access to the internet to those who are willing to worship the Antichrist. Using this process, he can effectively hold hostage access to money, friends, medical advice, family, employment, and education. Since the internet already subconsciously pushes the users to be more accepting of this world view, it will not take much of a push to transverse this boundary.

WE ARE BIG BROTHER

In order to govern the thoughts of the entire planet, a global government would have to be gargantuan and unmanageable. As any organization grows in size, it also grows in complexity. Bureaucracy tends to encumber itself, and a government run by humans is limited by the intellectual capacity of its leaders. For a government to manage the entire world at an intellectual and emotional level, it would need to operate to a degree of efficiency and intelligence never before seen among the kingdoms of men.

This seems like an impossible feat, unless the people can be caused to govern themselves. If society can operate according to an agreed-upon set of rules, power can be given to the people to dispense justice and rewards for their actions. The government would then only need to use a fraction of the power and the people could be guided culturally rather than authoritatively.

To an extent, this has already happened. The politically correct cancel culture that has reared its head in recent years has deployed the people against themselves. Anybody can now express any opinion about anything to anybody else through the internet. The online rage mob can, with the right prods from the right people, be deployed against anyone who goes against the progressive liberal agenda. The mob is merciless and totally without loyalty. It brings with it the threat of being shamed, bullied, and harassed off of social media. It brings threats of hacking, identity theft, and the release of personal information to people who might be willing and able to pay you a visit. Depending of the severity of the transgression and the social position of the offender, it can cause protests, firings, loss of sponsorships, and physical violence. The "fake" world of social media has very real consequences.

This rage mob, despite their efficacy on social media, lacks potency against the common man. It tends to drive more popular individuals to go along with the flow, but a person with little influence is unlikely to draw on the wrath of the rest of the world for having a wrong opinion in their little world. They may draw criticism proportional to the size of their followers, but most working-class people do not have to worry about losing sponsorships or acting contracts. It is unlikely that they will get fired from their job due to mounting social pressure, and the most that may come of it would be an unpleasant relationship with friends or family members. Cancel culture does an excellent job of running the political, sports and entertainment worlds, but to the common man it holds little threat.

Unless, of course, popularity on social media becomes more than just "likes" on a screen. The social credit score implemented by China permits access to small perks dependent upon how socially acceptable individual behavior is. This system, if implemented at a global scale, would have the potential to govern individuals to the lowest level. If the prices of commodities could be raised to levels that would require government assistance, that assistance could be dependent on the social credit score of the individual. People who espouse anti-progressive tendencies would have their scores lowered until they are no longer able to afford the basics. The quality of life can be controlled through how they choose to express themselves. Furthermore, if a person with a high social credit score would interact with a person with an undesirable social credit score, it could negatively impact the high credit score. In time, this would force the nonconformists into the lowest class of society where they would be strong-armed into espousing more favorable opinions. After all, Job 2:4 still applies.

To further ratchet up the pressure, social programs and federal monies could eventually become dependent on the overall scores of people in designated areas. Areas with higher overall scores would become the object of government-funded civil projects, while areas with lower scores may see increased tax rates. This would pressure individuals to police not only themselves but also their neighbors. By making the success of the whole dependent on the opinions of the individual, conformity can be enforced by blaming the oppression of the government on the resilience of those who refuse to surrender their individuality.

As a one-world government emerges, the dispersion of international aid could become dependent on the social credit scores of entire countries. Sanctions and tariffs would be leveraged against underperformers, while the high scorers would be permitted to host the Olympics, apply for loans as developing countries, get the backing of the UN in wars, or receive relief after experiencing a natural disaster. The potential of social credit scores on an international stage flexes its muscles from the top down and would allow the ruling government to determine what was acceptable from the federal to the personal level.

THE GLORY OF MAN

In Psalms 19:1-2, David says, "The heavens declare the glory of God; and the firmament sheweth his handywork. Day unto day uttereth speech, and night unto night sheweth knowledge." Throughout the word of God, the writers make many references to the fact that "In the beginning, God created the heaven and the earth" (Genesis 1:1). His creation shows His heart because the things found in nature are directly made by Him. Mankind can only take nature and bend it to his will. He does not create, he only manipulates. He takes the natural and forms it into the unnatural. Anything that is created by man is something that mankind has made by imposing his own will onto what God has created.

This concept may seem to devalue invention and progress as a whole. To an extent, it does, but that is not to say that all invention is evil. Inventions, again, are not good or evil of themselves; they simply enable humans to live more convenient lives. Some inventions help people live longer, others increase the yields of crops, and some provide entertainment. Without invention, humanity would still be naked, wandering around the perimeter of the garden of Eden, and looking for fruit trees. Inventing is natural to mankind, and all inventions can be used for good.

The problem lies in that each invention carries the potential to further remove man from God's domain and make his own hand more visible than that of God's. As inventions grow in complexity, they add additional layers of processing to the natural elements and better show the capabilities that humanity has. If a person fully embraces the inventions of man, his ability and tendency to understand God will begin to fall away. This is why the word "invention" has such a negative connotation in the Bible. It is used five times in the Bible and all five uses place the word in a negative light. Ecclesiastes 7:29 states: "Lo, this only have I found, that God hath made man upright; but they have sought out many inventions." The contrast given in these two statements is that God has put a certain amount of goodness in mankind, but it is diminished by the inventions that he creates. As man creates more inventions that display his brilliance to a greater degree, the creation of God is ignored, and the truths that can be learned from what He has made are lost.

This is why the Bible points out that cities are not good for mankind. God takes care to note that the first city ever founded by man was founded by Cain, a murderer, who was "of that wicked one" (Genesis 4:17, I John 3:12). The first city founded after Noah's Flood was Babel, which was so in violation of the laws of God that God himself chose to destroy the city by confounding mankind through language, which is an obstacle that has not been overcome in more than 3000 years. In Isaiah 5:8, he says, "Woe unto them that join house to house, that lay field to field, till there be no place, that they may be placed alone in the midst of the earth!" God understood that when mankind bands together to form cities, the natural creation must be dominated to a greater degree, reducing how much of the glory of God is displayed, and increasing the show of what humanity can do. This explains why cities are much more progressive than rural communities. Cities place mankind in contact with other humans and their inventions. The country gives people maximum exposure to nature where God has displayed His hand, and the solitude necessary to contemplate His existence. Cities do not just attract progressively minded individuals: cities generate them because they are cities.

The problem with the internet is that there is absolutely nothing natural about it. It is an invention that exists only as light created from electricity. The internet may exist as data stored on hard drives, but it is incapable of being observed without screens. These screens emit a light that is unlike anything that can be observed in the natural world in terms of its intensity, variation, and reactivity to the inputs of the viewer. Screens are remarkable, but, unfortunately, they can only create representations of reality, not reality itself.

The internet has been made entirely by man. Everything on it was created using computer code, written by people and programmed to form functioning systems. Mankind has created every document, website, advertisement, video, and photo. Anything generated by AI was created by a program that was originally written by humans. Humanity has even created worlds of its own in videogames, varying from archaic high-fantasy worlds to sci-fi futures, and everything in between. Social media websites present content generated by people or the bots that they have programmed. Google searches through what people have made to give the most relevant result. Everything in some way or another is created by man and viewed on an artificial screen. The internet is truly the crux of invention, as it is entirely separated from any naturally existing material. Because of this, the hand of God cannot be seen on the internet unless it is tainted by the hand of man. There is nothing about the internet that was made by God in Genesis 1, and it operates on a totally different set of rules than nature. This is part of the reason why humanity turns further from God as it spends more time on the internet. Even if the internet were a bastion of truth and purity, it would still corrupt a user's understanding of who God is and how He works. There is a continuous *subtle* understanding gained of who God is that is spent by observing His creation. There is an equally *subtle* understanding that is lost by leaving it. Mankind first ran from God by building a city to shut Him out. Now, the internet has become the last, great city, whose builder and maker is man.

CONCLUSION) WHAT TO DO ABOUT YOU

I felt that the conclusion should be written in the first person because there are many things that need to be said that are deeply personal to me. I have learned many lessons about this subject that I feel could be a great help to Christians young and old who are trying to navigate the internet and understand how it relates to their own personal walks with Jesus Christ. The topics of Internet Culture and modern communication technology to this day remain relatively unexamined in the Christian literary world. In my efforts to research this subject, I found no reliable books that detailed how these inventions have affected Christianity at a personal or collective level. There is some information available about the news media, and a few well written evaluations of the television, but I found nothing about the internet, social media, cell phones, search engines, or advertising revenue from a spiritual perspective. If such sources exist, they are hard to come by.

When I started researching, I made a concerted effort to find books written in favor of what social media is doing for society. I have heard preachers rail against some of the subjects that I have covered since texting became a thing and Myspace went viral. I know that I already said this, but I wanted to make sure that I went into this objectively. If these influences on Christianity as a whole were positive, I wanted to be honest enough to agree with the data and analysis provided by the sources. Since very few things are objectively all good or all bad, I wanted to make sure that I did not condemn this new movement entirely since there would likely be a balance of both helps and harms. An argument that something is exclusively good or bad can be dismantled by a skeptic (honest or dishonest) by citing exceptions. I have been very cautious about making dogmatic blanket statements about any subject in order to strip the dishonest skeptic of anything that could be used to argue the spiritual, philosophical, and scientific information presented. This will inevitably happen, but it is my goal to remove as much of this ammunition from them as possible so that any arguments made against the conclusions arrived at will come across as somebody obviously grasping at straws. Since technology and culture advance so rapidly, there is sure to be something that is outdated before this is even printed.

In selecting my sources, I found books written about what social media is and what it is doing to our culture. Many of these sources referenced other sources and scientific studies, which I would then read in order to further develop an understanding of this subject. I cannot emphasize enough what I found from more than 20 sources of mostly *unsaved, liberal, progressive authors.* Their conclusions were almost *unanimously in agreement* that the ubiquity of smartphones and Internet Culture in the developed world was more harmful than helpful. Through their various perspectives, they conclude cohesively that the social and technological wave sweeping across our society corrodes the naturally occurring and historically-supported process of cognitive development that help us to mature and thrive as individuals in a healthy society. The conclusions state that as a whole, our modern society is in decline. Many of them wrote works that are heavily slanted towards progressive ideologies. Many of them wrote in order to directly attack Donald Trump. Some wrote about big tech versus small business, and many wrote against the news media organizations that they had represented in times past. But all of them concluded that based on the current trends and recent developments, we are headed to some form of a collapse. Some more socially-oriented sources noted that society is becoming more prone to a totalitarian government takeover.

The most important thing to understand is that the Bible, modern mainstream science, and philosophy all align on the issue of the internet. They agree that there are major problems associated with the trending social movements that are causing harmful changes in society. They also all agree that the worst changes are passive in nature. As Christians, we should be aware of these issues and combat their effects in our own lives in relation to our walks with God. Having a healthy walk with God is the most important thing that a Christian can do. Prayer, Bible reading, church attendance, and witnessing are all critical to the walk of a Christian. Internet Culture and smartphone usage attacks all of these at some level, even if only through over-use, which crowds out the time left to spend with God.

In my personal opinion, the greatest detrimental effect that all of these components have on a Christian is the loss of little moments. Because smartphones enable access to perpetual entertainment, be it through games, socializing, texting, or light reading, people who use them to excess miss out on the myriad of spiritual opportunities that surround them. A perpetual access to frivolous entertainment feeds the mind at a superficial level while consuming literal years of time in increments sometimes less than a second long. The Devil is not consuming the lives of Christians by shutting them away for years at a time in prisons or killing them outright. He is consuming their lives on a second-by-second basis by making distractions always available. This is a spiritual "death by a thousand cuts". He is crippling them through a thousand small impacts rather than a single, heavy-handed blow. After all, "a soft tongue breaketh the bone" (Proverbs 25:15).

Simply because it is convenient, Christians are choosing to spend their moments with a phone and the rest of the world instead of with their Maker. Pulling my phone out whenever I have to wait on anything is a habit that I have begun to fight in my own life. It is a lifestyle where the little moments of prayer and communion with God are lost to what is sometimes literally just scrolling through lists of information that I have no intent of reading, interacting with, or watching. In these lost moments, God may be directing a Christian to pray, change their plans, or pass out a tract. The walk with God is purely an organic experience that must be learned by living it across as many moments as possible. It cannot be rendered to a formulaic strategy that applies to all Christianity. It must be learned through practice and experience. How many times have you seen an older person eating at a restaurant while a young person who is with them spends the whole time on their phone? The older person pays for the meal but is ignored by the younger person who has found something that is more entertaining but less rewarding. That is a perfect illustration of the entire life of a smartphone-addicted Christian. Most of the time spent on the smartphone is a pointless waste of time, and it could be better living in the moment with God, just as Nehemiah did. An interrogation from the king should not be the only reason that you take a moment to run to the Lord in prayer. A walk with God comes from spending every available moment with him. Smartphones are amazing time-saving devices, but then we spend all of our newly-preserved moments by creating combustible wood, hay, and stubble (I Corinthians 3:12). If this is all that it does for us, there really is no point in saving that time, is there? The number of moments lost in a day that could be spent communing with God can number in the hundreds. Over a lifetime, the treasures lost at the Judgement Seat of Christ are innumerable. I cannot claim total victory over this in my own life. The habit of losing moments to entertainment is a cultural dogma that operates in force on all those around us. It preys on how the brain naturally operates and feeds us with mental sugar that bloats the mind and crowds out the Spirit of God.

Hopefully, God has illuminated something in your life that should be changed in order to further enable your walk with God. The culture that has come about via the internet has changed modern society in a way that it will never recover from, and, as a Christian, it is easy to fall into the hurtful trends that this world brings into vogue without realizing what is really going on. It is likely that if you are reading this, that you have begun to develop doubts about your own life and are looking for the knowledge to understand what is happening on a spiritual level. I hope that this has armed you with enough material to win the victory in whatever battles you may be facing. If you are a preacher who has been saying for years what I have written here, I am hoping that this provides you with the scientific, philosophical, and, most importantly, spiritual ammunition that you need to further support your preaching, as long as it is in accordance with the word of God.

To everybody reading this, I hope that at some point I made you feel nauseated. The extent to which the internet has corrupted human societies is so insidiously crafted and effectively executed that one could cautiously say that the entire setup is brilliant. When the reformation broke Satan's grip on the western's world, he immediately pivoted and began using the printing press, which was the power behind the Philadelphia Church Age, against the world. He dynamically shifted his plans towards a culture into power that has been 400 years in the making. This culture effectively dismantles mankind's desire to fulfill its spiritual purpose and bends them to desire the reign of the Antichrist before he even steps onto the scene. When he rises to prominence, the world will be so corrupted that he will be welcomed in as a celebrated hero, rather than a vicious and oppressive warlord. He has conquered the mind of the world, and now the only thing he must do to rule over the entire planet is simply to be himself. As a Christian, this should utterly abhor and disgust you, and you should be becoming notably different from the lost world on a daily basis. Becoming a Christian is rapidly becoming the most unique thing that anybody could possibly do. Soon, it will be the only form of diversity that is not celebrated or encouraged.

I have compiled a few lessons at the end that I have learned along the way. The internet is new, it is big, and it is here to stay. I hope that you find this information useful in your walk with Christ.

WHY DO YOU NEED TO KNOW?

Consider on a daily basis what you really and truly need to know. Does Prince Harry really matter? Does learning the new features on next year's Chevy Equinox matter if you aren't going to buy a new one? Why does a snowstorm in Colorado matter unless you live there? Did a politician from a state that you do not reside in make an outrageous and offensive remark? If they did, how does this change anything about your day other than making you momentarily mad and possibly starting an online argument with a person whose mind you will not change? The biggest question you should ask is, does this matter in eternity? There is so much available out on the internet that has absolutely no bearing on your life at all. Celebrities do not matter. The only thing that they can do is something so offensive that you will refuse to watch their content in the future. Politicians will lie as they have since before Acts 23. The world will continue to degrade into a sinful, socialistic, globalized society that embraces the rule of the devil incarnate. Christians have known this since John wrote Revelation in 96 AD. Learning which celebrities are coming out in favor of trans rights is only a detail of the inevitable conclusion. Why worry?

Resistance against things that have no bearing real life and worry have taken the modern church by storm. You do not need to know all of the details of what is going wrong it the world because of sin. Christians are commanded to pray for those in authority "that we may lead a quiet and peaceable life in all Godliness and honesty" according to I Timothy 4:2. This command supersedes all need for great political action by Christians. A Christian is commanded to pray for the government in power, that they would be allowed to live as Christians and propagate the gospel in peace. It is all too often that Christians lose sight of the goal. Too many Christians live their lives to politically restore America to a great place for Christians to be, all while not living the Christian life that they should. What is the point of living in a Christian society if you aren't going to live as a Christian in the one that you have? What is the point of fighting for your right to freely preach the gospel if you don't preach it now? If more Americans devoted their time to growing spiritually and being fishers of men, there would be a lot more spiritually successful Christians in America, which would be more beneficial for our country than any form of political activism.

This argument boils over into personal conversations as well. Political talk often does little more than stoke self-righteous indignation against a lost and dying world. Bashing Hollywood can be appropriate as it is a key player in driving the spirituality of the world into the ground. Conversely, understanding all the ins and outs of every last wicked thing that comes out of it serves no purpose. It is good to understand the concepts and execution, but once you end up deep in the details, it is easy to lose the plot. Any Christian with half a mind knows that Hollywood is wicked. That has been preached since Hollywood became known for the silver screen. So what? Any actor or producer that you have any regard for will eventually fall to the world system or to cancel culture, so why waste your time emotionally investing in the personal life of a celebrity wouldn't know or care if you died tomorrow?

Sports figures do not matter. They are good at their respective sports, and that is all. No sports figure or Hollywood actor has any understanding of how the political world should be operated, so why get mad when they display their ignorance on the world stage? For those readers that went to public school, actors and athletes are the grown-up versions of the jocks and theatre kids, both of which are known for making poor life decisions. The only difference is that they have some years of college to liberally indoctrinate them, millions of dollars to warp their perspective, and contracts that are dependent on them staying in line with the progressive liberal agenda. Why would you expect anything less than unfiltered filth and disappointment?

Moving on from bashing the ignorant, let us move on to you, Christian. In what way has your understanding of politics or pop culture contributed to your reward at the Judgement Seat of Christ? I will answer for you that it hasn't. There are no rewards listed in the Bible for political activism or, as what most Christians are involved in, political complaining. Armchair political discussion has about as much impact on politics as armchair quarterbacking has on an NFL game. The only thing this does is stir emotional discontentment about losing rights that you don't use as it is. Witnessing to a person on the street does a lot more good than arguing with your liberal cousin online.

Christians need to learn to think about what they are talking about. We all have our hobbies that may not be spiritually grounded, but we enjoy greatly. I am not talking about this right now but will a little later. What Christians need to do is to understand that sitting around talking about things or going online and arguing about things that do not result any spiritual development are purely irrelevant. Many Christians have deluded themselves into thinking that being mad about something is good for them. Unless it results in action that furthers the Kingdom of God, it does not.

SHOULD I HAVE A FACEBOOK?

If you still believe that there is any merit to having a personal social media account, there is nothing else I can do for you. At this point you have set up an idol in your heart and you are going to get the dishonest answers that you want according to Ezekiel 14. I do not know why you are still reading this, and I am surprised you have read this far. There is nothing that is accomplished on social media that could not be done better by living a Godly, separated life and actively witnessing to others. Even accounts that are spiritually based are prone to the same pitfalls as personal accounts, and the drive to gain more followers and likes and reshares will always provide a negative, subtle impact on the content posted. Christians are not commanded to grow their own popularity. He must increase. You must decrease. End of story.

You are to go into all the world and preach the gospel to every creature. The word go means move, not sit at home and type up inspirational Bible messages to write across photos of mountains.

This is where I know many people will disagree with me. The argument in favor of spiritually based social media accounts always comes with a vast supply of testimonial evidence to the contrary about how encouragement, witnessing opportunities, or even conversions may have happened through the internet. To counter that point, I argue that while the number of people that can be reached with internet increases, the quality of the witness or encouragement decreases. The argument for quantity versus quality has already been discussed, and Jesus always chose to exposit the Scriptures to the individuals who chose to come to Him personally and learn of Him. His messages to the masses, without the explanations, are largely incoherent. People tended to follow him en masse because of His ability to create a limitless supply of bread, and possibly put the Jews in charge of the world by force (see John 6). If you want to touch a person, do it in person. Good can still be accomplished when a person does not complete the will of God perfectly in their life. This is why there is a good, acceptable and perfect will of God shown in Romans 12:2. Good things absolutely *can* be accomplished over the internet. But the good done over the internet will never compare with the greater good that can be done personally with a Christian or lost soul. As dumb as this sounds, there is nothing that can be said through a screen that matches the comfort and love that can be given through a hug. The difference is that giving somebody a hug requires a lot more effort and can be a lot more uncomfortable.

I will concede to spiritual involvement online in one aspect. The world now lives on social media and looks for answers using search engines. I believe, with a strict, single condition, that churches should have a Facebook page. If a lost person is looking for a church that can give them absolute truth, they are going to look online, and Facebook is the universal social media platform. Most young people today are not active on Facebook, and use other platforms to communicate, but they know that Facebook is the platform for "old people." If this offends you, read Psalms 119:165. They will look for a church on Facebook, much like people of years gone by would look in a newspaper for ads for churches. This is where the caveat comes in. The Facebook page should be purely static. By this, I mean that there should be no posts, no private message boards, and absolutely no private or public comments section. The only thing that it should have are enough photos and recent information to show that the church is still active, and a link to the church's website or phone number. There should be no way for anybody, saved or lost, in the group or not, to interact with this page at any time. It should purely be a sign directing them to either the web site or a good means of contact with the head of outreach. It should be just like an advertisement in a newspaper that shows were you are, when you have service, a brief statement of faith, and nothing more. It is the modern version of a newspaper ad. I cannot emphasize how important it is for there to be NO comments section. The website should have all of the important information about the church, doctrinal positions, upcoming events, etc. as well as a convenient way for an interested party to privately send a message to somebody in the church who can help them. The entire goal of a church's online presence should be to get people to attend in person, so they can be dealt with in person. It is my firm belief that in absolutely no case should a church have an account with Instagram, WhatsApp, or, God forbid, a Twitter. These platforms are not worth the damage that they cause, and the damage done by being active on these sites far surpasses any spiritual benefit that can be gleaned from them. Simply having one may be enough for people in the congregation to create an account for the sole purpose of following the church. It will end with them being an addict to the platform. If you have one of these accounts, I would implore you to take it to God and ask, out of an honest heart, if he has directed you to keep it. I have given you all the information that I have. The rest is between God and you.

I will also add in a final exemption. If you are the owner of a business, social media accounts are the best way to market your business. This is where the most people are, and you will get more business by staying active online than anywhere else. As a side note, your church, though it may be a 501c3, is not a business at its heart. It is not a tool to help you grow your attendance. Beware that you keep the account purely business oriented, and do not take time wandering down some pointless rabbit hole that yields no return. I personally do not own a business, and this is not a conversation that I have had to have with God. If you do, I advise you to first pray about it, and then act on the direction that God gives you. Simply knowing the dangers does not make you immune to them, so handle this cautiously.

CONSIDER THE LILIES

This is a point that I feel I made fairly obvious in the section "The Glory of Man," but it is too important to leave out at the end. The internet is a world that man created and poured his heart into. Nature is a creation of God that He poured His heart into. Psalms 19 makes it very clear that the natural world teaches us things about God and His glory. Nature is nothing like the internet, and the more time you spend in either one will determine whom you conform more towards. God does call people to serve in cities, and it is absolutely His will for some Christians to live in them. I offer this advice to everybody, but especially those who live in the more developed areas of the world: Go outside. There are benefits that you gain from nature that are just as subtly good for you as the internet is bad.

Romans 1:19-20 states: "Because that which may be known of God is manifest in them, for God hath shewed it unto them. For the invisible things of him from the creation of the world are clearly seen, being understood by the things that are made, even his eternal power and Godhead; so that they are without excuse." This passage shows that God demonstrates the spiritual significance to through His creation. Nature teaches many things to man that are antithetical to how the internet works. I will list a few. In nature, things die; on the internet, data is preserved forever. In nature, patience is required for any growth; on the internet, everything is instantaneous. Nature is abundant with discomforts, such as temperatures, bugs, rain, and distance. On the internet, all physical pain and discomfort is neutralized through a screen. In nature, decay shows the inevitability of death, and on the internet, continual updates teach the persistence of humanity. The more time that a person spends living in the manmade world of tech and the less time they spend in the natural world, the less they see the difficult lessons that God has tried to show man. God put humanity in a world with a curse, where there is pain, disease, discomfort, and death in order to show him that "it is appointed unto men once to die, but after this the judgement" (Hebrews 9:27).

Beyond the hard lessons, nature also teaches the beauty and glory of God. This world, despite its fallen and corrupted condition, still has places of great beauty. The places that are most sought after are those that are untouched by man. This is why waterfront property is universally more expensive in first-world countries. In places without running water, natural water is a necessity. In places where humanity's basic needs are met, waterfront property is a luxury. People take vacations to "get away from it all," or "slow down." To do this, they get away from people and into the natural world. This is because, according to Ecclesiastes 3:11, "He hath made every thing beautiful in his time: also he hath set the world in their heart, so that no man can find out the work that God maketh from the beginning to the end." He put it into the heart of man to want to see nature, and He did this as a mercy to draw men to His creation so that they could understand God better (this also shows why evolution is so critical in Satan's plans). The allusions to God through His creation are innumerable and are displayed throughout the Scripture. The rising and setting sun is a picture of both the death and resurrection of Jesus Christ (Matthew 27:45, Psalms 19:4-5). The sunset can also be a picture of the coming of the Antichrist (John 9:4), and the dawn can be a picture of the second advent of Jesus Christ (Malachi 4:2). The rainbow is a promise that the world will never be destroyed again by water (Genesis 9:13-15). The care that God gives to His creatures shows that His provision is sufficient for His children (Matthew 10:29-31, Luke 12:24). All of these things show the hand of God. In Job 37:14, it says, "Hearken unto this, O Job: stand still, and consider the wondrous works of God." In Matthew 6:28-29, it says, "Consider the lilies of the field, how they grow; they toil not, neither do they spin: And yet I say unto you, That even Solomon in all his glory was not arrayed like one of these." This is not a suggestion. It is a command. You can ignore the spiritual application if you want to miss a blessing, but God ordered people to think about the lilies in order for them to better know their Creator.

I do not know how many times I have sat and stared at a screen for hours on end, only to look up and feel like I'm coming back to the real world. There is an adjustment period between when we go from living on a screen to living in the creation of God. I do not know spiritually what this entails, but I do know that it is easier to silence the voice of God when I am watching a screen than anything else. The fast-twitch online world offers such an easy and quick distraction from the important things of life that it is tempting to use it to drown out the world and spend your life kicking the can down the road. I also know that it is easiest for me to silence the temptations and wickedness of this world when I am alone in the woods. There is nothing that makes it easier to dwell on thoughts of God and gain some relief from the spiritual warfare that wages in my mind than a ride on my bike through the woods. The contrast between the online world and nature is so opposite that it was shocking when I moved out of the city and got an outdoor hobby. On a personal level, I cannot overemphasize how good this has been for me spiritually. If you do not have any hobby that you like to do that puts you in some way in touch with the natural world, I would encourage you to ask God to give you one. He did this for me, and the spiritual benefits to it are both humbling and astounding. And when you go out there, turn your phone off. Even better, leave it in the car or at home. That *thing* has spent so much time tethered to each of our front right pockets that we feel naked without it. If you don't think that you have a problem, leave it at home, take a ten-minute walk, and notice how uncomfortable and exposed you feel.

As a side note to this, a personal observation of mine is that most of the Christians that I know who have a real touch from God on their lives tend to have at least one of the three following hobbies: hunting, fishing, or gardening. Throughout the process of time, God has laid his creation on their heart, and they have found that the serenity gained through any of these activities has benefits far beyond the meat or vegetables that they gather. I think that the points made in this section have proved this, and if you don't believe this, try it. The results may surprise you.

As a final note, I would ask one thing of every reader. Go outside and look at the stars. Psalms 8:3-4 says: "When I consider thy heavens, the work of thy fingers, the moon and the stars, which thou hast ordained; What is man, that thou are mindful of him? and the son of man, that thou visitest him?" Go outside at night and look up. David did this, and it made him consider the relationship that mankind has with the God of all things. It gave him a proper perspective. It showed him, somehow, that God would choose to visit man, and that man held value to God. We are His creation, and yet, somehow, we can please Him. There are all kinds of doctrinal implications about stars and angels and spirits and fire and the war of Revelation 12 and the gap in Genesis 1:2. For a few minutes, forget about all of that that. Go outside. Look up. And talk to God.

YOUR BRAIN: USE IT OR LOSE IT

Reading the Bible should be a given. There is no Christian that has a good relationship with God who does not habitually read their Bible. The only exception to that rule would be a person who is unable to read due to intellectual disability, a physically debilitating condition, or some form of persecution that has forcibly removed them from access to the word of God. Since you are reading this, none of these exceptions apply to you. The excuse "I have no time" is invalid. You have time for what you want to have time for. Serving God required sacrifice, and you cannot please him without giving Him your time and attention. Keep in mind that, as a Christian, you are a part of the Bride of Christ. If the Bride is too busy to listen to the groom talk or give him time every day, she does not actually love him. If you have a tight schedule, ask God for time.

In trying to find time to read the Bible, you will find a few things. One, God honors prayer, and two, it doesn't matter how much you read as long as you are reading as much as He wants you to. Ask God for time and He will show you when you should be reading. If you put your heart into the time He gives you, you can get more out of a single chapter than a self-righteous Christian gets out of reading ten with a bad heart. I can speak from personal experience and say that God has blessed me many times when I have only read a few chapters because it was the best I could give God at the time. I will also add that my life has been busy trying to fulfill all of the work that God has given me, and that leaves little time for anything beyond the essentials. You may need to cut back hours of sleep, hours at work, or time with your family. What is more likely is that you will need to cut back hours of watching the news, surfing the net, or watching YouTube. You have the time. Make sure you are prioritizing what will last in eternity.

Beyond just the Bible, read books. Not newspapers, not Wikipedia articles, and not status updates. Find a book with a hard back and pages that smell funny. Go to a library. Buy it on the internet and have it shipped to your front door. For years, people have been saying "Readers are leaders." Books do something for you that no other media can do, which is why God preserved His words in a book. God gave man the 10 Commandments in tables of stone, but the majority of the commands to Israel were preserved by Moses in a book, sprinkled with blood, and read to the people. The first book of the law is given in Exodus 17:14, and the 10 Commandments show up Exodus 20. God chose this format because He wanted to give His people the best possible means of understanding Him. Throughout history, it has been proven that a literate public is more spiritually minded than an illiterate one. The Philadelphia Church age was brought about by the consolidation and translation of the Bible into English. The printing press helped to break the stranglehold of the Catholic church by making the Bible more easily accessible to the general public.

The book of Proverbs emphasizes the importance of knowledge and wisdom. Proverbs 1:4-5 says that the purpose of the "Proverbs of Solomon" are "To give subtlety to the simple, to the young man knowledge and discretion. A wise man will hear, and will increase learning; and a man of understanding shall attain unto wise counsels:" In order for a man to be wise, he must have knowledge to be wise about. Simply having knowledge is not enough. In the last times, Daniel is told in Daniel 12:4, "But thou, O Daniel, shut up the words, and seal the book, even to the time of the end: many shall run to and fro, and knowledge shall be increased." The knowledge spoken about is frivolous knowledge that does not help the knower in any way. II Timothy 3:1, 7 state: "This know also, that in the last days perilous times shall come...Ever learning, and never able to come to the knowledge of the truth." To put this into modern terminology, "'Knowing' the facts took on a new meaning, for it did not imply that one understood implications, background, or connections... intelligence meant knowing of lots of things, not knowing about them" (Postman, 1986, p. 70). The pure acquisition of knowledge does not help a person to draw nearer to God. That knowledge must come with wisdom. According to Solomon, "The fear of the LORD is the beginning of wisdom: and the knowledge of the holy is understanding" (Proverbs 9:10). If the knowledge does not accommodate a fear of God, the knowledge is useless. Romans 1:21-22 says, "Because that, when they knew God, they glorified him not as God, neither were thankful; but became vain in their imaginations, and their foolish heart was darkened. Professing themselves to be wise, they became fools." The denial of God in the wisdom acquired causes God to darken the heart of a man. When man tries to take the glory away from God, God takes the mind away from the man.

This is not to say that nothing should ever be looked up online. Search engines are good for providing a small amount of information, but this needs to be kept in context and not overused. They do not figure out what the right answer to a question is and show it to you. It provides you with the most common answer that the algorithm thinks you will click on, based on what it knows about you. It is only a machine that makes a profit for its developers, and, unfortunately, it is being substituted for honest research. It cannot provide any context for the information other than what is said on the page. In order for an article to fully explain a situation in an honest manner, it would have to be labor intensive, lengthy, and boring. Given what has been presented in this thesis, if such an article even exists, it is not going to show up very high in the search results. If search engines could be programmed to find truth, the truths would be based on the trends of the world, and therefore would not be true. The problem comes in most evidently through the fact that all search engines try to give short, popular answers. If a person only learns by searching online, they lose the important supporting knowledge that explains why something is the way that it is. They learn only the what, not the why. The simple acquisition of basic knowledge cannot provide an understanding of any subject. The point is, there is nothing wrong with using search engines if you only need to know a small amount of information about something, but it is useless for understanding something. It may tell you how to fry an egg, but you aren't going to learn why cooking it using different fats and seasonings changes the consistency, flavor, and appearance. YouTube may show you how to change the air filter on a specific car, but it won't explain how a combustion engine works so that you can find the air filter on a different model. You have to consider how much you need to understand something, and then learn about it accordingly. Learning to fry an egg is one thing. Deciding who to vote for as the leader of the free world is another.

This is why a healthy amount of wisdom and knowledge are essential to the Christian life. God wants us to understand Him better. He reveals Himself through His words and His creation, and as we get to know both better, we begin to understand Him better. The parable of the sower and his seed means a lot more if you work in a garden. The Bible holds deeper meaning when you actually understand what words like "importunity," "lasciviousness" and "supplication" mean. Furthermore, in Proverbs 22:21, Solomon tells his son that he has written all of these things to him "That I might make thee to know the certainty of the words of truth; that thou mightiest answer the words of truth to them that send unto thee." Knowledge and wisdom allow a Christian to turn any knowledge gained back to the creation of God and understand Him better with it. It also allows a Christian to sift out any knowledge that contradicts the Bible as false and reject it. In a world that is saturated with a glut of questionably reliable information, understanding the Bible as the absolute standard of truth gives the believer of it a little more ground to stand on. While the spiritual approach should always be the primary way of directing a lost soul to Jesus Christ, having an understanding of outside subjects such as creation science, psychology, or false religions can help to supplement the knowledge provided in the Bible. It is not easy to disprove the Koran to a Muslim when you have never read the Koran, and it is not easy to attack evolution when you do not have an understanding of biology. It is possible, yes, but the more knowledge you have that can be related back to the Bible, the more you can support the truth while using a factual knowledge base to dismantle a lie.

As I have stated before, I do not believe that there is anything in this book that will be groundbreaking to a person who has studied the word of God, because preachers have been preaching against the internet and watching television since either of them have existed. They did this without the statistical data, the neuroscience, or the psychoanalysis of children. They did it by watching the spiritual effects that it had on people and recognizing the problems that it caused. This thesis is a tool to be used to support those claims and show that the world cannot do anything but prove that the Bible is true.

In reading up to this point, you have probably noticed that there are some books that I lean heavily on for support. Some of the material that I have read is a lot better written than other material, and some sources have proven to be much more relative to the Christian walk than others. If you are filled with a newfound desire to get off the web and read a book, I would recommend the following books to you if you wish to learn more about the topic that I have written on:

1. *"Amusing Ourselves to Death" by Neil Postman – This book was written in 1985 about television and everything that he says can be applied to the internet. He shows the progression of technology and how it changed society. He may have been saved and wrote mostly about how TV changed politics and religion for the worse. This is my number one recommended book for a reason, and it has something in it for every Christian.*

2. *"Alone Together" by Sherry Turkle – This book is written by a licensed clinical psychologist who is the founder and*

director of the MIT Initiative on Technology and Self. Her book is broken into an introduction and two parts. I recommend the introduction and part two. Part one is about how people emotionally connect with robots, and part two is about how technology changes the way that we think. It is gut-wrenching and unfiltered in its analysis of how tech has changed the world, and she puts an added emphasis on how it has changed parents and children.

3. "The Shallows" by Nicholas Carr – This was written about how the structure of the internet is detrimental to the human brain. He shows, through scientific research, how the internet changes the way we think and then dismantles us by being so helpful. It can be dense at times but provides hard, scientific evidence that technology is not as benevolent as the world would have you believe.

4. "The Big Disconnect" by Catherine Steiner-Adair – The author is a clinical psychologist who specializes in children and clinical instructor in the Department of Psychiatry at Harvard Medical School. She writes how cell phones, iPads, the internet, and social media have hurt children of all ages, beginning with infants and ending with teenagers. This is a must-read for anybody who is trying to navigate technology with their children. Some content is explicit.

5. "The Happiness Effect" by Donna Freitas – This book takes the testimonials of hundreds of college students regarding how social media has impacted them. The interviews reveal how fake social media is, how much it "pressure cooks" their minds, and how much most of them actually wish it didn't exist but are too afraid to quit. Some content is explicit.

6. *"Irresistible" by Adam Altar – Adam Altar has a PhD in psychology and his book "Irresistible" serves as the outline for Chapter 3. He breaks down what addiction is and how the human mind can be leveraged against itself to become addicted to things other than drugs. He helps to show how many things we are truly addicted to and what to do about it.*

USING, BUT NOT ABUSING

Most of the arguments made are made based on the results seen from heavy use of the internet or smartphones. That is why I often refer to the damages of "Internet Culture" and not just the internet. Many of the detrimental effects manifest themselves when a person immerses themselves in this culture and excessively implements it into every facet of their life. The more that a person uses it, the more that these effects come to light. This will immediately draw the reaction by some readers that "well I don't use it that much, so it isn't that bad for me." Chances are, if this is currently how you think, you are already under conviction (from God, not the science) for how much you use it and are looking for an excuse not to cut back or cut it off. This is a heart problem and not a head one, and that is something that only you can fix by spending more time with God and His word. There is a healthy way to use the internet, and if you are looking for it, I can offer some advice.

The negative impacts of the internet are largely passive, meaning that they eat away at you without being obvious about it. The internet is a lot like smoking. Your first cigarette will disgust and shock you. The more you do it, the more you adapt and the less damage it feels like it is doing. You may pick it up and put it down over time. Over a long period of time, it will give you cancer, and the doctor will likely tell you that you have to quit, or you are going to die, and once you quit smoking, your risk of a heart attack goes down within a week. This parallels how the internet impacts the brain. Over a long period of time, it will give you a spiritual cancer that can kill your walk with God. It may take more time for some than others, and some may not develop the cancer at all. But smoking at all gives you that risk. and smoking always doer irreparable damage to your lungs, hindering your ability to run. Quitting helps, but it wont undo some of the permanent damage. Its best to quit before the damage gets any worse. Unfortunately, too many Christians are smoking the internet through their trachea.

Where the example diverges from reality is in that internet use is becoming a requirement in our society, and, if managed correctly, does a lot less damage than a single cigarette. As our society adopts more technology, internet use becomes the only way to do some things. Manual functions are rapidly being phased out by it. I do my banking, make car payments, pay rent, and check the weather using the internet. At my job, all of our files are stored in the cloud. Since we have battery backups, a power outage does less impact to my workflow than an internet outage. Very few functions are actually done using physical documents, and they always have digital backups. If I were to cut all internet use out of my life, I would get fired in a few days for not doing my job. Everything that I have listed up to this point is actually a time saving tool that is better than doing it manually in most ways. The overall impact is a benefit to my productivity. The issues from internet use come from the abuse of the internet in your personal time.

Most of the content on the internet is useless to your Christian walk. It is little more than mindless amusement, and, if you ask God, He can give you something a lot more productive to do. If you view the internet as something that is constantly, passively wearing away at you, you can keep it in check by avoiding it as much as possible. By continuously reorienting yourself with healthy activities (see the previous section), reading the word or God, praying, and staying active for the Lord, you can keep it from consuming you. The goal of going on the internet should be to spend as little time on the internet as possible. If you can control it, it is the greatest time-saving tool ever created. If you can't, it will take more from you than you can imagine.

To help fight this temptation in your life, there are a few things that you can do to reduce the temptation to waste time. This draws from the conclusion made in Chapter 3, but the best thing you can do to resist temptation is to avoid it, which aligns with I Corinthians 10:13. If you cannot control your smartphone use, leave it in the car when you get home. There are apps that will tell you how much you use each app or how often you unlock your phone. They can also shut you out if you spend a certain amount of time on some apps. If you use the internet too much on your computer, cancel it and get a hotspot with limited data. If you go on websites you should not, get an internet accountability partner. There are programs that send your internet history to another person, which really helps to curb what you will look at online. There are many programs out there to help you measure and reduce your technological activity. Make use of them.

When it comes to children, the literature that I have read about technology and what it does to them has given me some very strong and well-supported opinions about it. I will say up front that I do not have children, and everything that I am writing comes solely from my personal experience and the books that I have read. Personally, I believe that no child should be given a smartphone before the age of 18. If a phone of some kind is necessary due to circumstances, a flip phone is best. No child under the age of 18 should have a computer or television in their bedroom. You may have a very spiritual child, but they are no match for the internet. Children have less self-control and a greater amount of curiosity than adults do. There is no child that I have ever met that I felt I could be given access to all of the information in the world, good and evil, and only use it for good. When you give them access to the internet with no parental oversight, you make them the gatekeepers of their own innocence, which will lose out against their curiosity. This world cares deeply about corrupting children for personal profit and to appease their conscience of sin. Do not give the world the access that they are looking for. Nobody can raise your child as well as you can as long as you have a walk with God.

Beyond just children, most adults honestly do not need a smartphone or lightning-fast internet. A major problem in modern Christian homes is the hypocritical double-standard that parents have with their children about their smartphone usage. If you don't think this is an issue in your household, ask your children, and they may surprise you. If you cannot handle your smartphone, I would recommend that you downgrade to a flip phone. Those still exist and this can help you to avoid sinful temptations by eliminating your ability to access them each time temptation strikes. In my apartment, I only have internet through a hotspot that is terribly slow. If you need to downgrade, do it. This reduces the amount of time that I spend on it for anything because I get frustrated just doing the bare minimum and am ready to be done when I finish my business. I do my online shopping at work after hours, along with personal email and paying my bills. I do not have a subscription to any TV or streaming service and have spent a lot less time watching videos on the internet since God gave me healthy habits to replace them with. Sometimes, I stop watching things and do something more productive just because my internet is slow and frustrating. The spotty connection is sometimes a gift from God because it gets me back to doing what I ought to be doing.

I do not say this to brag. I grew up with social media and spent literal years of my life as an avid online gamer. I did not remove these from my life in a day, a month, or even a year. It took me much longer to beat some habits than others, and I still struggle with some things. The old man refuses to die. The key that I have found comes from John 3:30 "He must increase, but I must decrease." I asked God not just for what he wanted me to do with my life, but for healthier hobbies. As he started giving me these, the desires for the old things began to fade away as I no longer had time for them. This is something that I had to do personally. If somebody had forced it on me, I would have resisted them and held on to them out of rebellion. As I have grown in my walk with the Lord, even throughout the process of writing this book, there are many things that I have slowly been able to lay down. This does not mean that I no longer think about them or want them. Resisting is still, and always will be a battle. But God has helped me through the temptations and he can do the same for you. There are very few things that I just quit, cold turkey, although that was needed in a few areas. I had to do it in a way that came as a result of my desire to draw closer to God. Your journey may look totally different from mine, but whatever your journey is like, it is a climb that is worth the effort. In talking about research for this book with other people, saved or lost, I have come across many people who wished that they could quit social media, but feel that they can't. I had one lost girl tell me she was jealous of me for not having any social media. This is because inside, the natural man still has an inborn desire to know God and be at peace with Him. This is stated in John 1:9. Most people know that there is a problem, but either do not know how to fix it, or are too afraid to take that step. I hope that the material presented has helped you to begin your own fight against the obsession that is overrunning our society. As a person who lived in the internet for years on end, had several active social media profiles, watched YouTube more than I care to think about, had been addicted to TV shows, and spent more time on video games than most people, I can promise you this: the more you climb, the better the view. With God, you can.

CLOSING

If I were to say that the contents of this book could effectively be summarized in a few paragraphs at the end, it would defeat the intent of a good portion of this book. I will, however, make a few closing remarks. Throughout this book, there are a few verses of Scripture that apply so effectively to the infection of Internet Culture and smartphone use into our daily lives that it would be appropriate to close with them. They have each run through my head hundreds of times during research, structuring, and writing this thesis, and they are proven through and through by the direction that the world is taking. To avoid belaboring the point further, they are as follows:

Genesis 3:1 – "Now the serpent was more subtle than any beast of the field which the LORD God had made..."

This verse shows that the Devil has been deceiving humans using subtlety since God put Adam and Eve in the garden. He rarely employs a direct assault on the life of a believer until he has sufficiently softened him up to where he can take him out with a single blow. The internet does exactly this to the human mind and has made the majority of people who spend their lives on it mentally soft. As the culture surrounding the internet becomes less intelligent and more anti-God, the world will shift into a mindset that accepts the Antichrist before he even comes on to the scene. The internet is breaking apart the good done to the world by the Philadelphia church age, and the Laodicean church has no response for it. It is falling away with the rest of the world. The only way to counteract the subtle influences is to maintain a healthy walk with God and His word.

I Timothy 6:10 –"For the love of money is the root of all evil: which while some have coveted after, they have erred from the faith, and pierced themselves through with many sorrows."

The reason that the internet is so full of filth is because man has realized that he can make money on the sinful nature of humanity. If human nature were pure, the internet would bring about a golden age of society where knowledge could be shared for the good of all. This is happening to a small extent but is overshadowed by the negative effects that it has on society. Every bit of false information, every news story that is convoluted for advertising purposes, and every addictive platform is designed to consume time, the only truly nonrenewable resource. The world knows that what it is doing is not good for them, but since somebody is always willing to raise the bar a little further, everybody else has to follow suit or get left behind. Satan may be playing the music, but mankind is choosing to dance.

II Thessalonians 2:9-10 – "Even him, whose coming is after the working of Satan with all power and signs and lying wonders, And with all deceivableness of unrighteousness in them that perish; because they received not the love of the truth, that they might be saved."

Mankind will choose to accept the Antichrist for a single reason: because they stopped loving the truth. A person who loves the truth above everything else will eventually come to a saving knowledge of Jesus Christ. A person who chooses to prioritize anything else over that will eventually fall to some form of deception. The architecture of the internet has sapped the belief that truth, as a concept, could even exist. The humanism that engulfs our society proclaims the gospel of finding your own personal truth, which is such a ridiculous concept that it becomes evident why Satan had to so deeply cripple the minds of this world before stepping in. The entire notion of relative truth has no basis in reality, but then again, most people live on the internet, not reality. As the world embraces this philosophy more and more, the only recourse for a Christian should be from Revelation 22:20: "Even so, come, Lord Jesus."

The title of this book, *Strangely Dim* comes from the hymn "Turn Your Eyes Upon Jesus¹". After all of the research, reading, analysis, and writing, I can only come to the following conclusion:

Either Internet Culture will dim your view of Jesus Christ, or Jesus Christ will dim your view of the world. There is no exception, and you must choose you this day whom ye will serve.

> *Turn your eyes upon Jesus*
> *Look Full in his wonderful Face*
> *And the things of earth will grow...*
> **Strangely Dim**
> *...in the light of his glory and grace.*

---

[1] *Turn Your Eyes Upon Jesus* | Helen H. Lemmel | Words: Public Domain

BIBLIOGRAPHY

Alter, A. (2017). Irresistible: The Rise of Addictive Technology andthe Business of Keeping Us Hooked. New York: Penguin Press.

boyd, d. (2014). It's Complicated: the social lives of networked teens. New Haven: Yale University Press.

Carr, N. (2010). The Shallows: What the Internet is Doing to Our Brains. New York: Norton.

Chapman, G., & Pellicane, A. (2014). Growing Up Social: Raising Relational Kids in a Screen-Driven World. Chicago: Northfield Publishing.

Conceptually. (n.d.). The Overton Window. Retrieved from www.conceptually.org: http://conceptualy.org/concepts/overton-window

Dijck, J. v. (2013). The Culture of Connectivity. Oxford: Oxford Press.

Federal Reserve Economic Data. (2020). Household Debt and Credit Report. New York: FED.

Foer, F. (2017). World Without Mind: The Existential Threat of Big Tech . New York: Penguin Books.

Frietas, D. (2017). The Happiness Effect: How Social Media i Driving a Generation to Appear Perfect at Any Cost. New York: Oxford Press.

Hagopian Institute. (2008). Quote Junkie B.C. CreateSpace Infipendent Publishing Platform.

Holiday, R. (n.d.). Trust Me I'm Lying: The Confessions of a Professional Media Manipulator. Penguin Books.

Jean M. Twenge, P. (2017). iGen: Why Today's Super-Connected Kids are Growing Up Less Rebellious, More Tolerant, Less Happy-and Completely Unprepared for Adulthood *and What That Means for the Rest of Us. New York: Simon & Schuster.

Kane, J. N. (1933). The Pocket Book of Famous First Facts. New York: Pocket Books.

Keen, A. (2008). The Cult of the Ameture: How blogs, MySpace, YouTube and the rest of today's uder-generated media are killing our culture and economy. Great Britain: Nicholas Brealey Publishing.

Kelly, K. (2010). What Technology Wants. New York: Penguin Group (USA) Inc.

Lazarus, N. (2017). The Connected Church. CreateSpace Independent Publsing Platform.

Mangen, A. (2008). Hypertext Fiction Reading: Haptics and Immersion. Journal of Research in Reading, 404-419.

McCarthy, J. (2020, June 1). US Support for Same-Sex Marriage Matches Record High. Retrieved from www.news.gallup.com: http://news.gallup.com/poll/311672/support-sex-marriage-matches-record-high.aspx

McLuhan, M. (1962). The Gutenberg Galaxy. Toronto: University of Toronto Press.

Miller, R. (2019). Social Media Marketing 2019: The power of Instagram Marketing - How to Win Followers & Influence Millions Online Using Highly Effective Personal Branding & Digital Networking Strategies. Middletown: Robert Miller.

Postman, N. (1986). Amusing Ourselves to Death: Public Discourse in the Age of Show Business. New York: Penguin Books.

Powers, W. (2010). Hamlet's Blackberry. New York: HarperCollens.

Pyle, D. H. (1792). The Taming of the Television. Murfreesboro: Sword of the Lord.

R. L. Paul, H. G. (1972). Alterations in Mechanonoreceptor Input to Brodmann's Areas 1 and 3 of the Postcentral Hand Area of Macaca mulatta after Nerce Section and Regeneration. Brain Research, 1-19.

Reifler, B. N. (n.d.). When Corrections Fail: The Persistence of Political Misperceptions. Political Behavior, 303-330.

Ruckman, D. P. (1982). The History of the New Testament Church, Volume 1. Pensacola: Bible Baptist Bookstore.

Ruckman, D. P. (1982). The History of the New Testament Church, Volume 2. Pensacola: Bible Baptist Bookstore.

Ruckman, P. (1960). The Mark of the Beast. Pensacola: Bible Baptist Bookstore.

Sales, N. J. (2016). American Girls: Social Media and the Secret Lives of Teenagers. New York: United States Vintage Books.

Schwartz, B. (2004). The Paradox of Choice. New : Harper Perennial.

Singer/Brooking. (2018). Likewar. New York: Houghton, Mifftin, Harcourt Publishing Company.

Steiner-Adair, C. (2013). The Big Disconnect: Protecting Childhood and Family Relationships in the Digital Age. New York: HarperCollins Publishers.

Tebbel, J. (1969). The Compact History of the American Newspaper. New York: Hawthorne Books.

Thoreau, H. D. (1949). Walden, an Annotated Edition. New York: Houghton Mifflin Company.

Truffaut, F. (1966). Hitchcock. New York: Simon & Schuster.

Tungate, M. (2013). Adland: A Global History of Advertising. London: Kogan Page.

Turkle, S. (2011). Alone Together: Why We Expect More From Technology and Less From Each Other. New York: Basic Books.

Vaidhyanathan, S. (2018). AntiSocial Media: How Facebook Disconnects Us and Undermines Democracy. New York: Oxford University press.

World Economic Forum. (2015-). Deep Shift: 21 Ways Software Will Transform Global Society. Retrieved from www.weforum.org: http://www3.weforum.org/docs/WEF_GAC15_Deep_Shift_Software_Transform_Society.pdfDuring the Kingdoms of Israel and Judah in the Old

TRUSTHOUSE
PUBLISHERS

Trust Publishers House,
the trusted name in quality Christian books.

Trust House Publishers
PO Box 3181
Taos, NM 87571

TrustHousePublishers.com

CPSIA information can be obtained
at www.ICGtesting.com
Printed in the USA
LVHW061049160723
752518LV00003B/294